A Lancashire Triangle Reviewed

Dennis Sweeney

Triangle

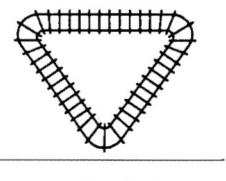

Publishing

Copyright © D.J.Sweeney 2015.
First Published 2015 by Triangle Publishing.
British Library Catalogue in Publication Data.
Sweeney D.J.
A Lancashire Triangle Reviewed.
ISBN 978 0 09550030 73
Printed by The Amadeus Press Ltd, Cleckheaton.
Written, compiled and edited by D.J.Sweeney.
Cover design by Scene, Design & Print Ltd, Standish.
Designed and Published by
Triangle Publishing,
509 Wigan Road,
Leigh, Lancs. WN7 5HN.
www.trianglepublishing.co.uk

All rights reserved. No part of this publication may be reproduced in any shape or form or by any means electrical, digital, mechanical, photographed, photocopied, e-mailed or stored in any retrieval system without prior written consent of the Author and/or Triangle Publishing

Front Cover. B.R.Standard class '9F' No.92019, with driver Cliff Davis at the controls, waits for the right of way from Jackson's Sidings, Tyldesley, c1965/6 at the head of a coal train for Garston Docks. The smoke effect is one of Jim Carter's trademarks when he had the opportunity to stoke up the firebox. By this period the sidings were not in the best of shape and great care would have to be taken on departure. In the distance near the signal post, is Jackson's Sidings signal box.   *Author's Collection (Jim Carter).*

Rear Cover. A woebegone looking Royal Scot class '7P' 4-6-0 No.46140 *The King's Royal Rifle Corps* perfectly posed at Patricroft Shed in the mid 1960s. The condition of the engine is indicative of the era as steam power approached its finale the picture telling its own story; even the nameplate is rusty.   *Author's Collection (Jim Carter).*

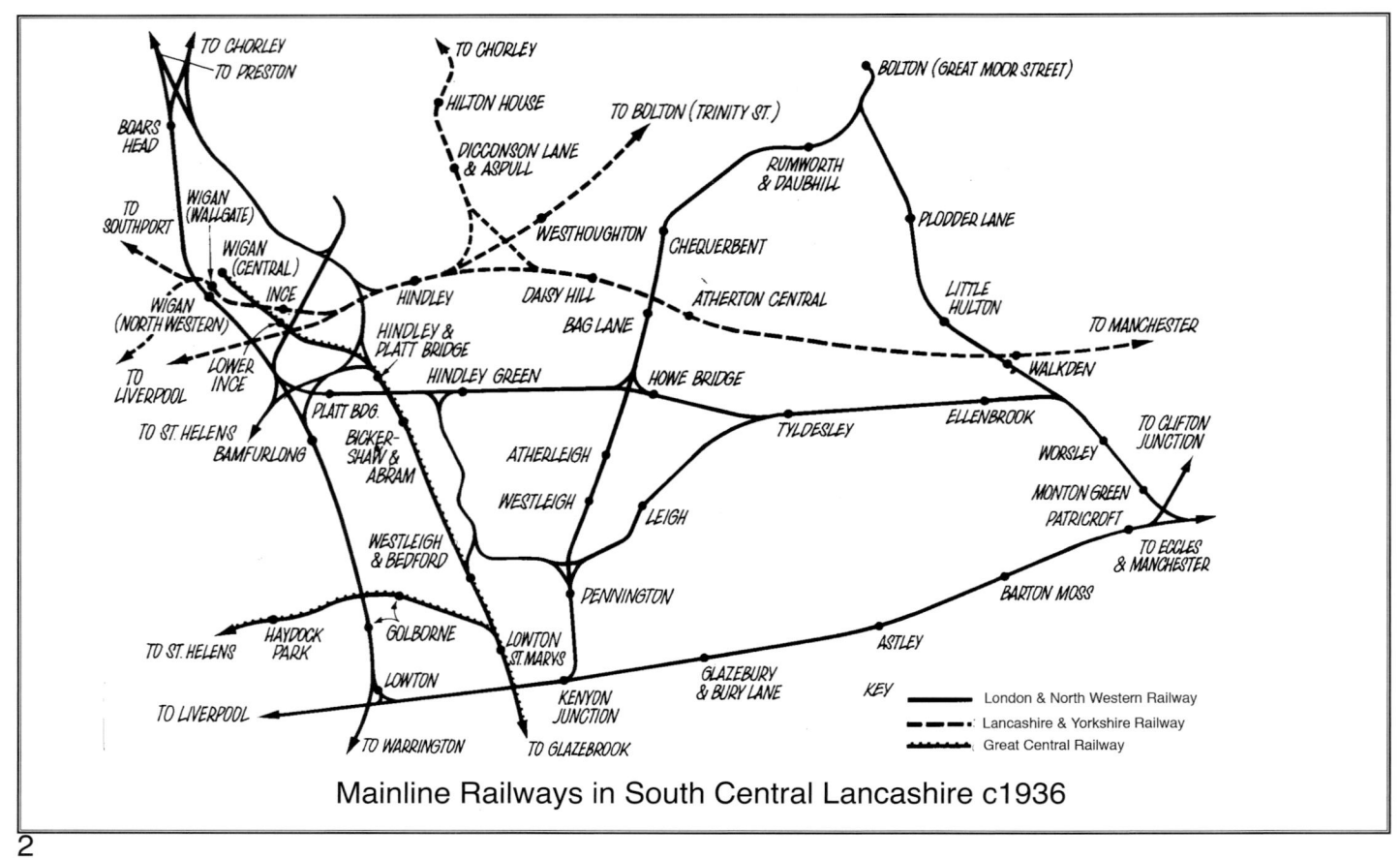

Mainline Railways in South Central Lancashire c1936

CONTENTS

	Page
Introduction & Acknowledgements	4
Wigan	5
Springs Branch Shed	9
Platt Bridge	17
Bickershaw Junction to Pennington	21
Hindley Green	36
Howe Bridge	40
Tyldesley	51
Ramsden's & Green's Sidings	61
Hough Lane	66
Ellenbrook	72
Roe Green Junction	83
Sanderson's Sidings	87
Worsley	93
Monton Green	97
The Black Harry Line	100
Patricroft	106
Eccles to Manchester	113
Tyldesley & Jackson's Sidings	129
Speakman's Sidings	145
Leigh	156
Pennington Junctions	168
Kenyon Junction	172
Timetables & Appendices	181
Bibliography & Abbreviations	189

INTRODUCTION & ACKNOWLEDGEMENTS

It is now over 18 years since the publication of my first book *A Lancashire Triangle Part One* appeared in print. In the intervening years it has become something of a collector's item and both the original edition and subsequent reprint have been unobtainable for some considerable time.

In 1996, when first printed, the process was to print from film. However, technology moves on and the digital age has taken over completely. The original film, having been destroyed, meant that the decision had to be taken either to reset the entire work in digital form or, print an entirely new book covering the same area. Given the fact that some of the original photographic material was no longer available due to a number of factors, not the least being that many of the contributors to the first imprint are no longer with us, I decided that a new work containing a complete set of previously unpublished illustrations, with but the odd exception, was the better option, despite repeated requests to reprint the original again.

The question then was, how much of the original text to use! All of it; part of it; or rewrite it completely? For the benefit of those who have been unable to obtain a copy of *Part One*, certain elements must be repeated in order to give accurate historical data; but for those who already have a copy and would like to see more photographs depicting the route, partial rewriting would seem to be the answer. Therefore, a combination of both aspects will be found herein.

Furthermore, I had decided remove the chapter dealing with the Bolton & Leigh Railway and cover only those railways which comprised the 1861 Acts i.e. the Wigan - Eccles-Manchester route, and the branch from Tyldesley to Pennington via Leigh, and its connection to the Liverpool & Manchester Railway at Kenyon Junction together with the various colliery railways and their mainline connections.

As an afterthought, a few pages are devoted to the 'Black Harry Line' which, even today, long after its demise, continues to be a talking point amongst railway enthusiasts for, if nothing else, the unexpected collapse of the tunnel through which it ran at Swinton.

I must express my sincere thanks to Gerry Bent, Eddie Bellass, John Ryan, Tom Pike, Ian Isherwood, Tim Oldfield, Peter Eckersley, Steve Carter Tony Oldfield and Peter Hampson who have provided so much material for inclusion. Special mention must be made of John Hall, now residing in Canada, who has made great efforts in scanning and sending over sidings details from his extensive collection of documents salvaged from B.R. in the 1960s which otherwise would have been destroyed.

I must also mention the late Jim Carter who has left a rich vein of railway images taken during his time spent working on the footplate, images which few can equal, let alone better. It was my privilege to have known Jim for a number of years and I was fortunate enough to obtain a number Jim's photographs after his untimely death. For me, those shots taken at, or near Jackson's Sidings, Tyldesley, are the most treasured, bringing back to life visions of the elemental railway remembered from my early years growing up around the mines and railways of the area.

Neither must I forget the late W.D.Cooper, 'Wilf' to his friends, who also has left us with a unique catalogue of the steam engine from the late 1930s until the passing of steam in 1968.

Jim and Wilf were often to be seen photographing the steam scene, be it on Shap or at Patricroft where Jim would manoeuvre engines in position for Wilf to capture on film. Wilf was a steam man through and through and never, as far as I know, for I visited him many times over the years, did he take any photographs of diesel or electric traction. He had occasion to visit relatives at Haydock and he would call at Leigh on his way home to Cabus in his 1965 Rover for a chat and a cup of tea. He was a gentleman of the old school and it pleased me immensely to be called his friend. In his own words, *we had much in common*.

Gordon Rigby and Ian Pilkington have, once again, offered their services as unpaid proofreaders and words are inadequate to express my relief at such assistance being so readily proffered.

Lastly, to all of those too numerous to mention who have provided snippets of additional information and photographs I express my sincere thanks.

All scales and dimensions are given in Imperial Measure.

D.J.Sweeney,
Leigh,
Lancs, 2015.

WIGAN

Plate 1. Wigan North Western in the 1960s as one of the B.R.Standard '9Fs' passes through with a through van train, possibly fish from Wyre Dock. The station, seen here as rebuilt in the 1890s by the London & North Western, would undergo another transformation in the early 1970s with the onset of electrification. *Author's Collection, (Alex Mann).*

The history of the route, as with most other railways in South Lancashire, is entwined with the development of coal mining in the area and a host of other industries that had been spawned by the industrial revolution.

Although a number of railways had been proposed in the Leigh, Tyldesley & Atherton Districts, in particular by the Lancashire & Yorkshire Railway, or their predecessors, none had come to fruition.

It was with some local elation therefore, that the 1860 proposal by the London & North Western Railway to construct a line of railway through the area was received. From Eccles, where a connection would be made with the former pioneering Liverpool & Manchester Railway, the line would run via Worsley, Tyldesley, Howe Bridge & Platt Bridge to Springs Branch, Wigan - Manchester Lines Junction - where it would join with the North Union Railway, (formerly the Wigan Branch Railway) which at this period was still, at least technically, independent of the London & North Western and would remain so until fully absorbed by the latter on 7th August 1888.

Included in the proposals was a branch to Pennington, via Leigh, connecting with the Kenyon & Leigh Junction's lines and a spur from Howe Bridge joining with George Stephenson's Bolton & Leigh Railway of 1828 at Atherton Junction. Both of these early railways, along with the Liverpool & Manchester Railway, had become absorbed by the Grand Junction Railway on 1st July 1845. On 16th July the following year the London & North Western Railway was formed by the amalgamation of the Grand Junction, Manchester & Birmingham and London & Birmingham Railways.

Not to be outdone by the London & North Western plans, the Lancashire & Yorkshire Railway again put forward proposals for a new route. This was to leave their line at Hindley, pass through Atherton, near to the cemetery, thence through the Shakerley Estate to re-join the Lancashire & Yorkshire lines at Pendleton. In fact this is similar to that later opened by the Lancashire & Yorkshire in 1888 from Crow Nest Junction via Atherton (Central) to Brindle Heath and in some measure the resurfacing of a much earlier proposal for a 'North' line of railway first mooted in the early 1830s following on from the success of the Liverpool & Manchester Railway of 1830. The latter objected to it most strongly, eventually forcing its abandonment.

Over the following months various news items appeared in the local press regarding the benefits to the populace that the railway would bring. Nearly all of those referred to, and gave favour to the London & North Western plans.

By March 1861 the London & North Western Bill had passed its final reading in the House of Commons and would shortly be submitted to the House of Lords and although their competing Bill had been rejected, the Lancashire & Yorkshire publicly stated their intentions to oppose the London & North Western Bill at every opportunity.

Petitions had already been sent by the inhabitants of Leigh and Bedford to Parliament in favour of the London & North Western proposals and further petitions from Astley and Tyldesley were to follow. Consequently the London & North Western Bill successfully passed through the House of Lords without, as it happens, any hindrance, the Lancashire & Yorkshire withdrawing their opposition to the Bill at the last moment having made a 'compromise' after negotiations which terminated in a 'Quid-pro-Quo' that it was said, *had no immediate bearings upon the railway accommodations of the district*. The Eccles-Tyldesley-Wigan and Tyldesley-Pennington Railway Bill received the Royal Assent on 11th July 1861.

The route of the railway was laid out by Elias Dorning, an engineer with considerable knowledge of the South Lancashire Coalfields. Contractors for the line were Messrs Treadwell & Co., the London & North Western engineer was William Baker Esq., and the works were to be completed in the spring of 1863 as per the terms of the contract. However, the vagaries of the British climate would put paid to that date and the railway was some eighteen months behind schedule when it finally opened.

The official opening was on 1st September 1864, with stations at Worsley, Ellenbrook, Tyldesley, Chowbent, Hindley Green and Platt Bridge, with Bedford Leigh on the Tyldesley-Pennington Branch. Chowbent became Howe Bridge in April 1901, Bedford Leigh became Leigh & Bedford in 1876 and finally Leigh on 1st July 1914. Bradshaw Leach on the Kenyon & Leigh Line became Pennington on 1st February 1877. Monton Green, between Worsley and Eccles Junction opened in November 1887.

Plate 2. Stanier 'Jubilee' No.45635 *Tobago*, is seen on the approach to Wigan North Western in the early 1960s with what appears to be a Euston - Manchester train if the coachboard is to be believed. Perhaps the lines into Manchester Piccadilly are blocked , but why this way? It could have been diverted via Winwick and the Liverpool & Manchester line into Piccadilly, or even into Victoria or Exchange Stations. It may have something to do with the electrification of lines into Piccadilly which would be nearing completion but it's certainly going the long way round if it's going to reverse at Wigan or Preston to take one of the former Lancashire & Yorkshire lines to reach Manchester!
Author's Collection, (Jim Carter).

REPORT FROM THE BOARD OF TRADE DATED 15TH FEBRUARY 1861.

Empowers the London and North Western Railway to make:

(1) A railway, length 12 miles 22 chains, from a junction with the company's Liverpool and Manchester Railway, near Eccles (Eccles Junction) to a junction with the North Union Railway, near and to the South of Wigan.

(2) A railway, length 3 miles 39 chains, from a junction with railway (l) at Tyldesley, to a junction with the company's Bolton and Leigh line, at its Bradshaw Leach Station; and

(3) A railway, length 25 chains, to connect railway(l) with the B&L (Bolton & Leigh) at Atherton, in the parish of Leigh, all in the County of Lancaster and to be completed within five years.

And for these purposes to apply the company's funds, and to raise further sums of £350,000 by new ordinary shares and £115,000 by borrowing.

Board of Trade March 1861.

The North Union Station at Wigan would be the terminus for the ex-Manchester local trains. Tyldesley, having the largest population along the route, and the greatest potential mining output thereby contributing greatly to the revenue of the railway, was the premier station on the London & North Western's branch from Eccles to Springs Branch Junction, and the junction for the branch to Pennington.

At the Manchester end, trains would start from Hunt's Bank Station (Victoria) until the London & North Western opened a new station, Manchester Exchange, sited at the western end of Victoria in 1884.

A number of colliery connections would be made for the exchange of coal traffic. On the Wigan - Eccles section these would, initially, be at Scowcroft's Sidings at Bickershaw, Chanter's Sidings at Howe Bridge, Atherton and Sanderson's Sidings at Worsley.

Over the next few years additional connections were made with Low Hall Collieries at Bickershaw c 1886; James Diggle's Westleigh Collieries at Hindley Green c1868; Swan Lane Collieries, also at Hindley Green c1865; The Westleigh Collieries of the Wigan Coal & Iron Co. at Howe Bridge West c1882; Tyldesley Coal Co., and Shakerley Collieries at Green's Sidings Tyldesley c1864/9; and Bridgewater Collieries at Ellenbrook c1871. On the Leigh - Pennington section the Astley & Tyldesley Collieries date from 1864, whilst Speakman's Sidings, Leigh were instituted about 1882/3.

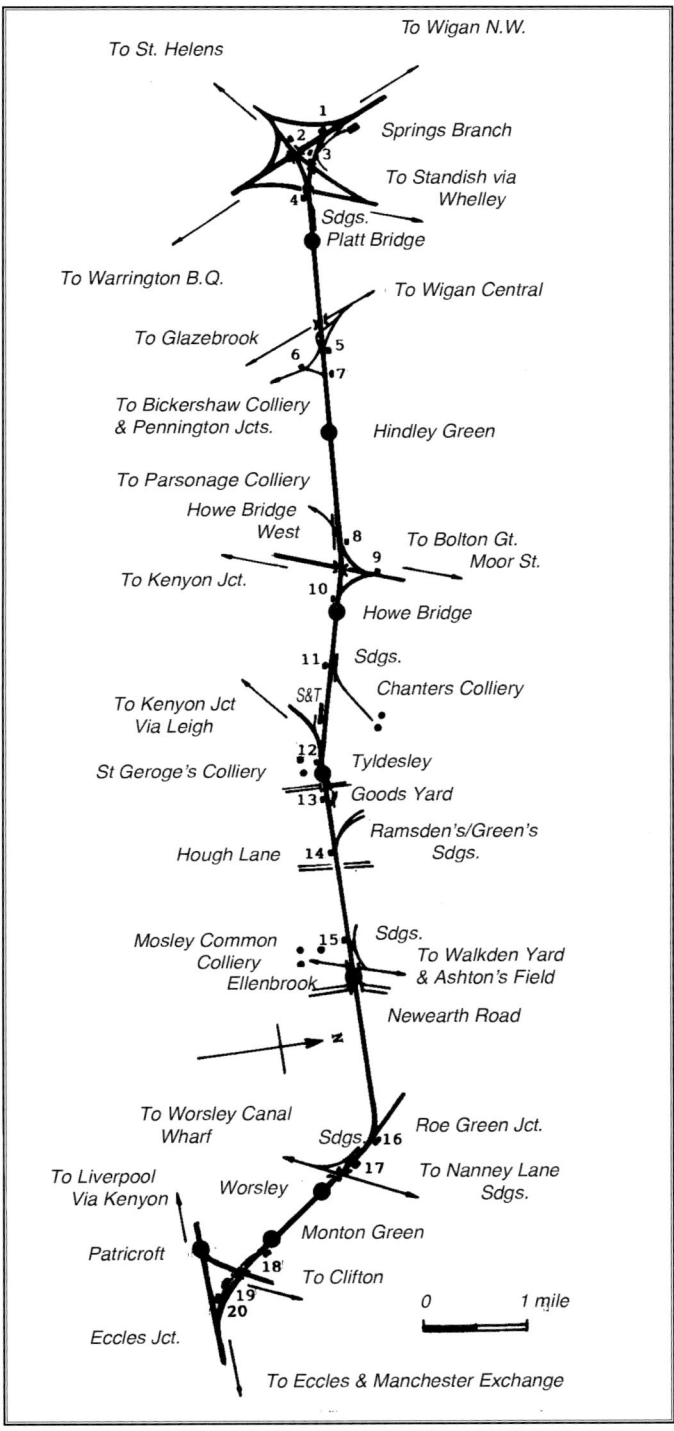

SIGNAL BOX KEY c1930

1	Springs Branch No. 1	11	Chanters Sidings
2	Fir Tree House Junction	12	Tyldesley No. 2
3	Cromptons Sidings	13	Tyldesley No. 1
4	Platt Bridge	14	Hough Lane
5	Bickershaw Junction	15	Ellenbrook
6	Hindley Field Junction	16	Roe Green Junction
7	Scowcrofts Junction	17	Sandersons Sidings
8	Howe Bridge West	18	Monton Green
9	Atherton Junction	19	Patricroft North Yard
10	Howe Bridge East	20	Eccles Junction

When the Wigan Junction Railway arrived on the scene with the opening of their railway from Glazebrook to Strangeways at Amberswood in 1879, it spurred the London & North Western into purchasing the Acker's - Whitley colliery branch at Plank Lane and by extending it northwards formed a new junction, Bickershaw, and by a southern extension to Pennington made a junction with the Kenyon & Leigh Junction Railway of 1831, thus allowing through running for traffic both ways, opening throughout in 1885.

Crompton's sidings connection to their collieries at Amberswood opened in 1864 and continued in use up to the early 1960s serving a nearby coke plant situated to the east of Warrington Road. If any mishaps occurred which prevented engine movements on/off shed via Cromptons, it was possible to come off at Springs Branch No. 1 end 'through the yard' working onto the loop lines.

Because of the steep gradient here, Crompton's box could not accept any train unless Springs Branch No.1 box also accepted it concomitantly. This was because of the close proximity to the main lines and any resultant overrun could have serious consequences. A heavy freight train approaching down the gradient would have the weight of perhaps 500 tons or more buffering up against the locomotive and on a wet, slippy rail, the engine's brakes would never hold the gathering momentum of all that weight.

Plate 3. A four car DMU takes the Up Goods line at Springs Branch. However, this cannot be a local service train as the Manchester-Tyldesley-Wigan service had ceased in November 1964. The destination blind says Rochdale; this implies either a diverted service from Wigan Wallgate due to engineering works or an accident or, as is more likley, refuelling. The new diesel shed at Spring Branch is built, having opened in 1967, but there are no steam locos on shed, as from 4th December 1967 it had closed to steam. There is however, a steam loco on the main line, the plume of smoke from which can be seen behind the signals. This narrows the date of the photograph to the winter of 1967/8.

Author's Collection (Alex Mann).

SPRINGS BRANCH SHED

The first engine shed in the Wigan area was believed to have been built by the Liverpool & Manchester Railway at, or near to Chapel Lane, Wigan in 1832. As the latter were working services on behalf of the Wigan Branch Railway who had opened their railway from Parkside East Junction to a station at Chapel Lane, it would seem to make sense to have an engine shed here.

The Directors of the Wigan Branch Railway agreed to a proposed merger with the Preston & Wigan Railway at a special General Meeting on 28th August 1833. The result of this meeting was the formation of the North Union Railway, the first between two Railway Companies to be sanctioned by a Parliamentary Act, incorporated by Royal Assent on 22 May 1834.

The North Union's Wigan-Preston line opened in 1838 and in September of that year, the North Union Secretary authorised the removal of the engine shed at Wigan to a more convenient location south of the Leeds-Liverpool Canal.

At what date the engine shed near Chapel Lane was removed is unknown, as is an accurate date for the first shed at Springs Branch, only that it was open prior to 1847 being brick built with two through roads. A turntable was provided which was located in the triangle between the New Springs lines and the main running lines and this is shown on the line plan of the North Union Railway c1864. On 9th December 1858, a shed was ordered to be built at Springs Branch and in the following May, the Chief Locomotive Superintendent, Ramsbottom, complained to the operating department of the London & North Western Railway that in effect the turntable as provided was not big enough for goods engines, pressing the Company to build a larger one, which he said would be a *great advantage*.

Evidently, little or no progress was made, for in October 1864, Ramsbottom again referred to the inadequate facilities existing at Springs Branch and that additional shed accommodation was urgently required, similar, he said *to the one now in progress at Ordsall Lane* which was to hold 24 engines. The present shed, it seemed, held only six engines when at least sixteen were in steam daily. The London & North Western Committee recommended enlargement at Springs Branch and a 'temporary' wooden structure was erected in 1864 located south of the two road (pre-1847) shed, which, complained Ramsbottom, was *worthless*.

Under the stewardship of a Mr. Worthington, the Committee made a more rational decision and in June 1867 presented a plan for a new steam shed on or near the site of the 'temporary' shed at Springs Branch, estimated at £12,500. Alterations to this scheme at the planning stage were to include a 64,000 gallon water tank.

By late 1868 the shed was still not complete and Ramsbottom recommended that the shed, planned to hold 24 locomotives *should be for forty now*. He goes on to say that *The original brick engine shed holds six(engines) only, is inconvenient and the present wooden shed is useless. There are twenty-five engines in steam and often ten extra at Springs Branch.* The Committee Members were unhappy about the extra £4,500 that would be required to enlarge the shed being built and referred the proposal to a 'Special Committee' who gave their approval to the extra works required in December 1868.

Plate 4. LMS 0-6-0 No.8309 is seen in steam at Springs Branch on 20th May 1938. This class of '2F' locomotives were built by Webb for the L&NW in 1873 and having seen 63 years of service when this photo was taken, looks to be in remarkably fine condition. It would later be renumbered to 23809, the new '8F' 2-8-0s taking the 8xxx series of numbers.

John Ryan Collection, (L.B.Lapper).

Plate 5. One of the ex-London & North Western 0-6-0 goods engines 'Cauliflower' No.28345 with a roundtop boiler at Springs Branch on 23rd May 1951. Note that the old No.1 shed to the rear is being rebuilt by the new owners of the railways. This was just one of a number of engine sheds to be rebuilt in the early post-war period by British Railways.
John Maconie Collection.

Plate 6. This 0-8-2T No.47887 of Bowen-Cooke design, first entered service in 1911 and at this period is one of only three that remained in service, the others being Nos. 47881 & 47884. It is seen alongside 28345 also on 23rd May 1951. *John Maconie Collection.*

Plate 7. A number of Class 'J10's were transferred to Springs Branch on the closure of Lower Ince Shed in March 1952 and were used on working the early morning workmen's services to Irlam from Wigan Central. No.65176 is seen at Springs Branch shortly after the closure of facilities at Lower Ince.
John Maconie Collection.

Plate 8. On 17th June 1967 '8F' No.48275 is seen in the company of B.R.Standard class '5' No.73071 laid up at Springs Branch. Trip workings to Howe Bridge West and Bickershaw were the preserve of Springs Branch crews and continued to be so until closure of Bickershaw Colliery in 1992. *John Ryan.*

Plate 9. The Class '2MTs' were introduced by the L.M.S in 1946 to a design by H.G.Ivatt, having a taper boiler, 5ft driving wheels and weighing in at only 47 tons 2 cwt, and intended for use on lines where heavier locomotives would be prohibited. The design was perpetuated into the B.R. era as Nos. 46000-46527. The later B.R. Standard design was virtually identical with modified B.R. fittings and introduced in 1953 with the running Nos.78000-78064, yet weighed in at over 2 tons heavier.

One of the L.M.S. built examples is seen having some attention at Springs Branch on 26th June 1950. *John Maconie Collection.*

The new shed, in the traditional building style with hipped roofs, opened the following year and had eight roads and, as it transpired, inadequate ventilation which was later rectified. This shed became known as 'No.1'shed and the two earlier sheds mentioned previously were demolished. However, some ten years later the allocation of locomotives at Springs Branch had increased to eighty or more as a result of the rapidly expanding coal trade. Therefore, in 1881, Locomotive Superintendent Webb sought approval for another new shed to be built alongside the 1869 building, apparently with more immediate success than his predecessor Ramsbottom had done. This second shed, also with eight roads, became known as No.2 shed and was built in the northlight style, much favoured in the use of industrial buildings, opening in 1882.

By the 1920s there were more than 100 locomotives at Springs Branch. In 1935 the shed was coded 10A under L.M.S. auspices, the principal shed in the area which included Patricroft, Plodder Lane, Preston and Sutton Oak (Lower Ince was added as a sub-shed in early B.R. days). The L.M.S set about a process of modernisation at many installations on the system and in 1935 new coal and ash plants were installed at Springs Branch, and in 1937, a new 100,000 gallon water tank. In the period after W.W.II., the LMS rebuilt No.1 shed in the reinforced concrete column-brick panel style, a pattern of construction much favoured by the LMS in the 1930s & 1940s when many sheds on the system were reconstructed in the drive for efficiency. During the rebuilding, No.1 shed was reduced to a six road, dead-end shed.

In 1955, B.R. re-roofed No.2 shed in the corrugated sheeting style, as were many more sheds now under 'New Management.'

Plate 10. A nicely posed shot of Stanier Class '5' No.45431 seen outside No.1 shed at Springs Branch in the mid 1960s. *Tom Sutch.*

Plate 11. Stanier 2-6-4T No.42462 is captured on shed at Springs Branch in the early 1960s with another unidentified member of the same class. Springs Branch worked a number of turns over the Wigan-Eccles lines including all the coal traffic originating off the Bickershaw Branch and traffic from Howe Bridge West Sidings. *Author's Collection (Jim Carter).*

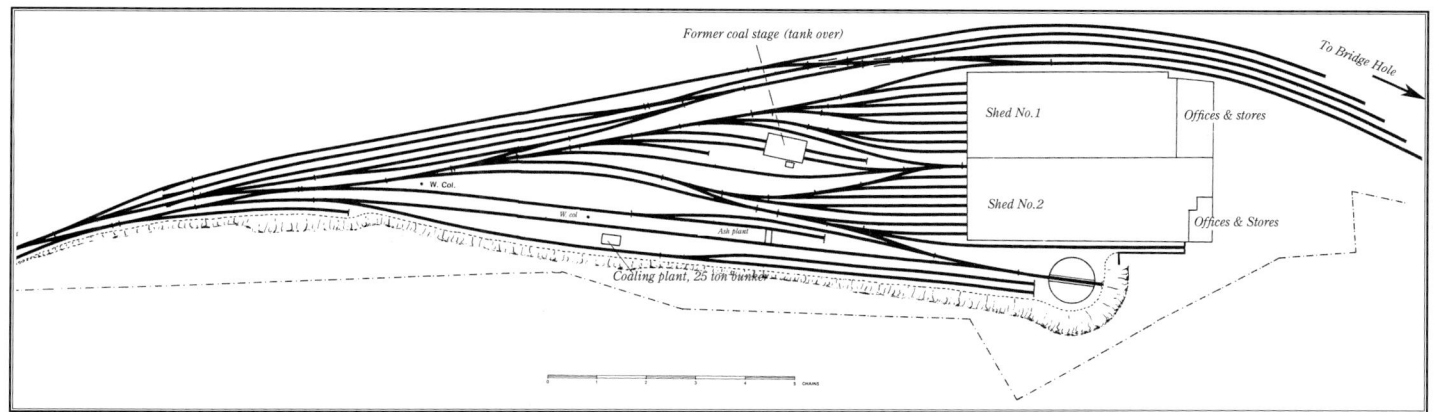

Fig 1 This layout of lines at Springs Branch Shed dates from the L.M.S. period and represents the final arrangement until the end of the steam era.

Plate 12. The new order at Springs Branch in the shape of type '4' No.47 366 seen in the early two-tone green livery outside the L.M.S re-built No.1 shed about 1974.

Tom Sutch.

Plate 13. This was the scene at Springs Branch on Friday 3rd June 1983 when a MGR train from Bickershaw Colliery for Fiddlers Ferry got itself into a heap of trouble blocking the up and down goods lines and ripping up the track on the Bickershaw line. One wagon has been re-railed and a second is about to be lifted.

Neville Bond.

13

Plate 14. An unidentified '9F' takes the Up Fast Manchester line at Springs Branch with a long van train c1966. Note that the loco has lost its number plate. On the left is Springs Branch No.1 signal box.
Author's Collection, (Alex Mann).

Plate 15. One of the Fowler Class '4' 2-6-4 tank engines, No.42374 is about to go on shed when photographed from Taylor's Lane Bridge on 3rd September 1965. The lines towards Tyldesley and Eccles, on a gradient of 1:49, can be seen to pass under the former Lancashire Union lines which had opened in 1869. The gate beyond the houses, left, once gave access to Fir Tree House Sidings and Crompton & Shawcross' mineral lines at Amberswood. The traffic movements here were controlled by Crompton's Sidings signal box out of shot on the right. *Eddie Bellass.*

Fig 2.

SPRINGS BRANCH
Manchester Lines Junction

AS AT 1950

CROMPTONS SIDINGS
TAYLOR LANE
UP GOODS
DOWN GOODS
UP FAST
DOWN FAST
TO ECCLES & MANCHESTER
CROMPTONS SIDINGS S.B.
PLATT BRIDGE 555 YARDS
TO SPRINGS BRANCH ENGINE SHED
ENGINE SHED SIDINGS
OVERBRIDGES
SPRINGS BRANCH NO.1 S.B 197 YARDS
TO WARRINGTON & CREWE
UP GOODS
DOWN GOODS
UP FAST
DOWN FAST
UP SLOW
DOWN SLOW

☐ SPRINGS BRANCH NO.1 S.B.

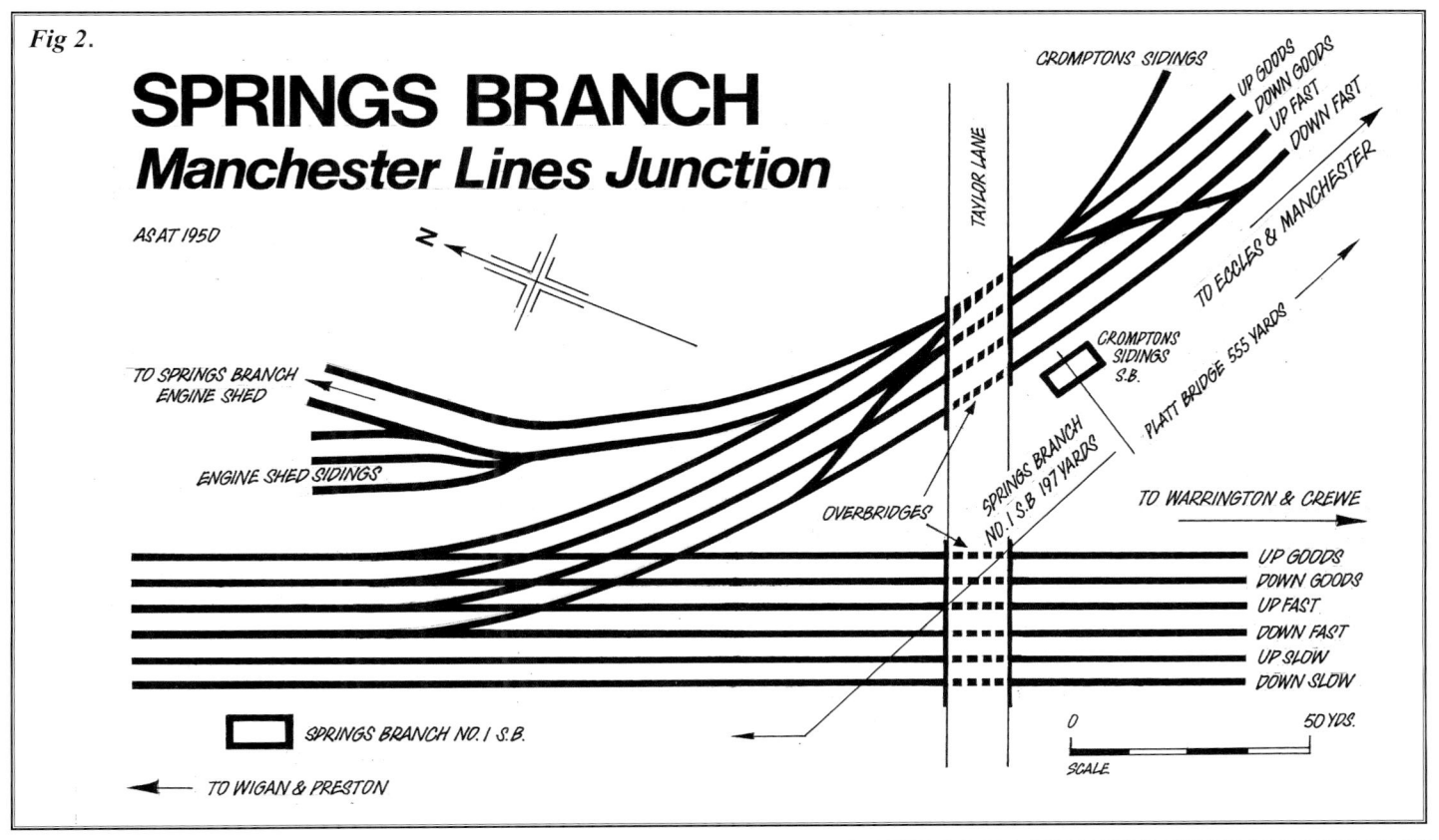

← TO WIGAN & PRESTON

0   50 YDS.
SCALE

Plate 16. By the time this photograph was taken c1971, the lines via Tyldesley to Eccles had been closed and only a single line remained to Howe Bridge West for colliery traffic from Parsonage and Bickershaw Collieries. A single lead junction with the Up Goods line is the only connection from the former through route from Eccles to the WCML.
Tom Sutch.

15

The branch to Crompton's Sidings connected with the Up Goods line opposite the similarly named signal box. This branch had, in fact, been constructed as a replacement for the original branch line from Amberswood Collieries which had connected with the North Union Railway some 600 yards south of Springs Branch, opening in the 1840s. These mines had been sunk by one Richard Blundell in 1842 but were eventually taken over by Crompton & Shawcross. Construction of the Springs Branch-Eccles route would cut across the branch as originally built west of Warrington Road, therefore this new outlet was provided at Cromptons Sidings.

The London & North Western would work some 800 yards of Cromptons branch, passing over Warrington Road by a bridge, to the exchange sidings at Fir Tree House. In the late 1870s a wagon works was established - Fir Tree House Wagon & Iron Co., alongside the branch, on the eastern side of Warrington Road. Wagon repairs were carried out at the works until shortly after W.W.II.

A coke cleaning and grading plant had been established alongside Fir Tree House Sidings in 1928 by the Liverpool firm of Messrs Hodgson. By the 1940s this was the only traffic being worked over the branch with trip workings every day by Springs Branch locos, coke wagons from the works deposited in Springs Branch Yard Sidings for marshalling. By 1962 these workings had ceased and the sidings agreement with Hodgson terminated.

' *Plate 17.* . By late August 1968 steam workings on Britain's railways had ceased, to be replaced in many cases by mediocre diesels. One of the more reliable designs was the type '2' later class '25' diesels. In 1971 type '2' No.5287 (no 'D' prefix) takes the single line enroute to Howe Bridge with empties for Parsonage Colliery passing Crompton's signal box which is in the throes of demolition. The Lancashire Union overbridge which spanned the Tyldesley lines here has already gone.
Alf Yates.

PLATT BRIDGE

In the years after the initial opening of the Wigan - Eccles route, Platt Bridge would be the recipient of more lines as the railways expanded to meet the demands of industry. In 1869, the Lancashire Union Railway which had been proposed in 1864 by Wigan Coal owners as a way of reaching East Lancashire markets was opened, crossing the WCML, and the Eccles route by overbridges. A short connecting curve was installed here, Fir Tree House - Platt Bridge Junctions, allowing freight trains from the Lancashire Union lines access towards Manchester and vice-versa. In 1888, the Platt Bridge Junction Railway was completed, connecting with the Lancashire Union at Amberswood West Junction and with the WCML at Bamfurlong, passing under the Eccles lines enroute.

The Bamfurlong Junction Railways Act of 1887 provided for burrowing lines from Bamfurlong Junction under the West Coast route and alterations to the recently completed Platt Bridge Junction lines. Further Acts of 1890 authorised quadrupling of the West Coast lines and construction of Bamfurlong Sorting Sidings which allowed a great deal of operational flexibility. All of these were completed by 1895 and it really was a time when the railways were the prime transport operators in the country.

Plate 18, right. This view at Platt Bridge Station probably dates from around the First World War period when women replaced many of the men who had joined up. An attractive looking girl, she poses alluringly between another railway employee, right, and a chap wearing clogs who is probably a miner, left. The adverts are of added interest. *John Ryan Collection.*

Plate 19. On an overcast day, a 'Britannia' Class 4-6-2, possibly No.70031 *Byron,* is signal checked at Platt Bridge on the low level lines with an express freight, having worked over the 'Whelley' lines from Standish Junction about 1966. Note that the engines nameplates have been removed, a common practice as steam workings began drawing to a close. This is a view from Warrington Road, Platt Bridge with the signal box on the Wigan - Eccles line just in view. *Mike Taylor.*

17

Platt Bridge Junction signal box was unusual in that it controlled traffic on two levels, the high level or Manchester lines and the low level or Whelley lines. On the high level were the Up & Down Goods and Main running lines between Crompton's Sidings and Platt Bridge with, in addition, the route to Fir Tree House Junction. The Goods lines were permissive and also worked wrong line, whereas the Main lines were absolute block. Both the Up and Down lines between Fir Tree House Junction and Platt Bridge Junction were permissive /wrong line worked. Adjacent to the Up Main line was Platt Bridge Siding which ran from Platt Bridge Junction towards Platt Bridge Station, this also controlled from Platt Bridge box and for a number of years used to stable the Royal Ordnance Factory (ROF) train stock. On the low level were the Up & Down Goods lines between Bamfurlong and Platt Bridge and the 'Up Flying Junction' line from Platt Bridge to Bamfurlong Junction. Any workings signalled on this line would join the Up Fast West Coast Main Line at Bamfurlong Junction, hence the term 'Flying'

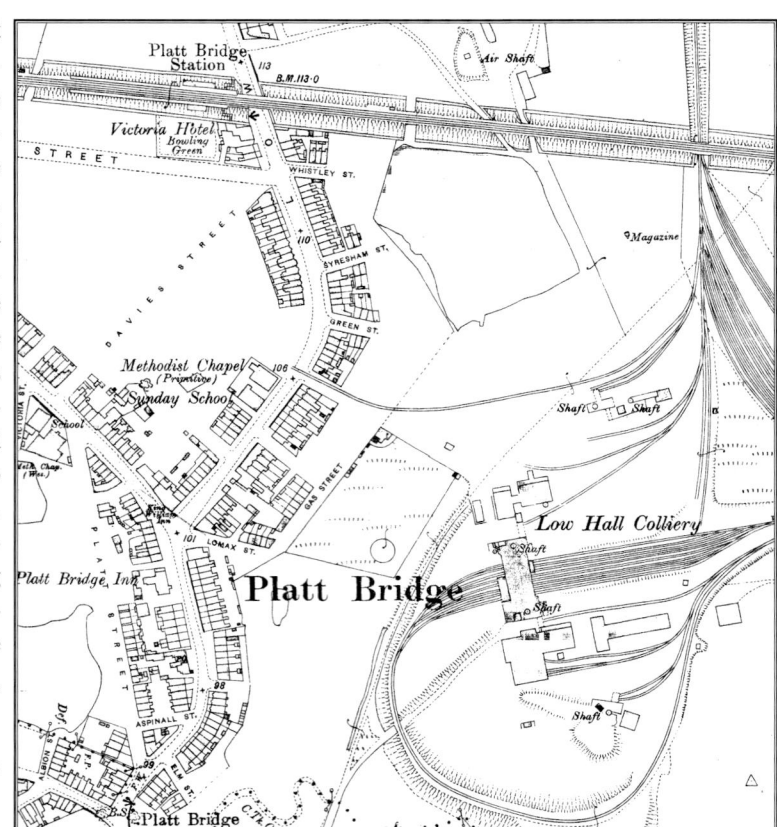

Fig 3, right. Low Hall Colliery and Platt Bridge Station are seen here from the 2nd series Ordnance Survey c1888/92.

Plate 20. Recent flooding events which have been headline news are, as can be seen from this photo on Lomax Street, Platt Bridge in August 1909, nothing new. However, the working classes of the age would certainly not have carried insurance for their contents and it is unlikely that the landlord would have offered any recompense. The floodwaters seem to have receeded by a foot or so by the time the picture was taken, the inhabitants marooned upstairs. The collieries in the background are part of the Low Hall complex. The location of Lomax Street can be seen in *Fig 3,* above.

John Ryan Collection.

Plate 21. Seen from the opposite side to *Plate 19*, a full view of Platt Bridge signal box as an unidentified 2-6-4 tank engine approaches from Wigan with a local service for Manchester Exchange in August 1964. As from November the same year this service was withdrawn. The original Platt Bridge signal box had been sited on the Wigan site of the Platt Bridge Junction lines and probably dates from the 1880s. This new box opened in 1961 and when the line to Howe Bridge was reduced to a single track it was demolished and the 55 lever frame from it was reinstated in Warrington Central box. *Eddie Bellass.*

Plate 22. This is the old Platt Bridge signal box seen in the early 1950s. It had begun to slide down the embankment being replaced by the modern B.R. flat roofed type as seen above. One of the L&NW G2/2A 0-8-0 freight engines is passing eastbound and appears to have one of the then, new, all metal, 16 ton mineral wagons in tow.
Peter Hampson.

Plate 23. Platt Bridge Station *c.* 1951 as viewed in the Wigan direction. At the end of the Up platform on the right is Platt Bridge Siding and in it some of the stock for the Wigan-Chorley ROF works service. Platt Bridge Station closed on 1st May 1961, the station buildings were later destroyed by fire.
Stations U.K.

Plate 24. Stanier Class '5' No.45425 is seen between Platt Bridge and Bickershaw Junction in September 1964 working the 16.20 Wigan N.W. to Manchester Exchange with two Stanier coaches and what appears to be an ex-LNER brake coach. Much of the old industrial Wigan is seen in the background, together with the terraced housing on Liverpool Road (A58). In the foreground are the lines to Low Hall Collieries.
Tom Sutch.

BICKERSHAW JUNCTION TO PENNINGTON

Bickershaw had become a junction in 1885 when the through route from Pennington South Junction was opened after the London & North Western had purchased the Ackers-Whitley private mineral railway from Plank Lane in 1881, extending it to form a junction with the main lines west of Scowcroft's Junction, the latter having had a much earlier connection. The line throughout was brought up to passenger standard and after the Pennington Loop lines were completed in 1903, for some years there were through trains from Manchester to Blackpool, Talbot Road. Bickershaw was also the junction for connections with the Wigan Junction Railways at Hindley & Platt Bridge station enabling through workings onto the Lancashire Union Railways Whelley Branch at Amberswood Junctions.

In 1883 the London & North Western Railway had applied for powers to construct their own line, The Hindley Junctions Railway, from Amberswood East to Bickershaw Junction. This railway was intended to run alongside, and be independent of, the Wigan Junction's line but the relative Acts as passed by Parliament obliged the London & North Western to meet the Wigan Junction Railways south of Hindley & Platt Bridge Station, at Strangeways East Junction, with running powers being granted to the London & North Western over the Wigan Junctions lines.

The new lines as authorised, consisted of a burrowing junction from Bickershaw, passing under the Wigan-Tyldesley line in the Down direction and a south to east curve in the Up direction, all being completed in 1886.

Plate 25. A second shot of No.45425 as the train approaches Bickershaw Junction. I used this train once each week when I was employed as an apprentice joiner, working on a site at Worsley Mesnes, Wigan. The contractors, Gerrards of Swinton, would let me leave the site early to attend night school, detraining at Tyldesley and then catch the 83 LUT bus service to home off Sale Lane. The train is crossing the former Wigan Junction's lines (Great Central from 1906) which ran from Glazebrook to Wigan Central. The next bridge just in front of the engine, is the Down Hindley Junctions overbridge, the Up line of which is marked by the line of fencing, far left. At lower left are the L&NW connections into the Low Hall Collieries from Bickershaw Junction, more of which can be seen in *Plate 24,* opposite. Although the Low Hall pits had closed some years ago this connection had been retained to give access to Maypole and Wigan Junction collieries, traffic from these often going out via Bickershaw. Scowcroft's dirt tip is prominent in the background.
Tom Sutch.

Through passenger express trains used the Bickershaw-Strangeways East - Amberswood East Junctions route from the summer of 1887 and the route continued to be used for regular passenger workings, particularly the Windermere 'Club' Express, until this train began to use the Lancashire & Yorkshire route via Walkden High Level and De Trafford Junction. Holiday specials consistently used this route to by-pass Wigan, latterly from 6th July to 7th September 1968. Great Central holiday specials from Sheffield and Nottingham to the Fylde Coast also worked the 'Whelley' via Manchester and Glazebrook.

Travelling eastwards from Bickershaw Junctions, Scowcroft's Junction is soon reached. John Scowcroft, who had a number of mines in the area, was quick off the mark in having a connection from their Engine Pit, sited south of the main lines, at the end of Coal Pit Lane, Hindley Green, to the London & North Western's line, probably from the opening of the line, certainly by 1865. Shortly afterwards, via an overbridge, their collieries north of the Tyldesley-Wigan main line also received rail connections. It was also possible to work, via Scowcroft's Sidings, onto the Ackers Whitley private railway as far south as Plank Lane. The rundown of Scowcroft's mines began in the 1920s, the last of their collieries, Grange, closed in 1937. Hindley Field Junction to Scowcroft's Junction closed on 27th December 1944.

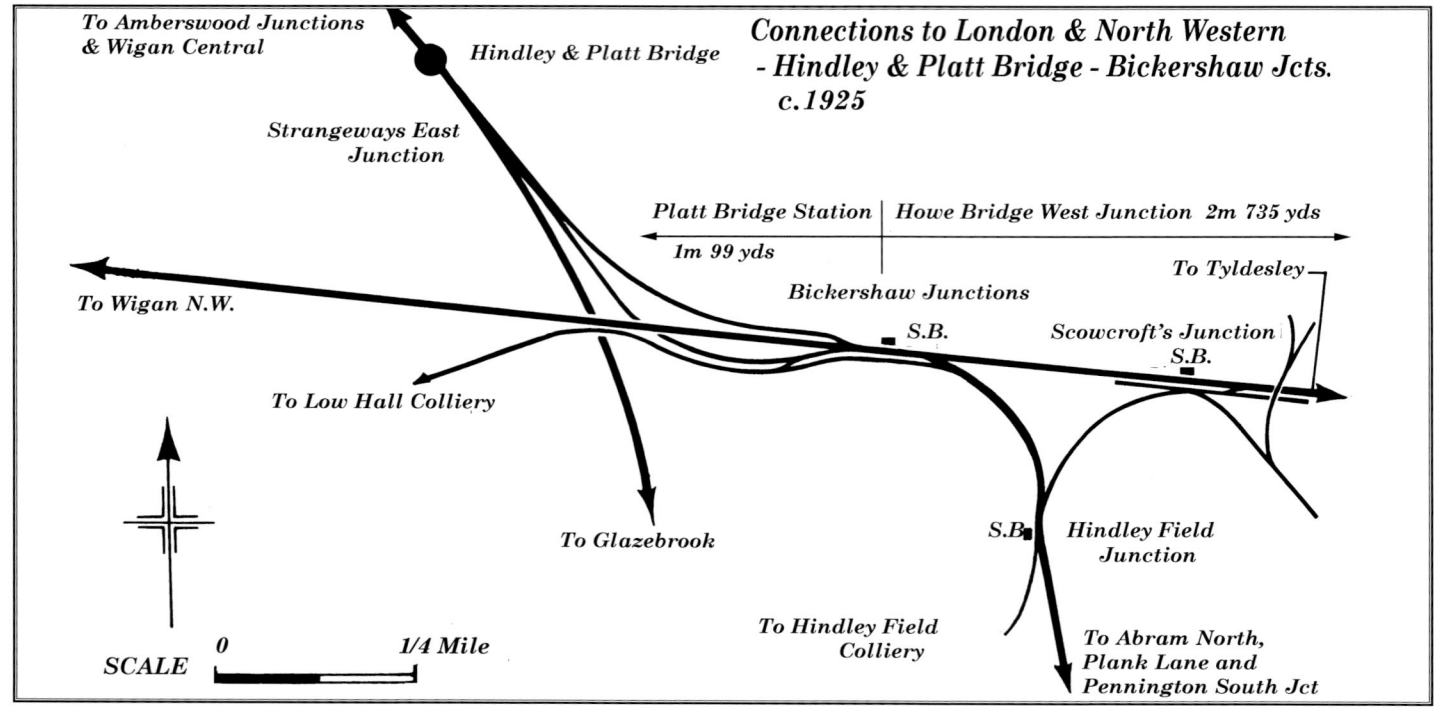

Fig 4. General layout at Bickershaw Junctions.

Plate 26. At Bickershaw West Junction in September 1964, an unidentified 2-6-4 tank engine reflects the setting sun whilst working a Manchester train. *Tom Sutch.*

Plate 27. An unidentified freight passes Bickershaw Junctions in 1964. Bickershaw Junction cabin, mostly hidden by the engine, was a Class '4' box and worked three shifts, opening 6am Monday until 6am Sunday. In the late 1940s about 80 trains per shift would pass through section during the morning and afternoon shifts.

The Great Central Shed at Lower Ince closed in 1952 and as a consequence, necessitated Bickershaw box being opened at 3.30am to work light engines from Springs Branch Shed to Wigan Central for the early morning workmen's trains to Irlam. Not a popular shift with the signalmen! *Tom Sutch.*

The sidings at Scowcrofts were retained after closure of Scowcroft's Collieries and used for storage of wagons due for repair at Earlestown and also for some traffic from Low Hall. Empties for Low Hall were often deposited in the sidings here on account of Low Hall having only two sidings which were regularly overflowing with 'fulls'. This being the case the Springs Branch trip locomotive would drop the empties at Scowcrofts, work engine and brake van to Low Hall Sidings, draw out the 'fulls' onto the Bickershaw curve, run round and right away to Springs Branch, deposit the 'fulls' returning engine and brake van to Scowcroft's Sidings to work the empties into Low Hall. Alternatively, from 1946 onwards, empties were usually worked in off the former Great Central route at Maypole Colliery and shunted by colliery locomotives to Low Hall or Wigan Junction Collieries.

At the latter end of its working life, 1940 onwards, Scowcroft's Signalbox was open two turns, 4pm-midnight/midnight-8am, with Sat Thurdays 8am-4pm/4pm-midnight.

Plate 28. Type '2' diesel No.D7635 is seen at Bickershaw Junction on 21st April 1971 and having worked empties to Howe Bridge West, is about to reverse down the Bickershaw Branch to collect a coal train from Abram North Sidings. At this period, track was single from Springs Branch to Howe Bridge. However, double track remained on the Bickershaw Branch until the new fast batching plant came into operation in 1985.
Ian Isherwood.

Trip workings to Howe Bridge West sidings would continue until 1974 when the remaining collieries in the area- Parsonage, Bickershaw and Golborne, were all connected underground and all rail dispatches of coal went out via Bickershaw. In 1984/5 a new rapid loading bunker had been erected at Bickershaw and the single track from Springs Branch relaid with welded rail throughout, eliminating the need for N.C.B. locos to work traffic to Abram North Sidings from the colliery head at Bickershaw for collection by B.R. This arrangement continued until 27th March 1992 when Bickershaw and Parsonage Collieries closed, although stocks continued to be moved for a few weeks afterwards. Golborne Colliery had closed in 1989.

23

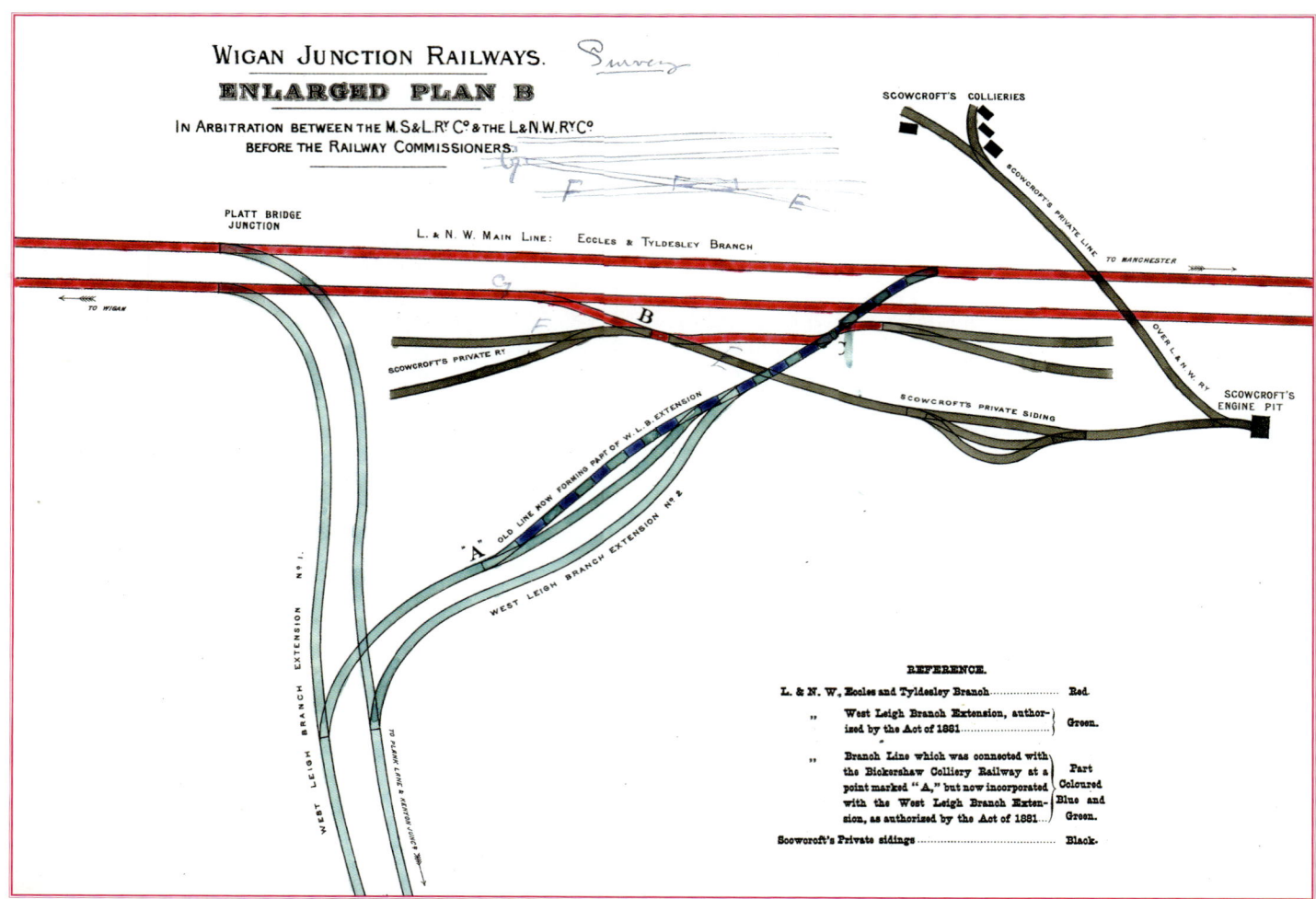

Fig 5. The original Scowcroft's Junction of 1864/5 and the later Bickershaw Junctions as planned, are shown here in this Plan of Arbitration between the London & North Western and Wigan Junction Railways. The former single line colliery branch of Ackers Whitley had previously connected with Scowcroft's Branch to gain a mainline outlet and, as already has been said, was purchased by the London & North Western in 1881 who doubled the track not only to Bickershaw as seen here, but also to Pennington South Junction, the whole opening in 1885. The Wigan Junction Railways had opened their line from Glazebrook as far as Strangeways in 1879, and to Darlington Street, Wigan, in 1883. The latter's railway is not shown here but was to the west of the North Western's lines.* The London & North Western's Hindley Junctions Railway plans of 1882 for lines parallel to the Wigan Junction s lines enabling connections with the Lancashire Union lines at Amberswood was not allowed by Parliament under the 1883 Act. Instead, they were obliged to make connections with the Wigan Junction's lines at Strangeways East. The Hindley Junctions Railway and its connections with the Wigan Junction Railways opened in October 1886 and the curve of the Bickershaw Branch as constructed to connect with the main lines were on a much gentler radius as shown in *Fig4*. It is thought therefore, that this plan must date from 1882/3, before the Bickershaw Branch line details were finalised and alterations to them, and also to Scowcroft's Junction, carried out, together with a connection to Low Hall Colliery from Bickershaw Junction.

Courtesy, John Hall.

* See **The Wigan Junction Railways** by the same author.

Plate 29. On 15th February 1992, Hertfordshire Rail Tours ran a special, *The Lune Ranger*, over the remaining single line to Bickershaw Colliery which is seen here on the inward leg worked by Class '47' No.47 489 *Crewe Diesel Depot*, with Class '20s' Nos 20 081/016 bringing up the rear. The train is seen east of Platt Bridge approaching Bickershaw Junction. *Steve Carter.*

Plate 30. Class '20s' Nos. 20 070/026 are seen at the head of a coal train from Bickershaw Colliery on 23rd July 1986 tailed by 20 016/177. Below is the Down Hindley Junctions trackbed from Bickershaw Junction to Strangeways East Junction. *Steve Carter.*

Fig 6. Scowcroft's Sidings c1916 quoting the original agreement date of 1865. *Courtesy, John Hall.*

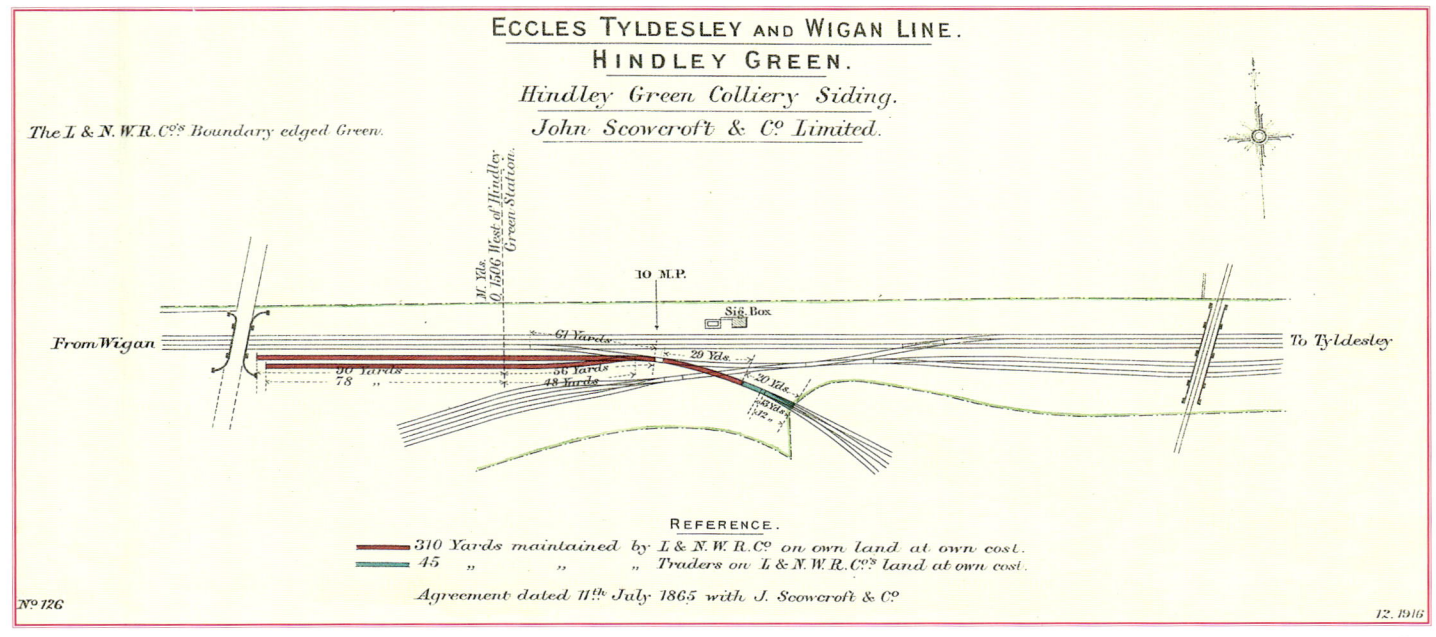

25

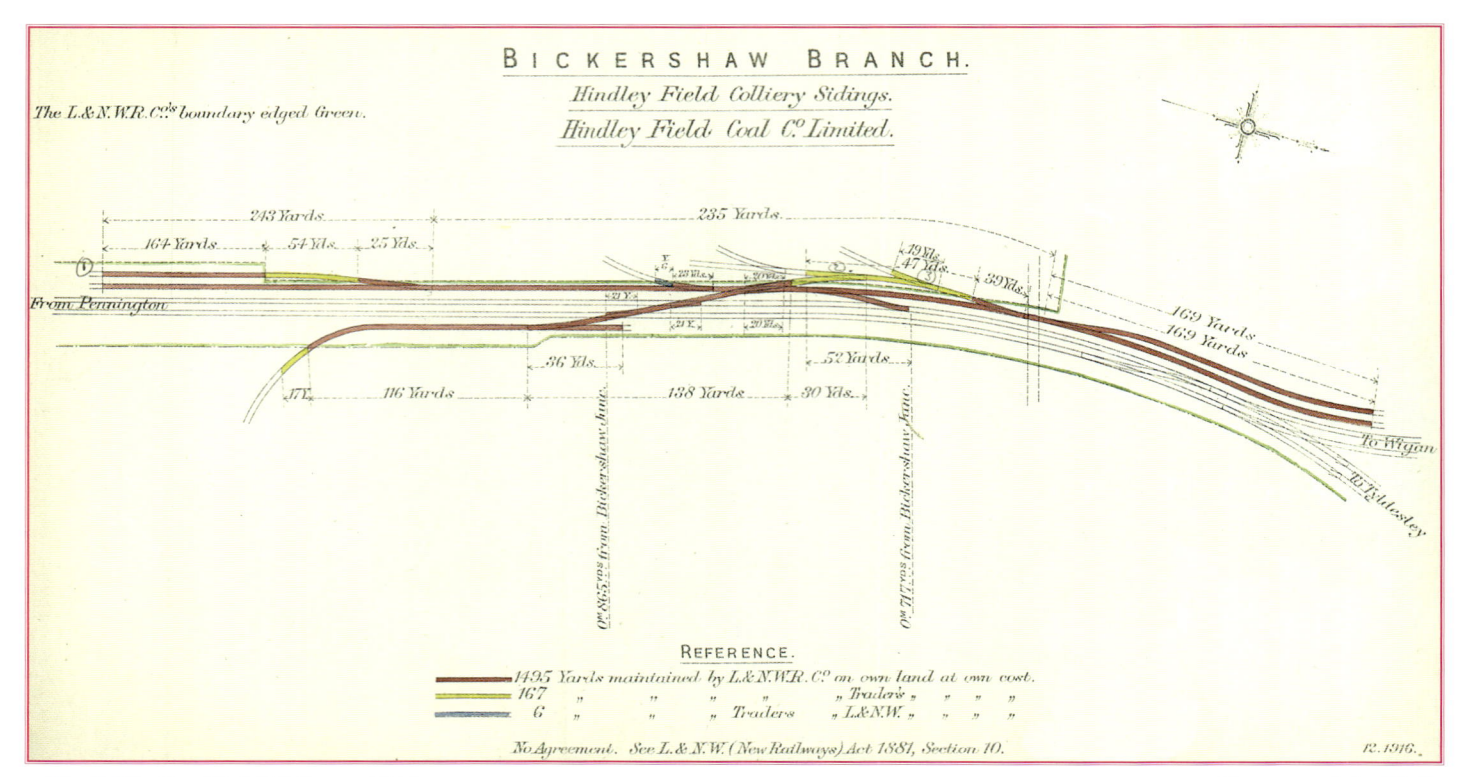

Fig 7. Hindley Field Sidings c1916. *Courtesy, John Hall.*

Plate 31. On a murky 8th January 1987 class '20s' Nos 20 071 & 20 157 are seen approaching Bickershaw Lane overbridge with empty MGRs from Fiddler's Ferry. The two brick pillars on either side of the tracks once carried a footbridge across the railway to Hindley Field Colliery which had mines on both sides of the railway. The colliery closed in 1927. See *Fig 7.* *Author.*

Plate 32. On 13th August 1966 the Wigan Area Railfans Society (WARS) ran a brakevan tour of lines in the Wigan Area begining at Springs Branch at approximately 09.25hrs, worked by Stanier Mogul 2-6-0 No.42986. After covering some 43 miles the tour passed through Hindley South to take the short curve of the London North Western's Up Hindley Junctions line to arrive at Bickershaw Junction around 14.45hrs where the engine was to run round and work the tour to finish at Wigan North Western. It is seen here at the top end of the Bickershaw Branch before detatching.
Brian Taylor, Courtesy of the Stanier Mogul Fund.

Plate 33. A pair of class '20s' Nos. 20 154 & 20057 are seen at the rear of a train of empties for Bickershaw Colliery having just passed under Bickershaw Lane bridge on 17th March 1992. Although the colliery had closed in March, coal stocks continued to be moved to Fiddler's Ferry until April. In the middle background is the Opencast Executive's batching plant alongside Bolton House Road, not in use at the time.
Steve Carter.

Plate 34. This view of 8th August 1959, is a from a point near Bolton House Road but looking towards the same track curvature as in *Plate 33* above, in the opposite direction. Behind the signal gantry is Bickershaw Lane, marked by the hedgerow. See also the track layout in *Fig 8*, page 29.
John Ryan.

Plate 35. A Class '50' at Abram North is a rarity indeed, but work Merry-go-Round trains they did as this example from the mid 1970s clearly shows. It is thought to be 50 005 ready to depart for Springs Branch, where the engine would run-round for the journey to Fiddlers Ferry. *Tom Sutch.*

Fig 8, below & opposite. Abram Coal Co's. Sidings are seen below and opposite as at 1916, much of which was still in evidence in the 1980s when steam haulage from Bickershaw Colliery to the Exchange Sidings at Abram was occasionally still used. This would all disappear with the installation of the new automatic loading plant and the relaying of the branch with welded rail throughout in 1985. *Courtesy, John Hall.*

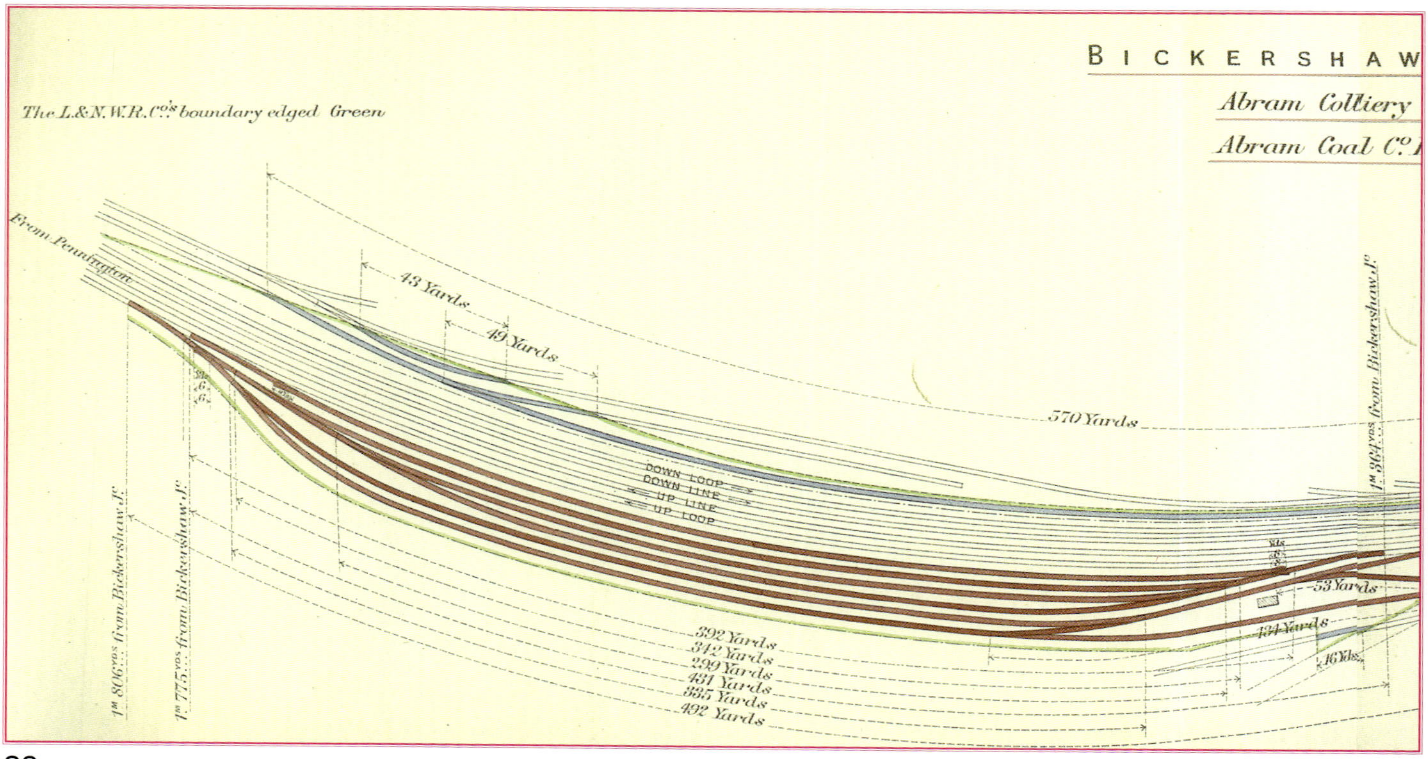

Plate 36. A couple of 0-6-0ST 'Austerities' get to grips with the gradient from Bickershaw Colliery to Abram North Sidings. The second engine is No.8 which had arrived at Bickershaw Colliery on 9th February 1977 from West Cannock Colliery and the photograph is believed to date from mid 1977 as by October the same year the number had been removed and the name *Bickershaw* added. However, by June 1978 the name had been removed and the No.7 added. The leading engine is unidentified but having a Giesl ejector fitted would have to be either *Warrior* or *Respite* at this date. *Tom Sutch.*

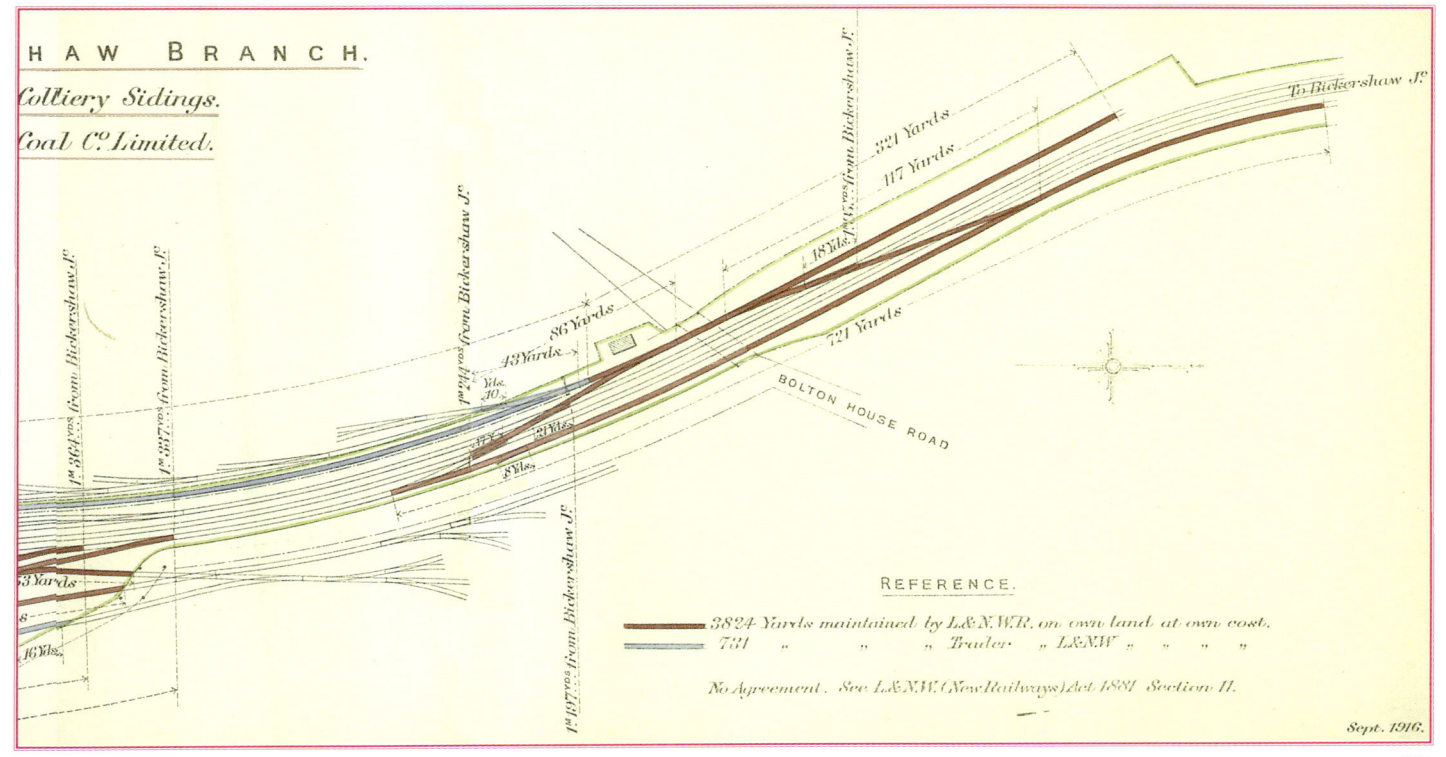

29

Plate 37. Ex-London & North Western G2/2A class No.48942 pauses alongside Abram North Signalbox on 8th August 1959 and at the request of the photographer, the signalman poses with the driver and fireman, a unique moment in the industrial history of this railway. The signalbox was sited opposite Bolton House Road, denoted by the line of fencing seen between the guards van and signalbox.

At the time the engine was shedded at '8C' Speke Junction. *John Ryan.*

Plate 38. Class '60' No.60 061 *Alexander Graham Bell* at the rear of a MGR train for Fiddlers Ferry seen on the approach to Abram North on 27th March 1992 with the mid afternoon departure from Bickershaw. Winter Hill broods in the background. *Author.*

Plate 39. During track laying operations when welded rail was laid between Springs Branch Junction and the colliery yard, 0-6-0 shunter No. 08 925 prepares for the return journey to Springs Branch with a short ensemble of stock on 8th March 1985 and is seen at Abram North.

In the left back ground is the Opencast Executive's dispatch plant for the Bickershaw opencast site operational for about ten years, last being used to store loaded MGR wagons during the 1984/5 miners strike. *Author.*

Plate 40. 'Austerity' 0-6-0ST No.7, HE/3776/1952, giving an impressive display of steam power climbing the bank from Bickershaw Colliery towards Abram North Sidings with loaded MGR wagons on 1st July 1983. Although the diesel 0-6-0s were here at the time they were often out of service for one reason or another. Before the new automatic loading plant was opened in 1985 the colliery locomotives worked the coal to Abram North Exchange Sidings for collection by B.R. *Author.*

Plate 41. On 1st March 1969 'Austerity' *Rodney*, HE/3695/1950, fitted with a Giesl ejector, is photographed in the pit yard at Plank Lane with a rake of 16 Ton minerals.

The driver is thought to be Harold Gillibrand.

John Ryan.

31

TIME		REASON FOR STOPPAGE	RECTIFICATION WORK CARRIED OUT
STOP	START		
9	21	TRAIN IN 1ST	
10	40	TRAIN OUT	WEIGHT — 1456-16
		BUNKER FULL	
13	35	TRAIN IN 2ND	
15	00	TRAIN OUT	WEIGHT — 1456-44
		BUNKER FULL	
04	39	TRAIN IN 3RD	
06	14	TRAIN OUT	WEIGHT — 1453.30
		BUNKER EMPTY	

Operational Log No. 22098. Disposal Point: Bickershaw. Date: 27/3/92.

Fig 9. The loading log for Bickershaw - Fiddler's Ferry M.G.R turns on 27th March 1992. These would have been some of the last scheduled trains to be loaded, although a few, as requested trains, ran in April to remove existing stocks.
Steve Carter.

Fig 10, below & opposite. This London & North Western outline of the Bickershaw complex shows the full extent of lines between Park Lane and the Leeds-Liverpool Canal, Leigh Branch. At bottom left is the connection to the newer shafts which had been sunk on the northern bank of the canal in more recent years, five in total sunk between 1872 and 1914, as opposed to those further north which had been leased to Hayes & Johnson - trading as the Abram Coal Co.Ltd. The main lines to Pennington Junctions cross, firstly, the marshalling Sidings, secondly, Crankwood Road where part the southern bridge abutment is still in situ, and thirdly, the Leeds-Liverpool Canal. Also shown is the location of the short-lived Plank Lane Station. On the far right is the connection to the Wigan Juction Railways at Westleigh & Bedford.
Courtesy, John Hall.

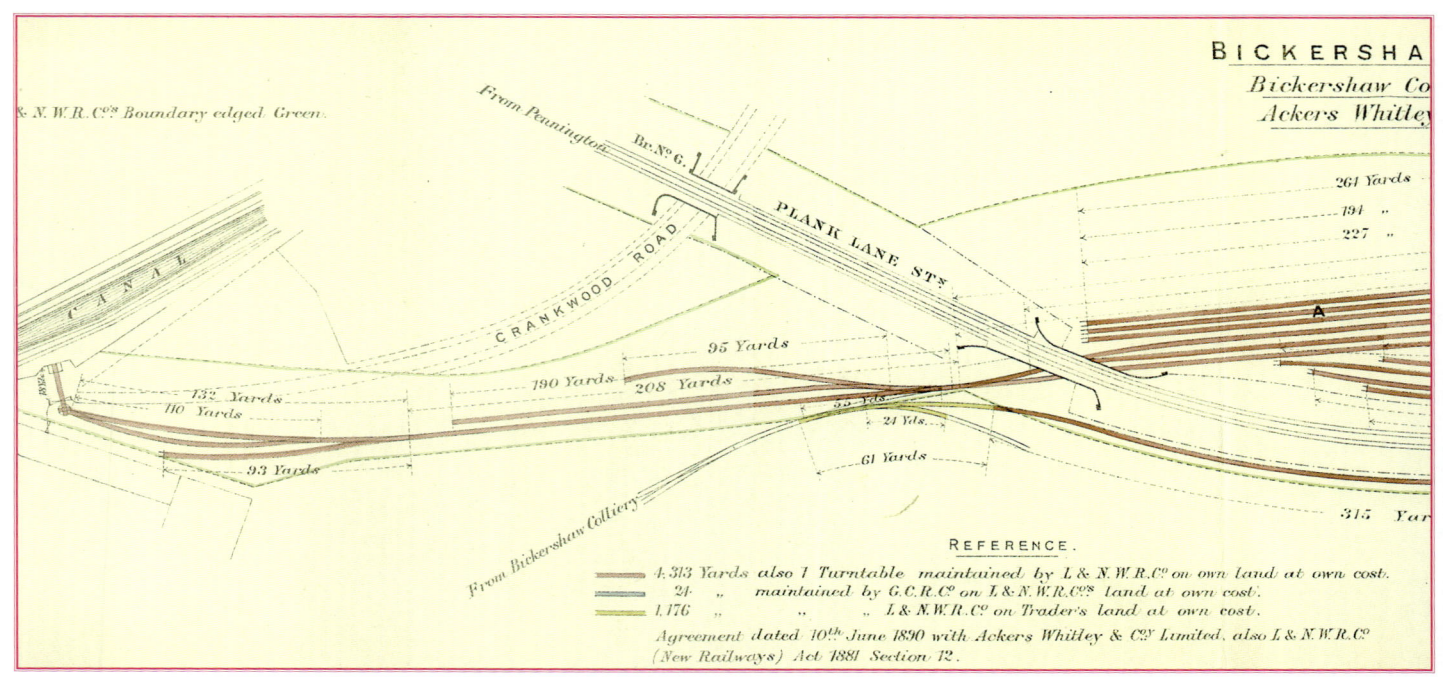

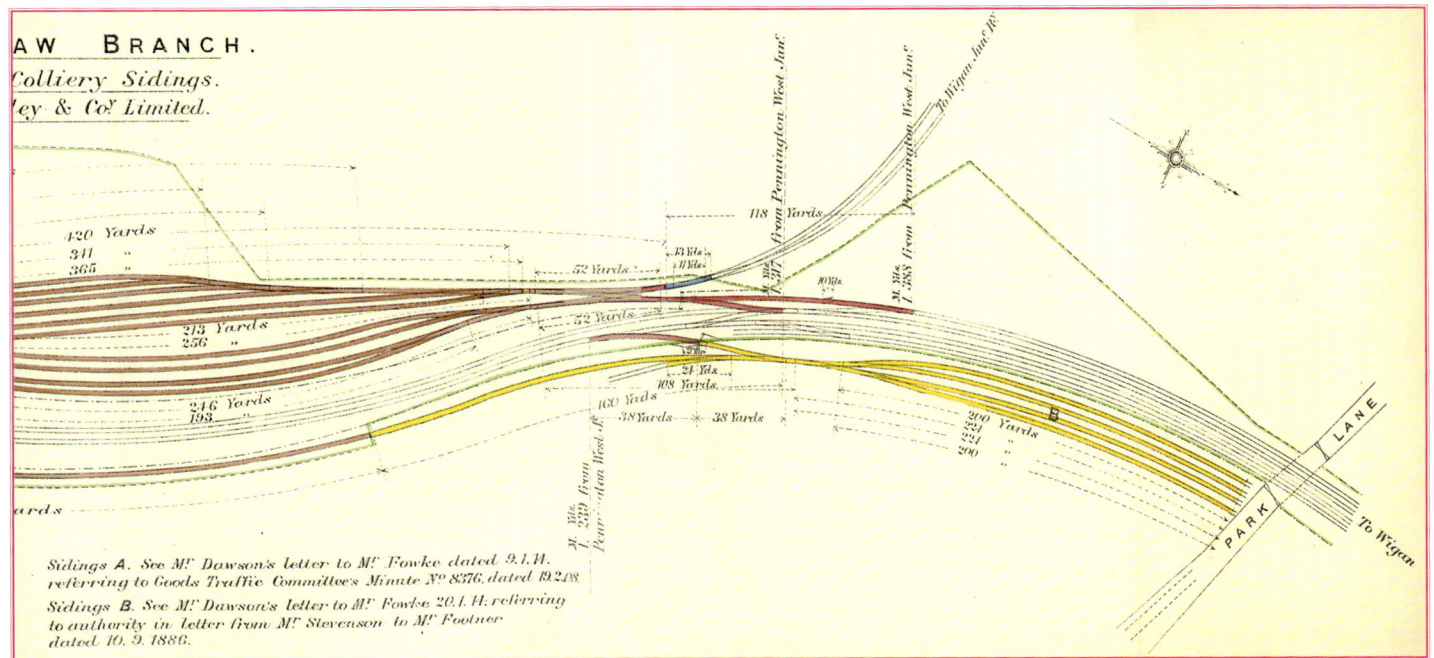

Plate 42. This undated photograph of Ackers Whitley & Cos. coal office is probably early twentieth century. The houses in the background are those on the north side of Plank Lane with the office itself, on Bickershaw Street. Behind the stone wall is a van on the railway tracks which looped round from the screens which were then sited between the canal and Plank Lane, still shown on the 1925 O.S. Revision. House building commenced on the Bickershaw Colliery site in 2015 eliminating any lingering traces of mining carried out here for close on two centuries.   *John Ryan Collection.*

Plate 43. This is the first shot of Bickershaw Colliery signal box I have ever come across and whilst not the best of images one that deserves inclusion if only for its rarity. The date is August 1959 looking south towards the colliery. The London & North Western lines to Pennington pass on the far side of the box. Can you imagine passenger trains using this route! It must have been a real voyage of discovery, a moonscape rather than a landscape. What were the thoughts of the passengers as their train rocked and rolled its way over these lines. They would certainly have seen some interesting mining history! *John Ryan.*

Plate 44. The two 0-6-0 diesel shunters *Western King* and *Western Queen* are seen at the end of the single track at Bickershaw Colliery on 23rd July 1986, now effectively out of use with the new batching plant being in operation.

These two locomotives were built by G.E.C at their Vulcan Works, Newton-le-Willows in 1979, works Nos 5479 & 5480. *Steve Carter.*

Plate 45. This is the view at Bickershaw Colliery as seen from the top of the loading bunker on 31st March 1992. Prominent are the 1930s built screening plant and the 1950s two road engine shed. Beyond the colliery complex the swing bridge at Plank Lane is visible, opposite which is the now demolished Britannia Inn.

Steve Carter.

Plate 46. A view of Plank Lane canal and bridge from the early Edwardian period. From the 1870s the mining activities of Ackers-Whitley & Co. were concentrated on the northern bank of the Leigh Branch of the Leeds-Liverpool Canal. This view from the south side of the canal shows the first of five shafts to be sunk here whilst the canal itself still has the lock in situ and the original bridge. By 1910, this would all change as subsidence necessitated the removal of the lock and the first, hand operated, swing bridge together with a new footbridge for pedestrians. Today's view is quite different as all the buildings here have gone and housing is being built between the canal and Plank Lane. *John Ryan Collection.*

Plate 47. The Locomotive Club of Great Britain (L.C.G.B) North-West Branch, ran their *South Lancashire Limited Railtour* on 21st September 1963 which included traversing the whole of the Bickershaw Branch from Bickershaw Junction on the Tyldesley route, through Pennington South Junction and onward via Kenyon to Parkside East Junction and back towards Wigan. Here the special, hauled by '8F' No.48178 runs alongside Leigh Flash near Pennington West Junction. Has the chap nearest camera got a migraine or is he concerned that the train might not make it to Kenyon over this decrepit stretch of railway? *John Ryan.*

Plate 48. Having traversed the perimeter of Leigh Flash without mishap, the L.C.G.B. special is about to pass under the Down Pennington Loop line, opened on 2nd June 1903 for freight and on 1st October for passengers when the London & North Western opened their new station at Plank Lane, allowing through services via Leigh including a Manchester Exchange-Blackpool service. Plank Lane station though was short-lived, closing in February 1915.

Regular passenger services via the Pennington Loops ceased as from 4th May 1942. However, holiday specials from Tyldesley and Leigh to Blackpool continued to use this route until the closure of Pennington East signal box on 28th October 1953; Pennington West having closed on 26th August 1951. Southbound coal traffic from Bickershaw Colliery used this route until September 1965. *John Ryan.*

35

HINDLEY GREEN

James Diggle, who owned a number of mines in the Westleigh area, had been instrumental in deciding the site of Hindley Green Station. His personal intervention in meetings with the directors of the London & North Western Railway in 1864 resulted in this location being chosen for its construction. There seems little doubt that it would have been extremely convenient for his personal use, being only a short distance away from his residence at Hindley Green Hall.

Diggle had arrived from Bury to manage Westleigh (Higher Hall) collieries in 1847 on behalf of the then owner John Hall, later becoming a partner of Hall and eventually, in 1858, outright owner. The colliery railway, originally narrow gauge, was converted to standard gauge c1864/5 and extended northwards to make a connection with the L&NW west of Hindley Green Station, provided for under an agreement of 25th July 1868.

Previous to the arrival of the Wigan-Tyldesley- Eccles branch, Westleigh Collieries had dispatched their coals to a wharf on the Leeds-Liverpool Canal, Leigh Branch, south of Firs Lane where discharge facilities were in place. In 1866 James Diggle sunk a new mine alongside his railway extension near to what was then Owen's Farm on Bickershaw Lane which it crossed on the level. This colliery was, however short lived, closing in 1877.

As a slight digression, when, as an apprentice joiner in the 1960s, I attended day release college and in the same class was another apprentice who then lived at Owen's Farm with his mother. Apparently, they never had to buy household coal as it was readily available near the site of the 1866 shaft, outcropping at the surface.

James Diggle died in 1880 and his mines offered for sale at auction, but with no immediate buyers, they were worked by his executors until sold in March 1884 to Mr. James Grundy and partners of Bickerstaffe who then worked the mines as the Westleigh Colliery Company.

By 1885, the colliery railway, always known as the Diggle's Branch, had been extended southwards towards Pennington Junction from the wharf at Firs Lane, to the rebuilt and extended Bickershaw Branch, formerly the Ackers-

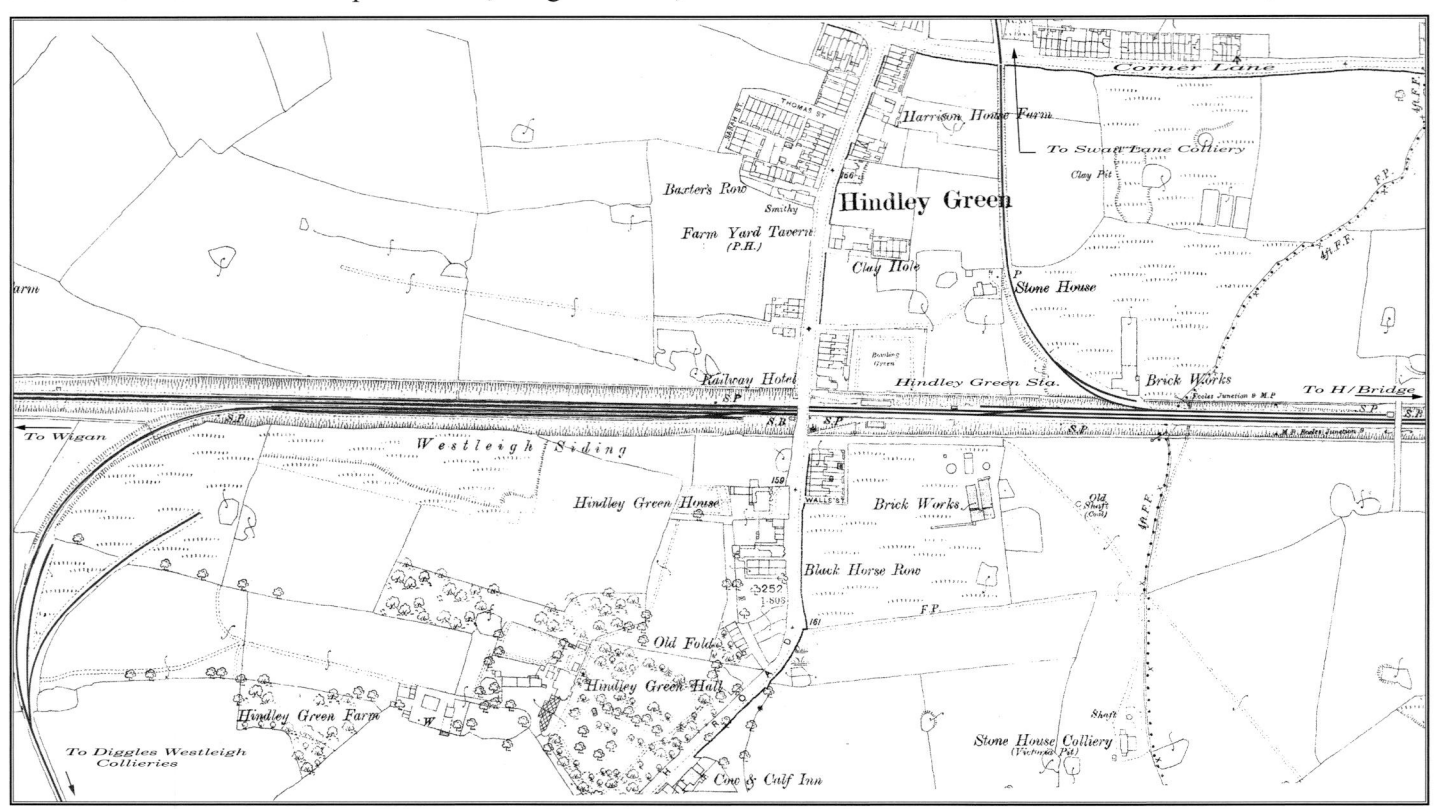

Fig 11. This is the Ordnance Survey from the second series c1888-92 showing Hindley Green Station and Diggles Westleigh Sidings connection with the London & North Western from his mines at Higher Hall and Lower Hall Collieries at Westleigh. The branch line east of the station is that to Swan Lane Colliery which crossed Corner Lane on the level. The trackbed eastwards from the station site is walkable although many, if not all of the bridges have been removed.

Plate 49. Hindley Green Station is seen here about 1950 looking East towards Howe Bridge. The station buildings seem to be in a reasonable state of repair and the embankments well tended and strikingly better than can be seen in *Plate 50.*   *Author's Collection.*

Whitley colliery line, which had been purchased by the L&NW in 1881. In 1903, construction of the Pennington Loop Lines necessitated alterations to the colliery branch.

The last of Diggle's collieries closed in the late 1930s but the sidings at Hindley Green remained for some years. At the Pennington end, Diggle's Branch, south of the canal, was retained for cripple storage and was still in use in the 1960s.

To the east of Hindley Green Station there had been a connection to collieries in the Swan Lane, Hindley area by a ¾ mile private railway under an agreement of 2nd December 1864 between the owner John Johnson and the L&NW. The branch crossed Corner Lane, near its junction with Atherton Road, on the level, immediately north of Hindley Green Station. Noticeably, No. 853 Corner Lane, Hindley Green, which was built after the branch line to Swan Colliery, has a skewed gable end which can still be seen to this day, matching the angle at which the line crossed over Corner Lane.

In 1874, nearby Long Lane Colliery and its brickworks were taken over by Edward Johnson, to whom Swan Lane collieries had passed in 1869. E. Johnson was declared bankrupt in 1886 and his assets came into the possession of one Moses Morris, trading as Swan Lane Brick & Coal Company. In the early 1890s, Morris sank the short lived Taylor Pit alongside the branch line just north of Corner Lane personificated in today's nearby Taylor Road. All of these concerns used the same mainline connection.

The colliery at Swan Lane closed in 1893 and the firm concentrated their efforts at Long Lane Colliery where another shaft had been sunk, opening in January 1897. In the interim, Moses Morris had set up the Swan Lane Nut & Bolt Works on the site of Swan Lane Colliery, probably in some of the outbuildings as the shafts here remained.

Morris had some financial problems and in 1899 Long Land Colliery was put up for sale. However, the nut & bolt works was retained as a going concern by Morris.

The new owners of Long Lane Colliery traded as the Swan Lane Brick & Coal Co. Ltd; and the sidings schedule records that a new agreement between the L&NW and Swan Lane Brick & Coal Co. Ltd; in respect of the mainline connections was signed on 16th September 1901. Further financial problems though brought about the closure of Long Lane Colliery and Brickworks in 1905.

A new company, Swan Lane Collieries Ltd; was registered in 1910 with the intention of re-opening Long Lane

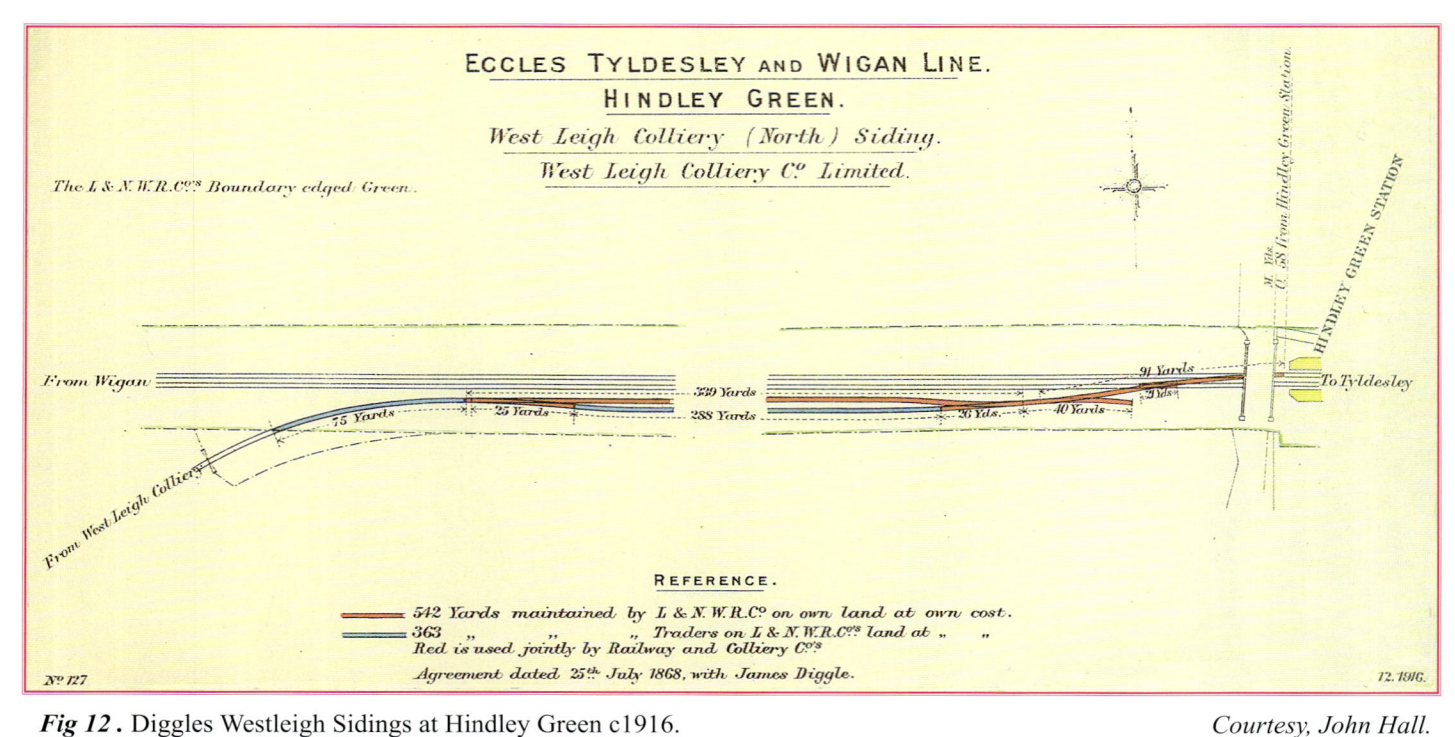

Fig 12. Diggles Westleigh Sidings at Hindley Green c1916. *Courtesy, John Hall.*

colliery, but a change of plan saw the older Swan Lane Colliery re-opened instead, the sidings agreement being transferred to them on 4th August 1911. The 0-6-0 locomotive *Rosneath*, in the possession of Unsworth & Cowburn, another local mining concern who had worked traffic on behalf of Swan Lane Nut & Bolt Works for a period, was purchased by the new company and a second engine, also an 0-6-0, *Arniston*, which latterly had worked at Bispham Hall Colliery, was purchased in 1922.

Swan Lane closed for good in 1927, being dismantled in 1929. Both the above engines were sold on, *Arniston* to the Brynn Hall Colliery Co; and *Rosneath*, firstly to contractors building a new dock for Lever Brothers at Bromborough and in the 1930s used on the construction of the A580, East Lancashire Road by contractor Sir Lindsay Parkinson.

The platforms at Hindley Green Station were accessed from each side of the road-over bridge on Leigh Road, the

Plate 50. A view eastwards at Hindley Green Station in 1964 as an unidentifed Stanier Class '5' calls with a Manchester Exchange-Wigan local train. The mill and mine chimneys of Atherton can be seen in the background.
Eddie Bellass.

38

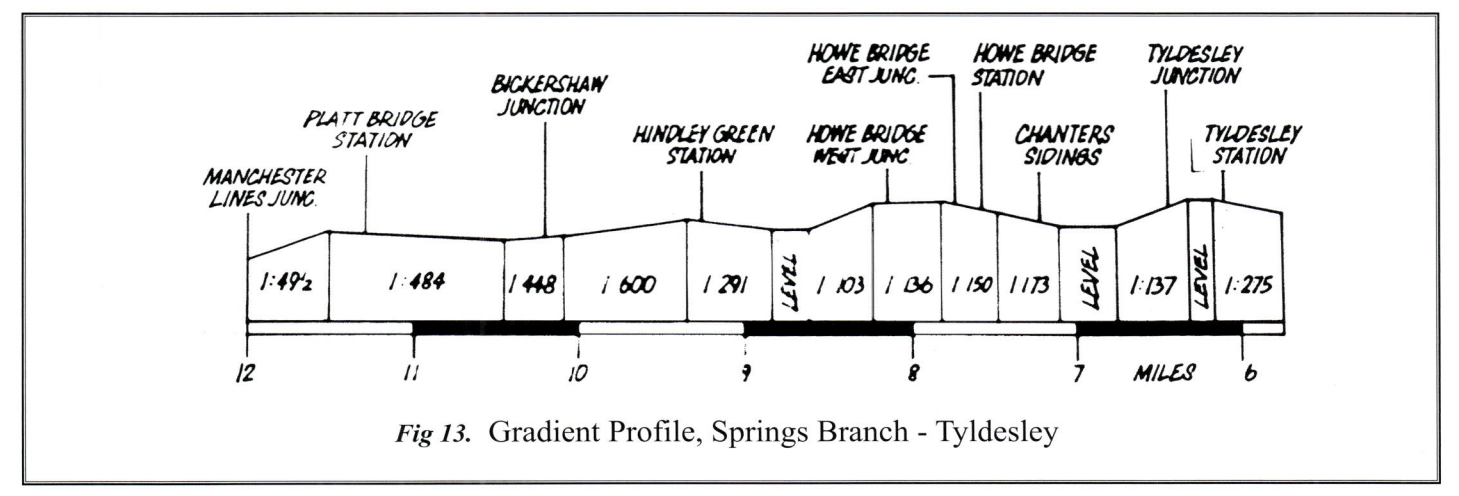

Fig 13. Gradient Profile, Springs Branch - Tyldesley

ticket office being on the Up platform for Manchester trains. By the 1960s though the state of neglect in evidence by this period did little to encourage passenger receipts. This was, however, just a symptom of a malaise which affected the railways in general. Nothing it seemed, could arrest the falling fortunes of a once great transport system. We all wanted our cars, and we got them; now though, there isn't enough road to run them on. I know, bring back the railway; some hope of that eh!

It hadn't always looked like it does in **Plate 50**, for in six consecutive years 1947-1952, Hindley Green won the best kept station competition in the Liverpool Lime Street District.

I think British Railways, as it was then, did their best, but they were beholden to the Treasury to keep the nationalised system going as cheaply as possible. The new dog on the block was barking louder and the oil lobby saw to it that they got funding for the motorways at the expense of the railways.

Conversely, in the newly privatised era which took effect in 1996, the railways have more than double the yearly funding as B.R. did in its latter years; much too late though for lines like these! Just to put matters into perspective the recent recession saw RBS get £45 billion of taxpayers money to keep it solvent. Just think what BR could have done with that!

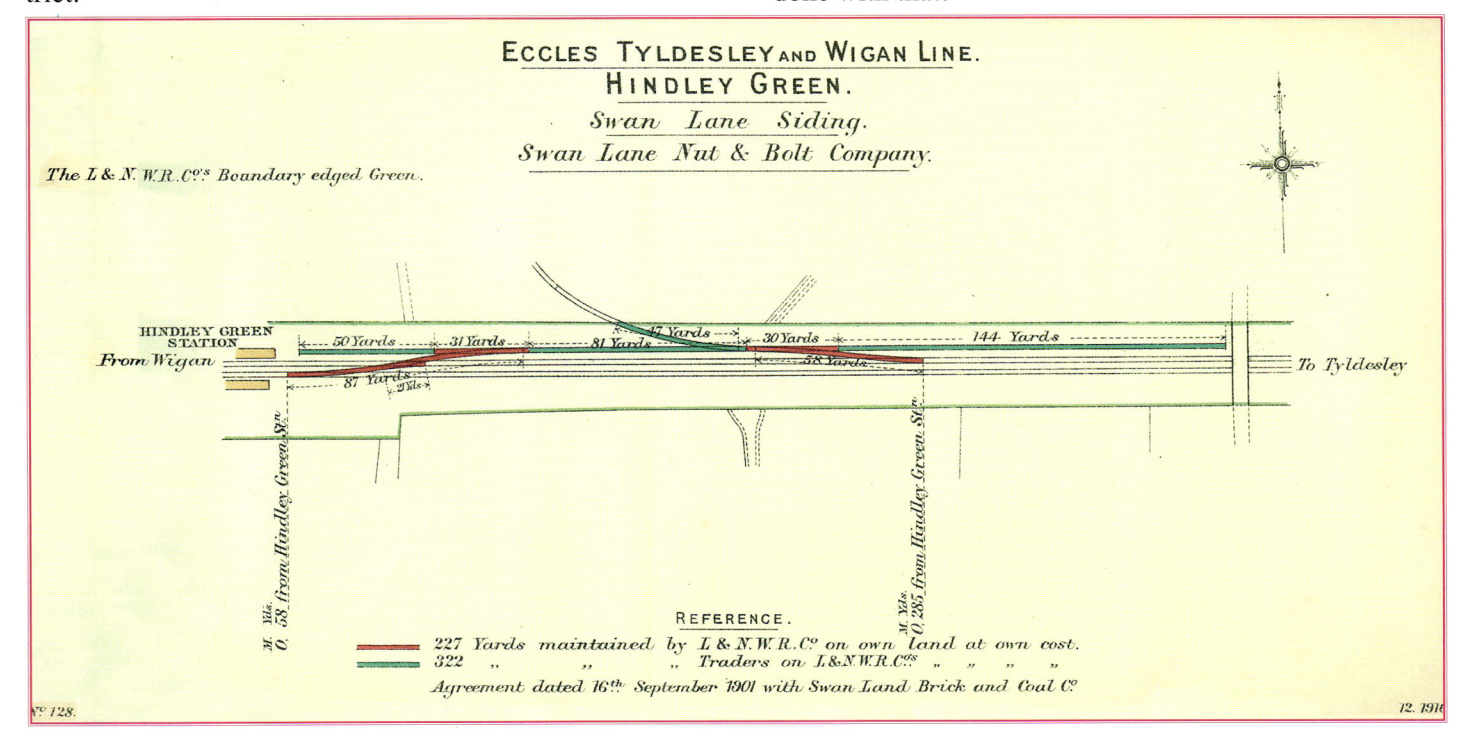

Fig 14. The former Swan Lane's Colliery Siding now registered to the Swan Lane Nut & Bolt Company c1916.

Courtesy, John Hall.

39

HOWE BRIDGE

There had been collieries at Westleigh from the late 18th century and by the mid 19th, much deeper mines were being sunk and as the century progressed a system of colliery railways developed to serve them.

The sidings at Howe Bridge West had been constructed in conjunction with the Wigan Coal & Iron Company's extension of their colliery railway carried out in 1882, from their Sovereign and Priestners Pits at Westleigh to the London & North Western Railway at Chowbent West Junction. During the line alterations to the Bolton & Leigh Railway authorised in 1880, a connecting curve from Chowbent West, later renamed Howe Bridge was built, to meet with the Bolton & Leigh Railway at Atherton Junction, opening in 1883. The signal box at West Junction also dates from this period.

Snapes Colliery, off Smallbrook Lane, had a connection with the London & North Western in the early years between the Westleigh Lane (Dangerous Corner) overbridge and Howe Bridge but by the early 1880s this had been removed, the colliery having closed.

A redundant signal box near this location was mooted as a possible station facility in 1882 by a body of Westleigh representatives which resulted in a meeting with their counterparts from the railway company at the site on 4th November that year. The suggestion though was not received with much enthusiasm by the railway company.

Originally named Chowbent, the station was renamed Howe Bridge in April 1901. It was a typical London & North Western all timber structure with access to the Up and Down platforms by a separate flight of steps. The booking office was on the Up platform with waiting rooms on both Up and Down platforms.

In the late 1940s and early 1950s it was not unknown for 400-500 persons to depart Howe Bridge on the Saturday morning holiday specials and extra staff were drafted in to help out. Pre W.W.II., there were also regular football specials from Tyldesley, via Howe Bridge East Junction, to Bolton Great Moor Street.

Fig 15. The traffic from Westleigh Wigan Coal & Iron Cos Collieries was transferred to the railway company at Howe Bridge West. This plan dates from 1916 but the sidings would have been open by 1882/3. *Courtesy, John Hall.*

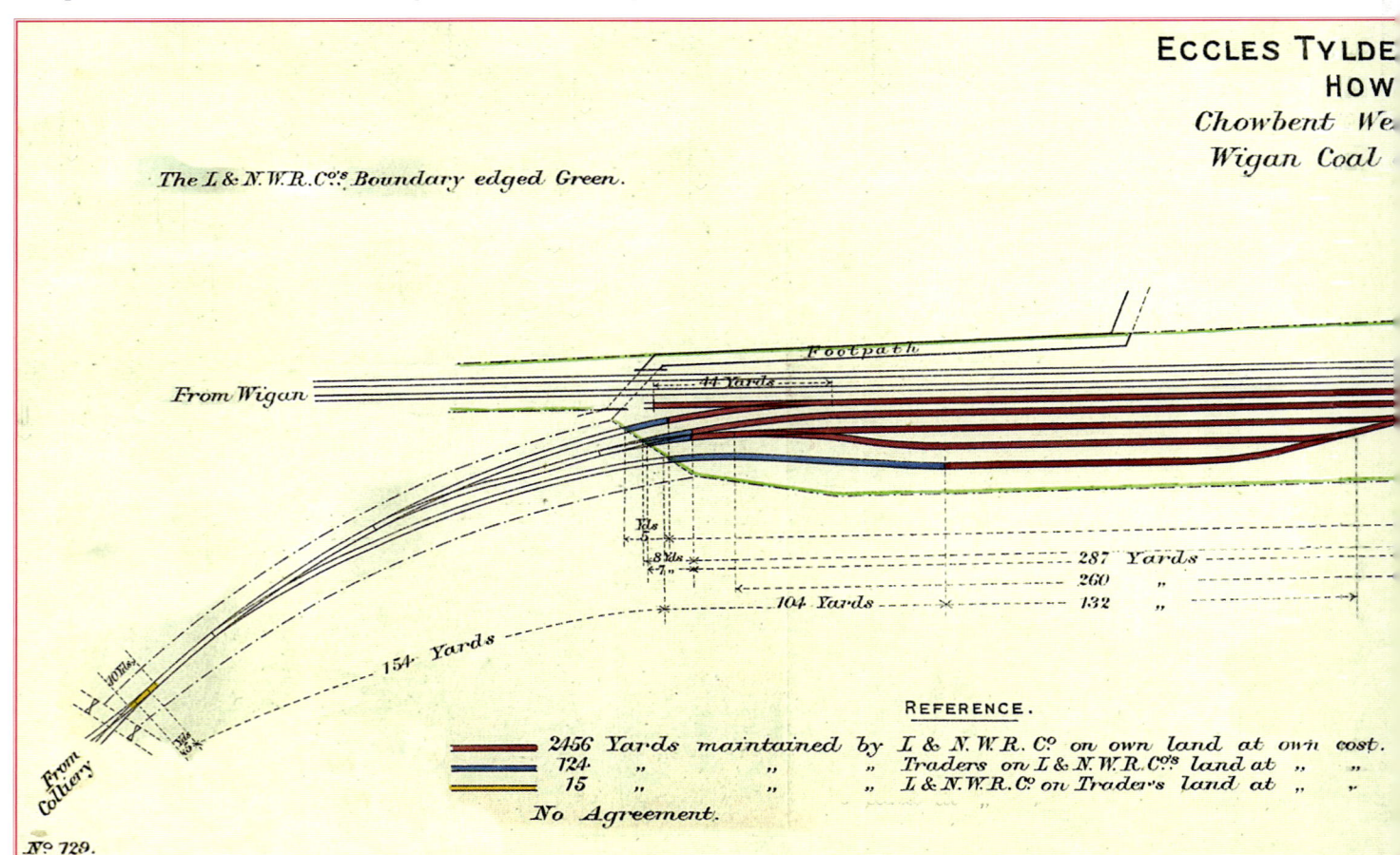

Plate 51. Chowbent Station photographed about 1900, just before the name changed to Howe Bridge, showing the Up platform for Manchester trains.
Author's Collection.

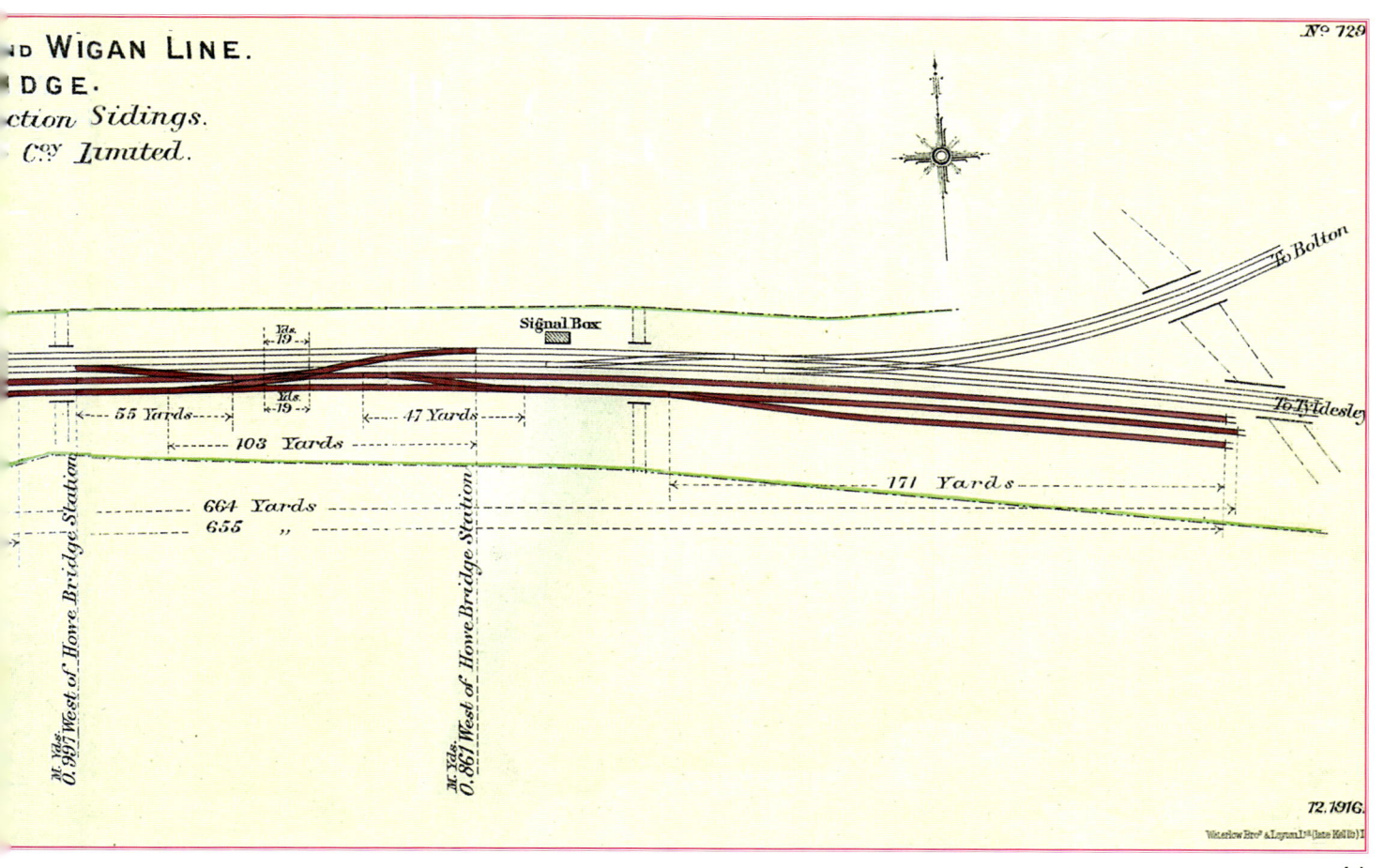

The early collieries of the Westleigh coalfield had been taken over by the Wigan Coal & Iron Company Ltd. on its formation in 1865, for one of the merging companies, namely the Kirkless Hall Coal & Iron Company had substantial operations within the Westleigh coalfield. In the late 1870s, Heart-o-th-Meadows Colliery, the sinking of which was begun by John Speakman Snr in 1870, was completed by the Wigan Coal & Iron Company in 1879. At the same period a new shaft had been sunk at Sovereign Pit, on the old Kirkless Hall Company's site. Heart-o-th-Meadows became better known as Priestner's Colliery and was served by a new spur off the colliery railway.

Such was the extent of the colliery rail system in the Westleigh vicinity it was possible for locomotives to work to Kirkless Works, the headquarters of the Wigan Coal & iron Company, from Westleigh, by a connection west of Daisy Hill station on the Lancashire & Yorkshire Railway and by way of Hindley No.2 Junction and a reversal, access their own colliery lines towards Kirkless. This route was last used about 1950/1 by Parsonage driver Henry Parkinson.

Sinking of the last mine in the locality, Parsonage, began in 1914 but was suspended during W.W.I., being completed about 1920. Parsonage Colliery had a steady flow of traffic to Howe Bridge West Sidings which could be seen crossing Westleigh Lane. Some of the coal traffic was worked to Preston or Southport from Howe Bridge and in addition there were numerous trip workings to Bag Lane Sidings. Coking coal went to the Lancashire Steel Corporation's Works at Irlam which replaced the ageing Kirkless, Wigan, plant as a centre of production. The latter was demolished in the early 1930s after the formation of Lancashire Steel and the Wigan Coal Corporation from the amalgamation of the Wigan Coal & Iron Company, the Pearson & Knowles Iron Company, the Wigan Junction Collieries, and the Moss Hall Coal Company. In the 1940s about 100 wagons per day were dispatched from Howe Bridge West.

Traffic from Howe Bridge West Sidings was, in BR days, either worked to Springs Branch for onward destinations or to Bag Lane Up Sidings. Any traffic for Garston usually went out from Parsonage via Westleigh Sidings and Kenyon Junction. This option was removed with the closure of the former Bolton & Leigh line between Pennington and Atherton Junction in June 1963. A fire which destroyed the screens at Parsonage in 1963 resulted in coal being sent to Bickershaw Colliery, via Howe Bridge West, for washing until August 1974 when the underground connection between the two collieries came into operation. However, some coal was still wound at Parsonage for road dispatch to local customers until May 1976.

The regular Manchester Exchange via Tyldesley to Bolton Great Moor Street service operated via East Junction until May 1942 when it was withdrawn as an austerity measure but never reinstated after hostilities ceased in 1945. However, freight trains, worked by Patricroft crews, continued to use the curve to reach Bag Lane Sidings where the train would be split into more manageable loads for the climb to Chequerbent Bank, thence onward to Hulton Sidings or Crook Street Yard.

Plate 52. This delightful scene at Howe Bridge dates from about 1910. Note the lower quadrant L&NW signals and the almost deserted roads, save the pony and trap, and a cabbie picking up at the station. St. Michael's Church is seen left, the vantage point from which *Plate 58* was taken.
John Ryan Collection.

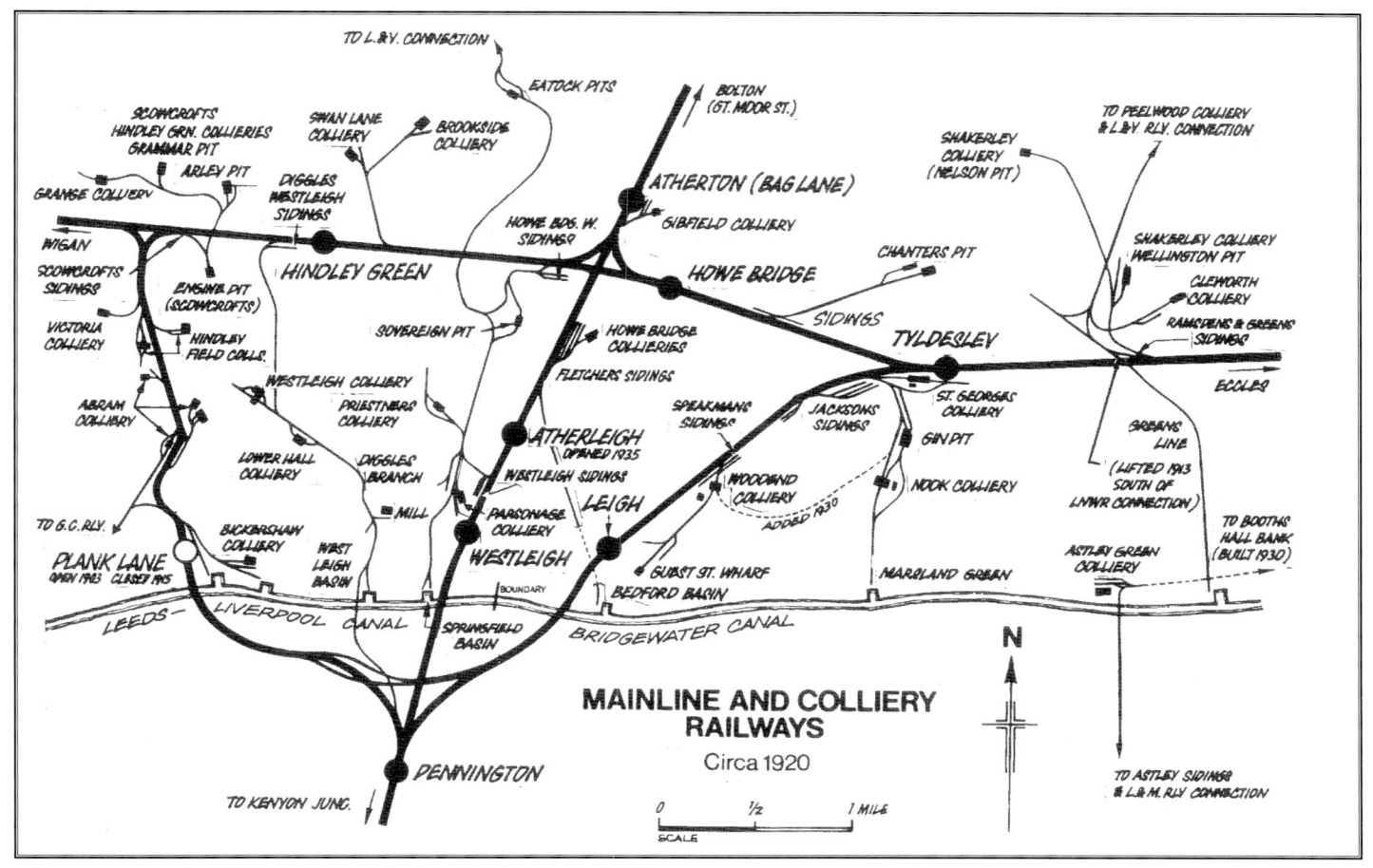

Fig 16. The colliery railways connecting with the Springs Branch-Eccles route between Bickershaw Junction and Tyldesley, are shown here as at 1920 when the combination of colliery and mainline railways were at their zenith. The dotted lines indicate extensions of the system at Gin Pit/Bedford and Astley Green after Manchester Collieries was formed in 1929. From the Westleigh Coalfield colliery locos worked to Kirkless crossing over the L&NW lines between Howe Bridge West and Hindley Green, passing Eatock's Pits on the way to connect with the L&Y lines west of Daisy Hill.

Not covered in this volume is the branch line from a point north of Atherleigh Station which ran to a loading wharf on the Bridgewater Canal at Bedford Basin, passing en-route, under the London & North Western's lines south-west of Leigh Station, then known as Bedford-Leigh. This branch line had been opened in the late 1850s for the transport of coal from the Gibfield Colliery of John Fletcher & Others, later known as Fletcher Burrows Atherton Collieries. It superseded a branch of 1830 which had run parallel to Leigh Road, Leigh, to terminate at Stock Platt Bridge Landsale Yard which bordered on the later Irvine Street, Leigh.

Plate 53. On 24th April 1968 at Howe Bridge West, ex L&Y 0-6-0ST No. 51456 is being made ready for transportation by B.R. to Ellenbrook Sidings and eventual preservation. From Ellenbrook, it is thought to have gone to Walkden Yard by the Central Railways system and later hauled to Astley Green Sidings from where it will be dispatched to the Keighley & Worth Valley Railway. The 0-6-0 diesel is probably YE/2717 built by the Yorkshire Engine Company in 1958 and sent new to Parsonage. *Author's Collection, (B.Hilton).*

43

Plate 54. The scene at Howe Bridge West c1952 as some track re-laying takes place. Of added interest is the Western Region brake van. *David Hill.*

Plate 55. One of the B.R. Standard Class '9F' 2-10-0 locomotives No.92052 is seen passing Howe Bridge East with a through van train on 29th November 1965. *Peter Eckersley.*

Plate 56. This view of Westleigh would appear to date from the mid-1950s, the only information written on the back of the print is *Westleigh School*, seen bottom centre. The colliery line which, en-route to Eatock's Pits and the Lancashire & Yorkshire Railway at Daisy Hill, crossed Westleigh Lane on the level to run alongside the school boundary has been lifted, last being used c1951/2. The remaning portion of colliery railway from Parsonage Pit to Howe Bridge West is seen in the top half of the picture, exiting far left. In the centre, to the left of new housing on Boston Grove, are the 'Barracks,' a much older housing development now demolished. See *Fig 16* for full extent of Westleigh's colliery railways.

Author's Collection.

Plate 57. The former Barton - Wright 0-6-0 class '23' tender engines of 1877 vintage were rebuilt by Aspinall from 1891 as saddle tanks, this example converted in 1896 at Horwich and numbered 752 by the L&Y, becoming LMS No.11456 after grouping in 1923. In May 1937 it was sold to Blainscough Colliery Co. to work at Welch Whittle Colliery. It is seen here at Parsonage Colliery in 1965.

John Ryan.

Plate 58. This remarkable eastwards view is taken from the *Yo-Yo*, a conical spoil heap adjacent to Diggles Lower Hall Colliery which had closed in the 1930s. In the immediate foreground is Diggles Westleigh Flash, with Edna Road Labour Club under construction, behind which are housing estates bordering on Wigan Road, Leigh c1951. May I draw your attention to the nearest chimney just right of centre which served the brickworks on Wigan Road itself. Behind that are the remnants of Priestner's Colliery outbuildings and its dirt tip, this being the only photograph known to date of that colliery. The white building partly visible in front of Priestners is the *Royal Oak* public house. On the horizon, above the dirt tip are the mills of Atherton with their chimneys jutting into the skyline. The smaller chimney to the right and further to the rear of the brickworks marks the location of the Lancashire United Transport's Depot at Howe Bridge. Further still to the right, with two chimneys close together, are Caleb Wright's mills at Tyldesley.

Back to the *Yo-Yo* though; apart from being a playground for the local kids, during W.W.II, it was also a training ground for American troops. It was removed when the Bickershaw opencast operations began in 1975.

Tom Edmondson.

Plate 59. Colliery locomotives had been granted running powers over the mainline railways from the very beginning of the railway era. Even if the original agreements could not be located the London & North Western found it impossible to rescind access to these lines by colliery engines due to the longevity of use. In June 1951, 'Austerity' *Humphrey* passes through Howe Bridge with a train from Gibfield Colliery, on the old Bolton-Leigh line, to Chanter's Washery. *Author's Collection, (W.S.Garth).*

Plate 60. Howe Bridge East Junction about 1950. This is the original connection with the Bolton & Leigh Railway at Atherton Junction, item 3 as given in the Board of Trade report in 1861 (see page 7) at 25 chains length. The all timber platforms were elevated and gave a good view of the surrounding area. *Author's Collection, B.R.*

47

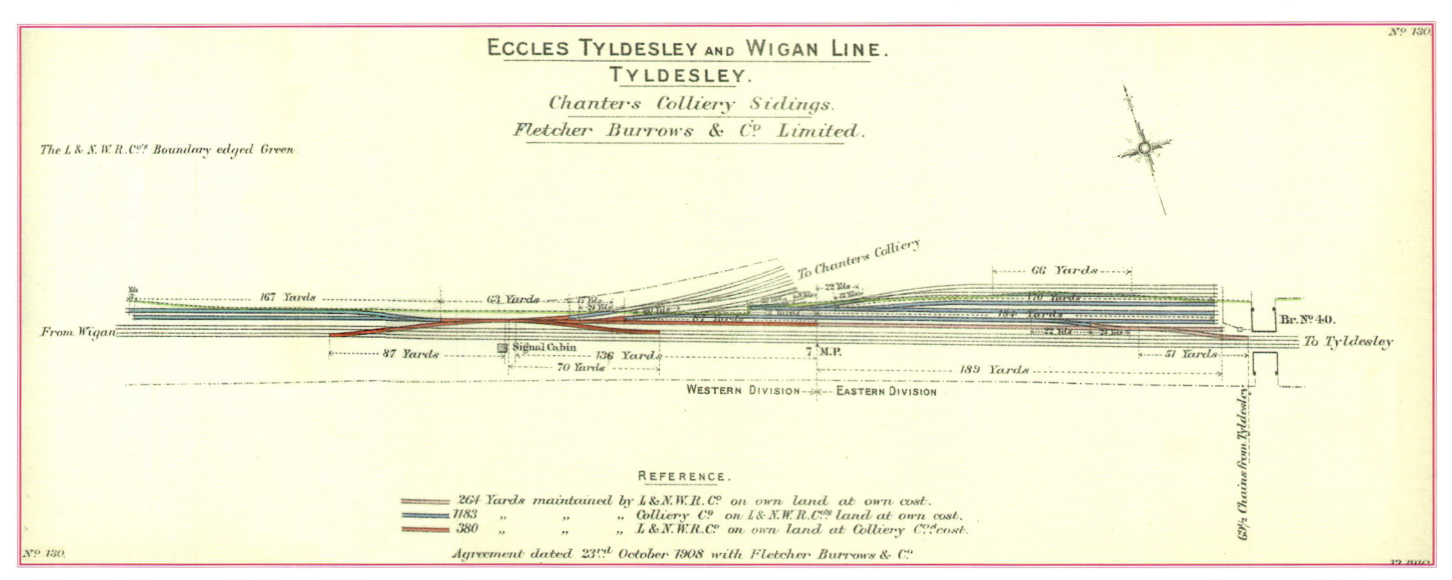

Fig 17. Chanters Colliery Sidings as at 1916. *Courtesy, John Hall.*

Plate 61. Howe Bridge from Leigh Road on 1st December 1954, looking towards St. Michael's Church. Note the absence of any traffic and the overhead wires of the South Lancashire Transport Company. The trolleybuses of the Company served a large portion of industrial South Lancashire connecting the towns of Leigh, Bolton, Farnworth, Swinton, St. Helens and Tyldesley, with their headquarters at Atherton. Operation commenced in 1930 and was not finally abandoned until 1958. *Author's Collection, B.R.*

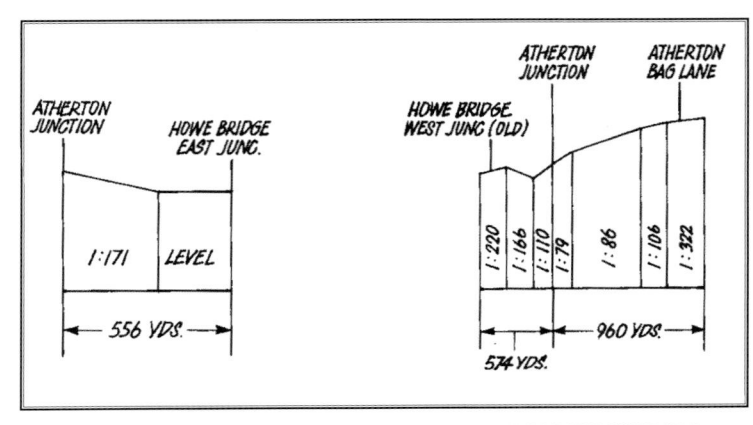

Fig 18. GRADIENT PROFILES: ATHERTON JUNCTION - HOWE BRIDGE JUNCTIONS

Plate 62, above. A Manchester bound train calls at Howe Bridge on a summers day in 1959. In the distance can be seen the headgear of Chanter's Colliery.
John Ryan.

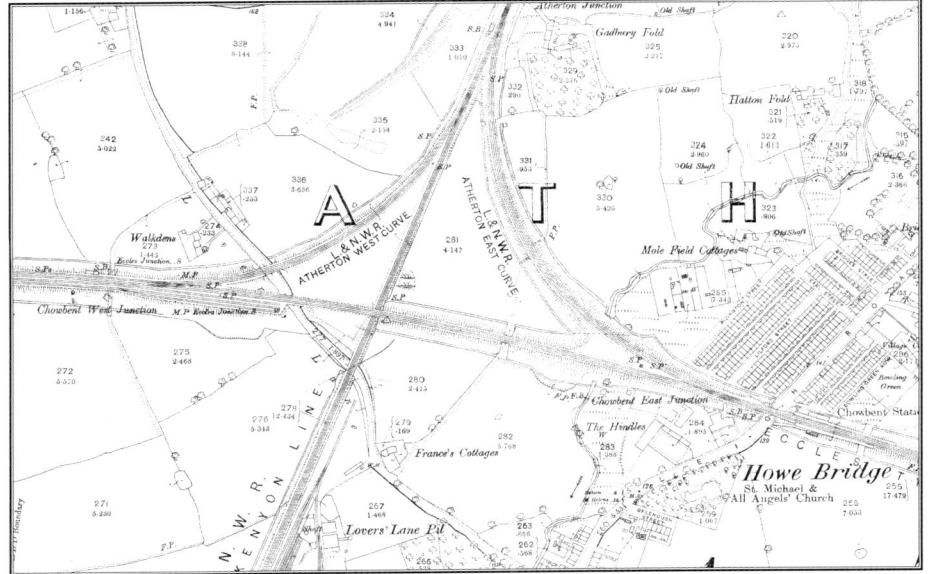

Plate 63. One of the London & North Western's heavy freight engines Class 'G2/2A' passes through Howe Bridge westbound about 1950 with a train of wooden bodied coal wagons from one of the local collieries.

Fig 19. Howe Bridge Junctions are shown here from the 2nd series Ordnance Survey c1888/92. The triangle of lines here are intersected by the Bolton & Leigh Railway of 1828/9. When the Wigan-Eccles route opened in 1864 it conected with the Bolton & Leigh by an east to north curve from Howe Bridge (Chowbent) Station, Howe Bridge East-Atherton Junctions. The west facing curve opening in 1883.

49

Plate 64. Chanters Colliery is seen here from the corner of Tyldesley Old Road, possibly in the years just after W.W.I. There are three versions of Atherton Collieries wagons on view, the most recent being the one on the right. *John Ryan Collection.*

Chanters colliery dates from 1854 on a much older site. There were two shafts here and both were deepened in the 1890s to reach the Arley Mine at over 1800ft. Chanters was one of the most successful of the Atherton Collieries Pits and continued working, in NCB ownership, until 1966, later becoming a training school for mining apprentices.

The branch line was approximately ¾ mile long and had been constructed at the same time as the main running lines by the contractor, Treadwell, and in all probability opened for traffic in 1864. Situated between Howe Bridge and Tyldesley the branch ran in an easterly direction passing under Tyldesley Old Road at Hindsford.

Chanters Sidings signal box was built specifically to serve Chanters Colliery workings and had 18 levers, 15 working with 3 spare; in LMS & BR days the box opened two turns, 6am-2pm/2pm-10pm. The ground frame here, situated at the Tyldesley end, was controlled from the signal box. Usually the colliery locomotive would be on hand to receive the returning empties worked direct from Fleetwood, Wyre Dock, Bolton or Garston Dock, Liverpool; if not the train engine would shunt the empties into the sidings. Some of the coal trains were worked by colliery locomotive working two turns per day with 12/15 wagons, to Bag Lane Up Sidings or, via the Howe Bridge triangle, to Westleigh Colliery Sidings. Others were direct workings, to Wyre Dock for example, whilst some of the traffic went to Springs Branch for northbound destinations. Up to 120 wagons per day was the average dispatch from Chanters Sidings. In BR days, Chanters had a contract to supply loco coal to the railways.

In 1965 the washery at Chanters had broken down beyond economic repair and as a result, coal was sent to Nook for washing and then dispatched via Jackson's Sidings to Garston Docks at Liverpool. Yes, we were still exporting coal then, whereas now we import it from half-way around the world.

Plate 65. This unusual view of Howe Bridge is taken from the bell-tower of St. Michael's Church with what appears to be a rebuilt 'Royal Scot' 4-6-0 working to Manchester Exchange c1953. *David Hill.*

TYLDESLEY

For decades, the people of Tyldesley had been badly served regarding railways, their nearest stations being on the Bolton & Leigh line at Bag Lane or Westleigh or, an even longer trek to Astley on the Liverpool & Manchester line. It was with some enthusiasm therefore that London & North Western's Act of 1861 was received. Despite the opposition of the Lancashire & Yorkshire Railway to the plans, their objections were overcome and in due course the first sod was cut by the Earl of Ellesmere at Worsley on 11th September that year.

Tyldesley would be the premier station on the route and at that period had a population greater that any other township in the Leigh Parish. The construction of the railway was followed with great interest by the local people who were eager for its opening. There were some major earthworks to consider; deep cuttings had to be cut at Worsley and Tyldesley, interlaced with embankments, numerous bridges and culverts. The weather proved to be a problem and the particularly wet summers of 1862/3 with work being suspended in the intervening winter.

Eventually though, the new railway was ready for opening. The works from Kenyon, through Leigh to Tyldesley, were inspected by Colonel Yolland on 17th July 1864, as was the Winwick cut-off line which had been under construction at the same time. On the following day an inspection of the line from Eccles Junction, via Tyldesley, to Wigan took place. Four engines were used to test the bridges. All was well, Colonel Yolland made his report to the Board of Trade and in mid August the opening day was announced.

Wednesday 24th August 1864, was, apparently, a day of bright and glorious weather, a day fit indeed for the ceremonial opening of the new railway, well prepared for by the local populace and London & North Western Railway Company alike.

A special train left Manchester, Hunt's Bank, at

Plate 66. On 9th April 1938 Stanier 2-6-4T No.2492 pauses at Tyldesley with a Wigan North Western - Manchester Exchange train. This two cylinder class of engine with the taper boiler was introduced by Stanier in 1935, being ideally suited to the 18 mile stopping turns between Wigan & Manchester on this route. *W.D.Cooper,(Cooperline).*

12.30p.m.,(Manchester Exchange Station was not opened until 1884) drawing 18 coaches and a luggage van, each coach being decorated with flags and bright coloured bunting. The Bells of Salford Churches gave their approval as the train gathered momentum. A stop at Eccles to take on some of the guests, thence to make its way upon the new metals. Small gatherings of people at Worsley and Ellenbrook welcomed the train as brief stops were made there. Tyldesley was reached at 1.09pm. and here was made the greatest effort to celebrate this connection at last with the Railway World. Every vantage point was occupied. Sunday School Children filled the open fields to the left of Waring St. Triumphal Arches spanned the roads and almost every house had some form of banner or decoration flying in the breeze. The Ellesmere Yeomanry Band provided the musical accompaniment as the train drew into a station overflowing with sightseers and bedecked with colour.

The view from Tyldesley Station was described as *magnificent* with *open country as far as the eye can see* and *fertile landscape relieved by masses of foliage*. Richard Moon must surely have been well pleased with the London & North Western's latest territorial conquest.

Following a brief respite at Tyldesley the train continued to Bradshaw Leach (Pennington) arriving at 1.33pm, where a waiting engine was attached, to depart at 1.38pm, arriving back at Tyldesley at 1.49pm.

A field battery employed nearby, had on returning here, been strengthened by the addition of two mortars, the gunners causing some amusement, retreating hastily after applying the fuse.

Departing from Tyldesley at 1.53pm, the train paused at Chowbent, where flags portrayed the motto "Welcome to Great Britain", a response no doubt by some local wit to a "where the hell's Chowbent" remark uttered by some luckless railway official who probably got an earbashing in Lanky dialect for his pains.

The *grimy faces* of some colliers were to be seen on reaching Hindley Green and after passing Platt Bridge the train continued to Wigan where, at 2.20pm, guests from the North boarded for the return journey to Tyldesley.

On arriving back at Tyldesley, the directors and guests alighted from the train to march in procession headed by the 60th (Atherton) Lancashire Rifle Volunteers Band, 2,100 school children, 800 members of friendly societies, Worsley Yeomanry Band, Tyldesley Drum & Fife Band and the Mosley Band.

Plate 67. Stanier Class '5' No.45455 comes off the Wigan line at Tyldesley on 3rd October 1966 with a train of 5 plank wooden bodied wagons which is quite late in the steam era as by now the steel bodied type had been used on coal workings for some years. Perhaps this is an engineers train working to Patricroft. In the triangle of lines is Tyldesley Signal & Telegraph Yard. *Peter Eckersley.*

Plate 68. The 2-8-0 heavy freight engines designed by Sir William Stanier were introduced by the LMS in 1935 and lasted right until the end of the steam era in 1968. No.48214 is seen working tender first through Tyldesley on 29th January 1967 with an engineers train engaged on track recovery from redundant sidings. In the background St. George's Church still stands proud, but the colliery of the same name which occupied the foreground has been reduced to rubble. The bridge, extreme left at the end of King William Street, gave pedestrian access to Gin Pit, Nook Pit and Astley & Tyldesley Collieries Cricket Club, passing over the eastern end of the colliery sidings.
Peter Eckersley.

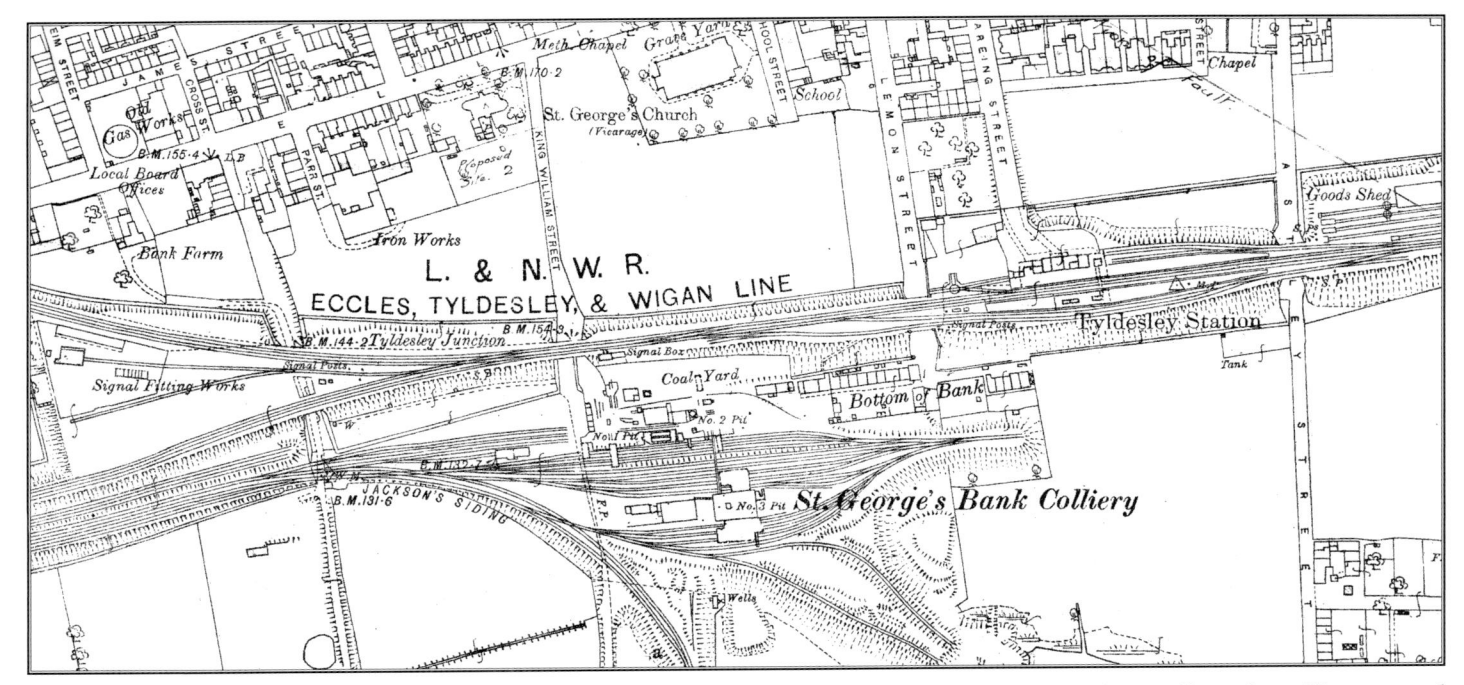

Fig 20. From the second series Ordnance Survey, Tyldesley Station and St. George's Colliery are shown. Since the colliery opened in 1862, there has been a big expansion in the sidings both at the colliery and nearby Jackson's Sidings. Note also that the turntable at the west end, near the junction for Leigh, has been removed and the Signal & Telegraph Department established.

Plate 69. Tyldesley Signal and Telegraph Dept., situated in the triangle between the Wigan and Leigh lines with, on the gable end, the time keeper's office, complete with geraniums in the windows and staffed by Jack Watson and George Hamp in the 1950s. Next to this was the Telegraph Inspector's Office of one Claude McCutcheon, followed by stores, tinsmiths and at the far end the blacksmith's shop. Note also "Britannia" re-sited on the gable end over the time keeper's office. *Author's Collection, B.R.*

Plate 70. Rebuilt 'Patriot' No.45535 *Sir Herbert Walker K.C.B.* passes Tyldesley goods yard with a morning express for Manchester Exchange c1948/9. Note that the locomotive is running without smoke deflectors *Peter Hampson.*

Plate 71. This aerial view of Tyldesley Station was taken in the 1930s and there appears to be plenty of activity. In the Down Loop, a tank engine and four coaches idles away whilst a train is departing for Manchester from the Up platform. The two lines in the bay are still intact, but the one upon which two L&NW vehicles are standing would be removed in 1941. *Author's Collection.*

The Signal & Telegraph Depot (S&T) began to be transferred to Tyldesley from Ordsall Lane, Salford, in the late 1880s, and the blacksmiths shop, as seen in the accompanying photograph dates from that period. Previously there had been a locomotive turntable on the site with a connection off the Down Wigan line. A single road engine shed, probably constructed here in the late 1860s, was virtually demolished in November 1878 during a light engine movement through Tyldesley. The engine in question was working to Platt Bridge on the Down Main, and unfortunately the Signalman at Tyldesley No.2 box had inadvertently set the points into the shed road. In the shed at the time was a dead engine which, when hit by the misdirected locomotive, was sent crashing through the gable end, down an embankment and ended up in a nearby garden; the beginning of garden railways! Scale 12in = 1ft.

The damage to locomotives and shed were said to be considerable and it is not clear if the engine shed was ever rebuilt. However, the connection into what became the S&T yard on the same site was re-sited onto the Up Leigh line prior to 1888 and the turntable removed.

Tyldesley Signal & Telegraph staff were responsible for maintaining the signalling apparatus and signal boxes over a wide area, the eastern boundary was, in post World War II days, marked by the A580 road-over bridge at Roe Green. The latter, Sandersons Sidings, Worsley, Monton Green and Eccles Junction installations all came within the Patricroft area. The southern boundary for the Tyldesley S&T gangs was the Kenyon Up Distant near Parkside East Junction, this an early conversion to colour light, controlled from Kenyon No. 1 box. From Roe Green, all the equipment on the Eccles-Wigan route as far west as Bickershaw Junction Signal Cabin came under the Tyldesley area, whilst the northern outpost was marked by the Bolton No. 1 and Fletcher Street cabins on the Bolton & Leigh line. On the Roe Green branch, the signalling equipment at Lever Street, Walkden Low Level, Plodder Lane, Little Hulton Junction etc, were again serviced by Patricroft gangs.

As previously stated, the western boundary for Tyldesley S&T was Bickershaw Junction. At the eastern end of the triangle of lines here was Scowcroft's Sidings and signal box. Scowcroft's mines had ceased production in the 1930s but their sidings remained in use for some years. The Hindley Field Junction to Scowcroft's Sidings curve had closed on 27th December 1944 and Hindley Field signal box abolished. Scowcroft's signal box had been suffering the effects of subsidence and became a problem, eventually being done away with, probably in the early 1950s and the block section extended from Bickershaw Junction to Howe Bridge West.

Howe Bridge West box was also in a precarious state by the late 1950s, gradually slipping down the bank due to subsidence. This posed extreme problems with the mechanical operations of the box and it too was demolished, to be replaced by a new 1943 standard pattern frame, 40 lever box built inside the triangle of lines at Howe Bridge and brought into use shortly after the new Tyldesley signal box.

The new signal box at Tyldesley, commissioned in 1963, was built on the site of the former cattle dock turntable disused since the early 1950s. This new box, also constructed with a 1943 standard pattern frame had 55 levers and replaced Tyldesley Nos. 1&2 boxes, the London & North Western absolute block system here being replaced with track circuits under the Whellwyn block system. In later years the resulting colliery closures would gradually see off the signal boxes at their relative locations so that by 1968 only Monton Green, Ellenbrook, Tyldesley and Leigh remained on the through Kenyon route.

The section of line between Tyldesley and Green's Sidings with Up and Down Main lines parallel to the Up Goods Loop, seems to have been an accident black spot as a number of incidents occured here pre-1890. One involved the Up 'Scotch Mail' colliding with a coal train from Springs Branch during shunting movements between the Up Main and Up Goods Loop. The inquiry into this accident blamed the Signalman at Tyldesley No. 1 Cabin, who it appears, had failed to ascertain that the Up Main was clear before he pulled off the signals for the Mail train, and by the Yard Shunter, who it was said, *ought not to have uncoupled sixteen wagons and left them standing on the Up Main without having received permission of the Signalman to do so.* Again there were quite a number of injuries and considerable damage, particularly to the Up Mail locomotive, and to the goods van and wagons of the coal train.

Plate 72. On 24th September 1966, the Railway Correspondence & Travel Society (RCTS) ran a railtour of lines in the South Lancashire area hauled by Class '5' No.45154 *Lanarkshire Yeomanry*. After arriving at Tyldesley off the Wigan line, the locomotive is seen running round before departing for Pennington Junction as the photographers line up for their shot.   *Peter Eckersley.*

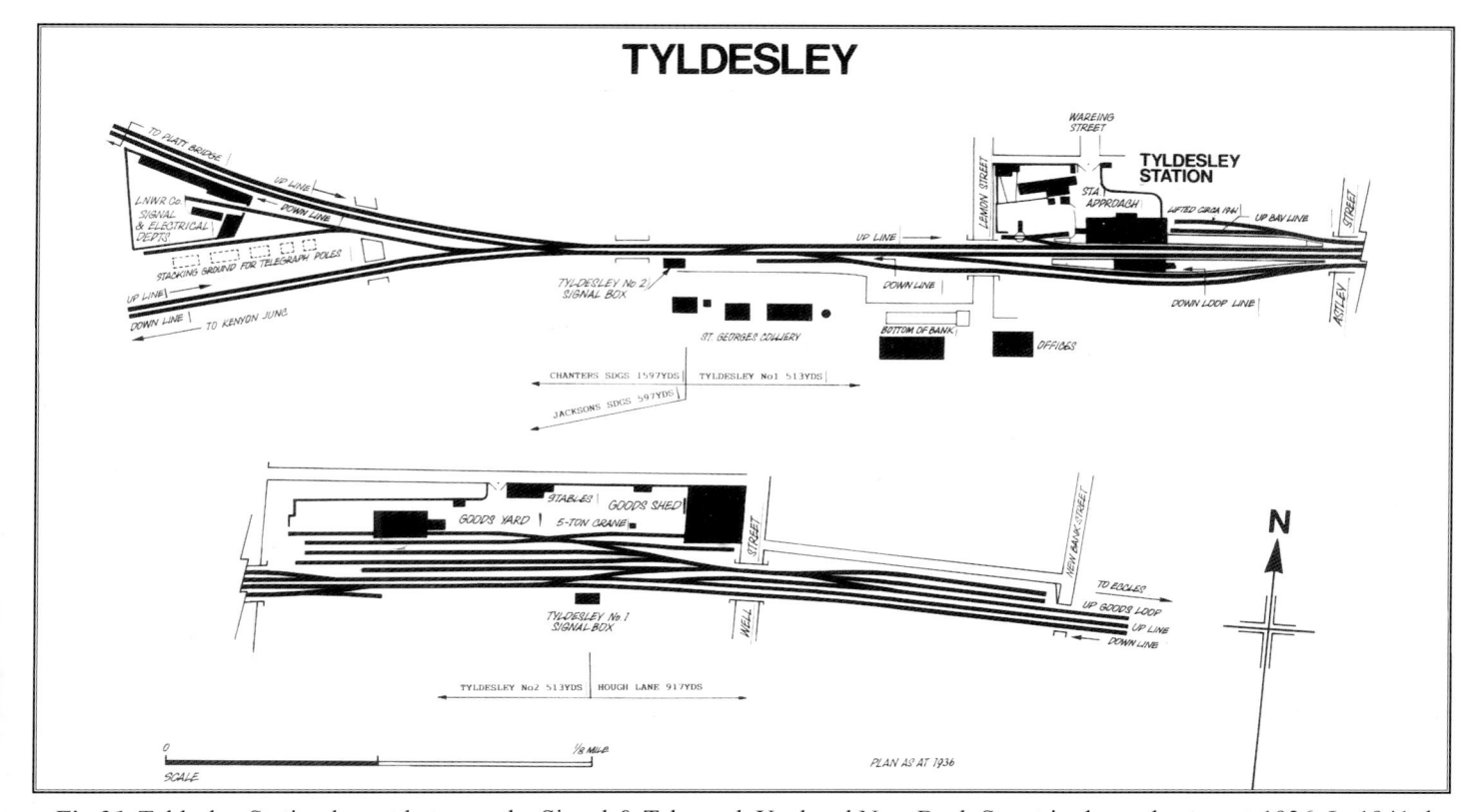

Fig 21. Tyldesley Station layout between the Signal & Telegraph Yard and New Bank Street is shown here as at 1936. In 1941 the most northerly of the bay sidings would be removed but the cattle turntable abutting Lemon Street remained in use until the mid 1950s.

Plate 73. Ex-London & North Western 0-8-0 No.49335, is seen shunting in Tyldesley Goods Yard c1950. *Peter Hampson.*

Tyldesley lost its regular passenger service to Wigan North Western in November 1964, with the last holiday passenger traffic working from Tyldesley via Wigan from 6th July 1968 to 7th September 1968. Tyldesley to Hulton Sidings via Howe Bridge East and Atherton Junctions closed on 6th January 1969. Through goods and parcels traffic ceased to use Howe Bridge East to West Junctions as from 7th October 1968. Passenger services between Liverpool Lime Street via Leigh, Tyldesley and Eccles Junction to Manchester Exchange, continued until 3rd May 1969. The last trains to use the route were returning BICC excursions from Blackpool on that date. Complete closure of the line from Kenyon Junction to Eccles Junction via Tyldesley is officially given as 5th May 1969.

The Minister of Transport agreed to the withdrawal of Wigan N.W.-Manchester Exchange local services in the Autumn of 1964 on condition that there was an increase in the number of trains between Manchester, Tyldesley and Leigh with improved bus services from these stations. This cut right across BR's intended follow-up proposal to withdraw services from Liverpool Lime Street via Kenyon, Leigh and Tyldesley to Manchester and the resultant closure of all intermediate stations. The Minister, it was said, noted this and required that if such a future proposal occured it must be based on a "census" to include "those passengers displaced by withdrawal of the Tyldesley-Wigan locals". Many relevant figures supporting retention of services were often deemed inadmissible on the grounds that they did not conform to the criteria as laid down in proposed closure procedures.

Plate 74. BR 'Britannia' Class No.70021 *Morning Star,* departs Tyldesley Station on 25th June 1966 with a holiday special for North Wales and appears to be emitting steam from all the wrong places, but to good effect. As the end of the steam era approached many of the locomotives suffered from neglect and the authorities saw little point in maintaining the engines to a high degree, seeing that they would be withdrawn for scrap in the next two years. *Peter Eckersley.*

Plate 75. This view looking north along Astley Street is early 20th century. A similar photograph appeared in Part One and it seems likely that both were taken by the same photographer. The 'Misguided' Busway, at present under construction, crosses Astley Street on the level, the embankments having been removed in the mid-1980s. On the left are the dirt tips of St. George's Colliery and a rake of L&NW stock appears stationary, presumably on a westbound train. Note the mistaken road name.

John Ryan Collection.

Plate 76. A number of the Tyldesley Signal & Telegraph staff pose for the camera on Tyldesley Market Square about 1966. *The late Tom Yates.*

Plate 77. Tyldesley Station frontage on Wareing Street is seen in this period view just after the first World War. All the station signs are London & North Western vintage which would change to LMS in the 1920s on the formation of the 'Big Four'.
Author's Collection.

Plate 78. Mr Wilfred Hunt, of Irlam, who had worked in the Tyldesley Section of British Railways, is seen receiving a barometer from his colleagues, on his transfer to Miles Platting c1956. Left to right are:- C.McCutcheon, H.Rigby, J.Watson (seated), J.Barlow, L.Mills, W.Hunt, H.Coop and S.Joynson.
Authors Collection.

Plate 79. Members of the British Railways Tyldesley and Leigh Ambulance classes receive awards at the annual distribution, held at the Railway Hotel, Tyldesley c1954. Identified Left to right are:- A.Haynes, H.Paul, 3rd, unknown, 4th unknown, P.Hanrahan, 6th, unknown, C.Collier, H.Parr and H.Scott.
Authors Collection.

60

RAMSDEN'S SIDINGS and GREEN'S SIDINGS

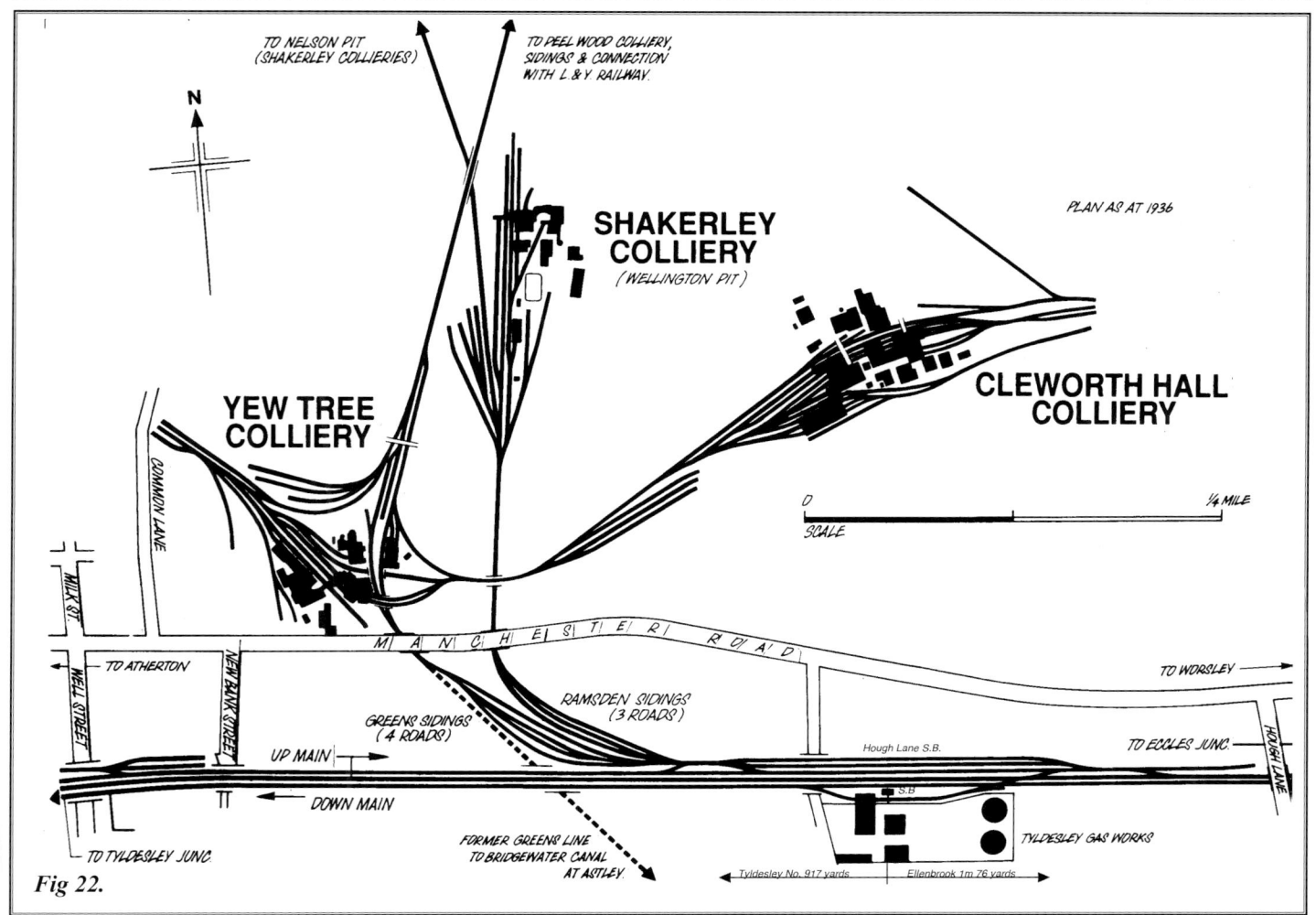

Fig 22.

Connections were made here with the London & North Western Railway to serve the collieries of George and William Green's Tyldesley Coal Company, and also the Shakerley Collieries of William Ramsden.

Coal had been mined on the Shakerley Estate at Tyldesley from the early 15th century. The sale of Shakerley Estate in 1836 is described as *land of excellent quality, tithe free. Abounding with young timber, inexhaustible coal mines of excellent quality, ready sales would be vastly increased if the projected North Line of Railroad between Liverpool and Manchester be proceeded with.* The North Line is a reference to the proposal in 1834 by the Manchester, Bolton & Bury Railway to construct a direct line between Wigan and Manchester, running to the north of Tyldesley, thereby reducing the distance travelled by the circuitous route using the Wigan Branch Railway's line to Parkside and thence the Liverpool & Manchester line to Manchester, by some six miles. This proposal was objected to by the Liverpool & Manchester Railway who again recruited C.B.Vignoles to carry out their bidding in opposing the Bill when it came before Parliament. Defeat of the Bill and subsequent events resulted in an extremely long gestation period for a line to the north of Tyldesley, running through the Shakerley Estate. In the event, Shakerley Estate was duly purchased by Jacob Fletcher of Peel Hall, Little Hulton, whose only heiress, a daughter Charlotte Anne, married Robert Wellington 3rd Viscount Combermere in 1866 (later divorced). Therein lie the origins of names given to the Wellington Pit of Wm. Ramsden's Shakerley Collieries and Combermere Colliery of George Green's Tyldesley Coal Company.

George and William Green are reputed to have begun sinking operations under Yew Tree Farm in the mid 1830s, but early information is sketchy. The first edition Ordnance Survey of the mid 1840s indicates a number of shafts on, or in the vicinity of Shakerley Common, including a 'Shakerley Colliery' about a half mile to the north of Elliott Street.

61

It seems more likely that coal of any quantity was not produced until the late 1840s from Green's collieries and by 1850/1 their tramway to the Bridgewater Canal at Astley was in operation.

At the Shakerley end, Green's tramway was rather steep so was cable worked. In fact the high ground here was known as the 'Banks', a derivative of which, namely 'Bongs', became the colloquial name for Tyldesley. Wagons were horse drawn over the remaining section to the Bridgewater Canal and here discharge facilities were built.

In 1864 connections were made with the London & North Western Railway, the main line itself passing over Green's line as the latter descended from the higher ground at this point. The tramway was converted to standard gauge during construction of the main line and sidings were laid for the transfer of traffic, on the lower ground, by the London & North Western. Locomotives were employed on Green's railway from 1867.

John Holland, who built some of the first railways in Ireland, joined with George & William Green whose colliery at Yew Tree became very successful. In fact he went to live at Pear Tree House, on the corner of Mort Lane and Sale Lane, Tyldesley, in 1858.

A new colliery was sunk at Combermere, to the north of Yew Tree in 1867 and the colliery railway extended to it. Combermere Colliery was short lived and closed in the mid 1890s, but on the same site Green's Tyldesley Coal Company established a brick works.

Tyldesley Coal Company's Peel Wood Colliery was a more extensive undertaking. Situated alongside the later Lancashire & Yorkshire line on Tyldesley's northern boundary it was worked from the early 1880s until 1928. The colliery railway was extended to Peel Wood, and additional connections were made with the Lancashire & Yorkshire Railway in 1888 when the line from Pendleton to Crow Nest Junction, Hindley opened.

Closure of Green's Line, South of the London & North Western connections occured in 1913, when the Tyldesley Coal Company gave notice to the Earl of Ellesmere, over whose land the railway passed, that the landlease would not be renewed. In the event, some of the track and plant at Astley was sold to the Clifton & Kearsley Coal Company who were sinking their Astley Green pits at the time.

William Ramsden appears to have taken over a 'Shakerley Colliery' in 1861 and this particular colliery was, in later years, more commonly known as Nelson Pit. Ramsden's Wellington Pit dates from the late 1860s and was situated about $1/4$ mile to the north of Tyldesley Coal Company's Yew Tree Pit. The exact date for the connection of Ramsden's Shakerley Collieries with the London & North Western, alongside Greens Sidings is obscure. William Ramsden was amongst the invited guests at the inaugural sod cutting ceremony of the Eccles-Tyldesley Branch at Worsley in 1861. He would undoubtedly have been keen to establish rail connections early on and it seems likely that by the time Wellington Pit opened it was rail served.

Plate 80. This view of Ramsden's and Green's Sidings dates from the late 1920s. The wagons in the nearest siding appear to be loaded with pit props and are a mixture of North Eastern., London, Midland & Scottish, and colliery internal user wagons marked with the letter 'X'. In the second siding are wagons of Tyldesley Coal Company and North Eastern. A Midland type 0-6-0 tender engine is getting ready to depart from the third siding with a coal train, probably after the ex-L&N.W. tank engine has passed with the local passenger train to Manchester.
Authors's Collection (H.Gillibrand).

The branch to Ramsden's collieries passed beneath Manchester Road, Tyldesley, by a separate underbridge from that of Green's Tyldesley Coal Company, and like the latter, Ramsden's colliery railway ascended the 'Banks' on a steeply graded incline. Ramsden's railway passed under the Tyldesley Coal Company's railway before reaching Wellington Pit and beneath it again en-route to Nelson Pit.

Shakerley Collieries were taken over by Manchester Collieries in 1935 when virtually worked out, for their quota of coal. Wellington Pit closed in the same year but Nelson Pit continued in operation until 1938.

In the mid-1950s opencast operations on the former sites of Shakerley Collieries Nelson Pit and Tyldesley Coal Company's Peel Wood removed any remaining traces of colliery workings. The site at Combermere, which had become a brickworks is still apparent, as is part of the trackbed of the colliery railway that served it, from a point north of the Wellington Pit site. The latter, and what remained of the Yew Tree site, were landscaped in later years after the closure of Cleworth Hall Colliery.

There had been a small signal cabin controlling Green's Sidings and this had been situated alongside the Down line, west of Hough Lane cabin. It was shown on the 1936 Ordnance Survey but probably abolished pre 1940.

Plate 81. Seen outside the Tyldesley Coal Co's. locomotive shed is *Shakerley,* purshased new in 1901 by Wm. Ramsden & Sons Ltd, works No. HE/736.

Manchester Collieries took over Ramsden's Shakerley Collieries in 1935 when their last colliery, Nelson Pit, was almost worked out, purely for its coal quota.

Having been transferred to work between Howe Bridge and Chanter's Collieies in 1938, *Shakerley* was transferred back to its former stamping ground in 1949 and remained to work Cleworth Hall Colliery until 1963 when rail traffic from the colliery ceased. Latterly, it had been overhauled at Walkden Yard in 1956, hence the lined maroon livery, Walkden's trademark in N.C.B.days. *The late Cyril Golding.*

Plate 82. Ramsden's & Green's Sidings were lifted in 1963/4, after the closure of Cleworth Hall Colliery. Taken from a similar viewpoint as **Plate 80,** the now vacant trackbed of the sidings is seen. In the background, just visible through the mist is Nook Colliery, and in the foreground the rugby field at the bottom of Well Street now covered by housing.
Authors's Collection, (H.Gillibrand).

Plate 83. Andrew Barclay 0-4-0 saddle tank *Carbon* of 1913 vintage is seen outside the Tyldesley Coal Company's engine shed on 1st August 1959. At this date only Cleworth Hall Colliery remained open, the line, far left, serving the colliery, passing over the lines of Ramsden's Shakerley Colliery on the way. In the next road is 0-4-0 *Jessie,* built by the Hunslet Engine Co. in 1927. Out of shot on the right was Yew Tree Colliery, or what remained of it by this period. Note the steepness of the lines passing under Manchester Road, far right heading south towards the mainline connections.

Cleworth Hall Colliery was the most successful of Tyldesley Coal Company's mines, opening about 1874 and continuing in production under NCB ownership until closure in 1963. Yet, only in 1959/60, a new reinforced concrete bridge was built on Manchester Road to accomodate coal dispatches from Cleworth Hall Colliery, replacing the existing original.

The sites of Cleworth Hall, Yew Tree and Wellington Pits are now covered by housing and little evidence remains of the mining activity that took place here for over a hundred years. However, part of the trackbed of Green's line to Astley is still walkable but the section between Henfold Road and Chaddock Lane is used as road access for industry. *Author's Collection, (C.A.Appleton).*

Plate 84. A 4-car DMU approaches Tyldesley c1964, near to the former Green's and Ramsden's Sidings. Note again the open aspect in the background which will soon be covered in housing, some under construction behind the gasworks wall, far left.
Authors's Collection, (H.Gillibrand).

64

Plate 85. 'Jubilee' Class No 45657 *Tyrwhitt* is seen a few yards east of the former entrance to Green's and Ramsden's Sidings about 1965. The gate, far left background, denoted the boundary to the sidings and in years past was closed on new years day to preserve the landowners right-of-way. On higher ground is Nelson Street, the viewpoint for *Plates 80, 82 & 84.* The locomotive has the yellow cabside warning stripe denoting that it is banned from working under the electrified wires south of Crewe. This is a typical Jim Carter shot having first stoked up the firebox for effect and made sure steam pressure was up.

Author's Collection,
(Jim Carter).

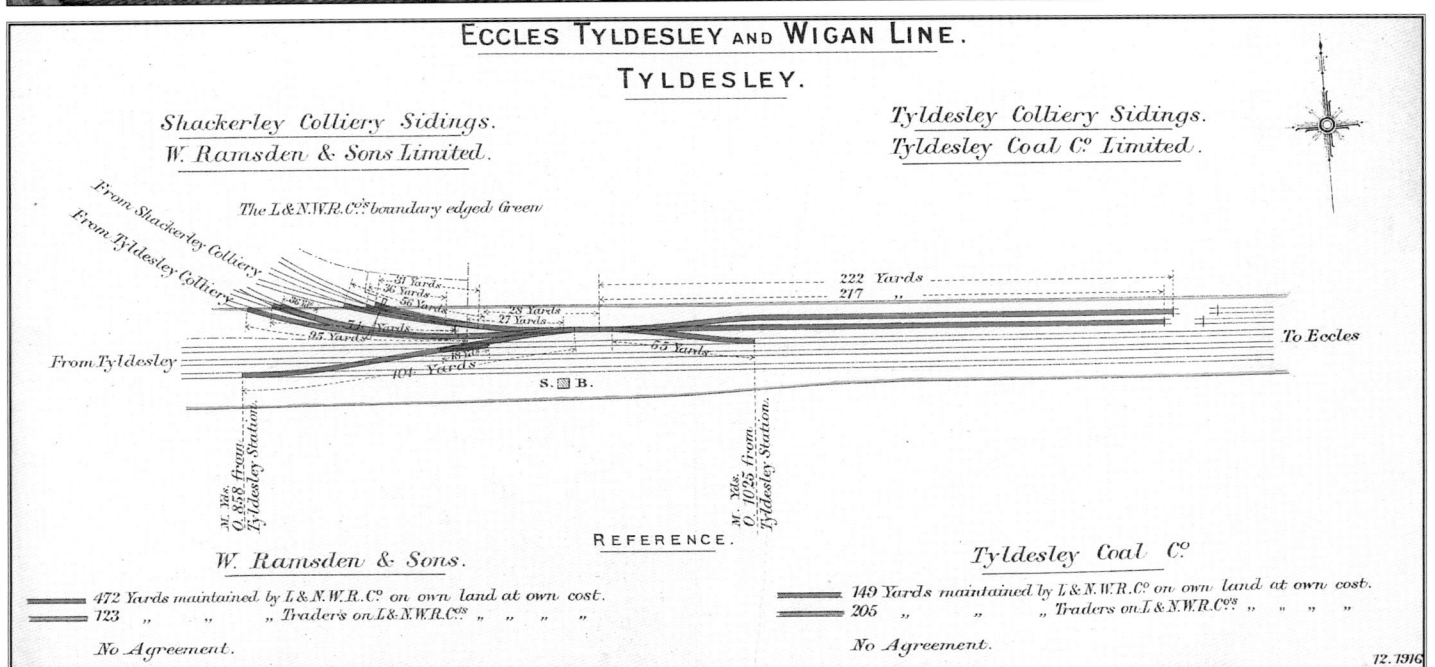

Fig 23. Green's Sidings signal box is shown on this 1916 arrangement at Ramsdens/Greens Sidings. *Courtesy, John Hall*

HOUGH LANE

As the railway progressed eastwards towards Ellenbrook and Worsley from Tyldesley, Hough Lane signal box was reached which, before the new box at Tyldesley opened in 1963, was 917 yards from the old Tyldesley No.1 box. The gas works, on the south side of the lines, opened in the 1880s, the foundation stone being laid by William Ramsden of Shakerley Collieries in 1880. He was also Chairman of the Gas & Water Committee on Tyldesley Council. Deliveries of coking coal to the Gas Works were deposited in a loop line off the Down Main which ran round the back of the box to rejoin the main line west of Upton Lane bridge, Upton Lane being the only road access to the gas works, built for the horse & cart era, preventing any vehicle of size passing through.

The Up Goods Loop ran from Well Street to Hough Lane where the Up Main line could be accessed. This allowed slow moving freights to be held whilst the faster passenger trains passed.

In the days when everyone went by train on their holidays, empty coaching stock was often stored in the sidings at Hough Lane.

Plate 86. This incredibly dirty photo taken from Nelson Street is a late 1920s view of the gas works, the earliest known. The gas works was built in the 1880s, road access to which was by Upton Lane, centre. There are a number of private owner wagons in the nearby sidings which extend to Hough Lane but only the LMS insignia can be distinguished.
Authors's Collection, (H.Gillibrand).

Plate 87. Hough Lane signalbox in the late 1950s. This was a London & North Western type '4' opening in 1911 which allowed the closure of the existing Hough Lane box. On opening it had 49 working levers and 15 spare, later increased in 1928 to 51 working.
Peter Hampson.

TRAIN MOVEMENTS THROUGH TYLDESLEY MID 1950S (WEEK DAYS)
UP LINE

am/pm	Time Arr.	Dept.	Train No.	Except	Class	From	To
am		12.13			K	Ince Moss Junction	Weaste Junction Siding
am		12.34		MO	E	Springs Branch	Liverp'l Rd, Manchester
am	1.37	1.37		MX	H	Preston	Patricroft
am		1.47	374	MX	C Fish	Law Junction, Scotland	Oldham Rd, Manchester
am		2.03		MX	E	Carnforth	Liverpool Rd, Manchester
am		2.17	382	MO	C Fish	Wigan NW	Oldham Rd, Manchester
am		2.24		T O	E	Carlisle	Cross Lane
am		5.57	24		A	Wigan NW	Manchester Exchange
am	6.08			SX	B	Wigan NW	Tyldesley
am	6.14	6.15			B	Leigh	Manchester Exchange
am		6.22			D	Carlisle	Liverpool Rd, Manchester
am	6.25		111	MX	K	Kenyon Junction	Tyldesley
am		6.56		SO	D	Carlisle	Liverpool Rd, Manchester
am	7.08			SX	B Motor	Wigan NW	Tyldesley
am		7.15	109	MX	K	Tyldesley	Hough Lane
am	7.14	7.16			B	Kenyon Junction	Manchester Exchange
am	7.27			SX	C ECS	Leigh	Tyldesley
am	7.41	7.42			B	Kenyon Junction	Manchester Exchange
am	7.57			SX	B Motor	Leigh	Tyldesley
am	7.54	8.03			B	Preston	Manchester Exchange
am	8.17		109	MO	K	Kenyon Junction	Tyldesley
am		8.23	352	MX	C Fish	Aberdeen	Manchester Victoria
am	8.15	8.30	111	MX	K	Bag Lane	Ellenbrook Sidings
am	8.52	8.53	188		B	Liverpool Lime Street	Manchester Exchange
am	9.30	9.32			B	Wigan NW	Manchester Exchange
am	9.43	9.55		SX	J	Garston Liverpool	Jacksons Sidings
am		10.14	204		A	Windermere	Manchester Exchange
am	10.23	10.24	40		B	Chester General	Manchester Exchange
am	10.45	10.46		SX	GEB	Jacksons Sidings	Ellenbrook Sidings
am		11.18	336	SO	A	Morecambe E Road	Manchester Exchange
am	11.20		109	SX	K Emt's	Kenyon Junction	Tyldesley
pm	12.05		109	SO	J	Kenyon Junction	Tyldesley
pm		12.06		SX	G LE G	Leigh	Patricroft Loco
pm	12.12			SO	G LE G	Leigh	Tyldesley (1.20/Leigh)
pm		12.09	398	SO	A	Blackpool North	Stoke-on-Trent
pm	12.43	12.46			B	Wigan NW	Manchester Exchange
pm	1.47			SO	C ECS	Leigh	Tyldesley
pm	1.56	1.58	84	SO	A	Windermere	Manchester Exchange
pm		2.07	110	SX	K	Jacksons Sidings	Patricroft N Sidings
pm	2.06	2.09		SO	B	Kenyon Junction	Manchester Exchange
pm		2.18		SO	G LE P	Tyldesley Ex 1.47	Patricroft Loco
pm	1.40	2.22	109	SO	K	Jacksons Sdgs	Patricroft N Sidings
pm		2.55	105	SX	K	Tyldesley	Patricroft
pm	3.03		290	nnSO	B	Blackpool Central	Tyldesley
pm		3.09		MX	G LE G	Jacksons Sidings	Patricroft Loco
pm		4.05	110	MO	K	Jacksons Sidings	Patricroft N Sidings
pm	4.12				B Motor	Leigh	Tyldesley
pm	4.22		113	SX	G LE G	Leigh	Tyldesley
pm	4.35		292	SX	K	Bolton	Tyldesley
pm	4.41	4.43			B	Wigan NW	Leeds City
pm		5.05	109	SX	K	Jacksons Sidings	Patricroft N Sidings
pm	5.11	5.11		SO	C ECS	Wigan NW	Tyldesley (5.45 K/Jct)
pm	5.34	5.35	C273		A	Blackpool Central	Manchester Exchange
pm		6.00			H	Carlisle	Ordsall Lane
pm	6.02				B Motor	Earlestown	Tyldesley
pm	6.22	6.23			B	Wigan NW	Leeds City
pm	6.12	6.27		SX	F	Bolton	Warrington
pm	7.25			SX	B Motor	Kenyon Junction	Tyldesley
pm	7.55		112	SX	G LE G	Leigh	Tyldesley
pm	7.33	8.15		SX	K	Atherton Bag Lane	Weaste Junction Siding
pm	8.22			SO	G LE P	Wigan NW	Manchester Exchange
pm	8.38	8.43		SX	B	Wigan NW	Manchester Exchange
pm	8.50	9.13	112	SX	K	Jacksons Sidings	Bolton
pm		9.25		SX	D	Garston Liverpool	Oldham Road/Phillips Pk
pm	9.23	9.28		SO	B	Wigan NW	Manchester Exchange
pm	9.42	9.45			A	Glasgow Central	Manchester Victoria
pm	9.55			SO	B Motor	Kenyon Junction	Tyldesley
pm	10.29			SO	B	Leigh	Tyldesley
pm		10.40		SO	G LE P	Tyldesley	Patricroft Loco
pm	10.50	10.52		SX	B	Wigan NW	Manchester Exchange
pm	10.52	10.54		SO	B	Wigan NW	Manchester Exchange
pm	11.07	11.15			G LE P	Leigh	Patricroft Loco

SUNDAYS

am/pm	Time Arr.	Dept.	Train No.	Except	Class	From	To
am		1.45	374		C Fish	Carlisle	Oldham Rd, Manchester
am		2.14			E	Carnforth	Patricroft N Sidings
am		5.57	24		A	Wigan NW	Manchester Exchange
am		7.14	352		C Fish	Aberdeen	Oldham Rd, Manchester
am	8.43	8.50			B	Liverpool Lime Street	Manchester Exchange
am	10.01	10.03			B	Wigan NW	Manchester Exchange
pm	2.16	2.18			B	Wigan NW	Manchester Exchange
pm	4.06	4.08			B	Liverpool Lime Street	Manchester Exchange
pm	7.15	7.17			B	Wigan NW	Manchester Exchange
pm	7.41	7.43	288		B	Liverpool Lime Street	Newcastle-on-Tyne
pm	9.15	9.16			B	Liverpool Lime Street	Manchester Exchange
pm	10.04	10.06	378		B	Liverpool Lime Street	Manchester Exchange

TRAIN MOVEMENTS THROUGH TYLDESLEY MID 1950'S (WEEK DAYS) DOWN LINE

am/pm	Time Arr.	Dept.	Train No.	Except	Class	From	To
am	12.35			MO	G LE P	Patricroft Loco	Wigan NW
am		1.22	177	MO	A Mails	Leeds City South	Wigan NW
am		1.22			A Mails	Stalybridge	Wigan NW
am		2.24			A News	Manchester Exchange	Wigan NW
am		2.59		MO	H	Ordsall Lane	Preston
am	2.50	3.28		MX	H	Ordsall Lane	Carlisle
am	4.09	4.42		MX	K	Ordsall Lane	Springs Branch
am	5.20	5.23			G LE P	Patricroft Loco	Leigh
am	5.56			SX	G LE P	Patricroft Loco	Tyldesley
am		6.17		SX	B Motor	Tyldesley	Wigan
am	6.26	6.33			B	Manchester Exchange	Preston
am	6.39		109	MX	G LE G	Patricroft Loco	Tyldesley
am		6.45		SX	B	Tyldesley	Leigh
am		7.05	111	MX	K	Tyldesley	Atherton Bag Lane
am		7.12		SX	B Motor	Tyldesley	Leigh
am		7.15		SO	B	Tyldesley	Leigh
am	7.28	7.30			B	Manchester Exchange	Wigan NW
am		7.39	109	MX	K	Hough Lane	Leigh
am		8.00		SX	G LE G	Tyldesley	Leigh (5.57 Ex Leigh)
am	8.23	8.25			B	Manchester Exchange	Kenyon Junction
am		8.30		SX	B	Tyldesley	Wigan NW
am		8.35		SO	B	Tyldesley	Wigan NW
am		8.42	109	MO	G EBV	Tyldesley	Speakmans Sidings
am	8.45	8.47	345	SO	A	Cross Lane	Barrow
am	9.30	9.34	315	SO	A	Cross Lane	Blackpool N via Leigh
am	9.43	9.55		SX	J Emt's	Garston Liverpool	Jacksons Sidings
am	10.45	10.46		SX	G EBV	Jacksons Sidings	Ellenbrook
am	11.24	11.26			B	Manchester Exchange	Wigan NW
am		11.41	110	SO	J Emt's	Patricroft Dn Sidings	Jacksons Sidings
am	11.33	11.44			F Emt's	Ellesmere Port	Chanters Sidings
am		11.48		SX	K	Ellenbrook	Kenyon Junction
am		11.52	293	SO	G LE G	Patricroft Loco	Atherton Bag Lane
pm		12.30	109	SX	G EBV	Tyldesley	Leigh
pm	12.35	12.36		SO	B	Manchester Exchange	Kenyon Junction
pm		12.45	109	SO	K	Tyldesley	Jacksons Sidings
pm	1.03	1.05		SO	B	Manchester Exchange	Wigan NW
pm		1.20		SO	B Motor	Tyldesley	Leigh
pm		1.42	110	SO	K	Tyldesley	Kenyon Junction
pm		1.52	291	SX	G LE G	Patricroft Loco	Atherton Bag Lane
pm	2.09	2.11		SO	B	Manchester Exchange	Wigan NW
pm		2.15	109	SX	G E&2BV	Tyldesley	Jacksons Sidings
pm	2.20		105	SX	K	Ellenbrook	Tyldesley
pm		3.20		SO	G LE P	Patricroft Loco	Tyldesley (3.49 Leigh)
pm		3.21		SO	C ECS	Tyldesley	Springs Br.(Ex 3.03 Up)
pm	3.30	3.30		SX	G LE P	Patricroft Loco	Tyldesley (3.49 Leigh)
pm	3.36	3.40		SO	B	Manchester Exchange	Wigan NW
pm	3.42	3.45		SX	B	Manchester Exchange	Wigan NW
pm		3.49			B Motor	Tyldesley	Leigh
pm	4.17	4.18	37		A	Manchester Exchange	Barrow
pm	4.24			SX	G LE P	Patricroft Loco	Tyldesley (to shunt)
pm		4.25			B Motor	Tyldesley	Earlestown
pm		4.34	39		A	Manchester Exchange	Glasgow
pm		4.43	112	SX	G LE G	Patricroft Loco	Leigh
pm	4.47	4.49			B	Manchester Exchange	Wigan NW
pm		4.50	113	SX	G LE G	Tyldesley	Jacksons Sidings
pm	5.38	5.40			B	Manchester Exchange	Wigan NW
pm		5.45			B	Tyldesley	Kenyon Junction
pm	6.12	6.18		SX	B	Manchester Exchange	Leigh
pm	6.12	6.27		SX	F	Bolton	Warrington (+1BV Tyd)
pm		6.30	292	SX	K	Tyldesley	Kenyon Junction
pm	6.39	6.41			B	Manchester Exchange	Wigan NW
pm		6.45		SX	B Motor	Tyldesley	Leigh
pm		6.45		SX	B Motor	Tyldesley	Kenyon Junction
pm	7.05	7.29		SX	D	Liverpool Road Gds	Carlisle Viaduct Yard
pm	7.32			SO	C ECS	Manchester Exchange	Tyldesley
pm		7.37		SX	G LE G	Tyldesley	Jacksons Sidings
pm	7.24	7.43		SO	E	Liverpool Road Gardens	Carlisle Viaduct Yard
pm		7.49		SX	K	Patricroft Sidings	Garston Liverpool
pm		8.05	112	SX	G EBV	Tyldesley	Jacksons Sidings
pm		8.20		SO	K	Patricroft Sidings	Garston Liverpool
pm	9.46	9.56		SX	B	Manchester Exchange	Wigan NW
pm	9.56	9.59		SO	B	Manchester Exchange	Wigan NW
pm		10.05		SO	B Motor	Tyldesley	Leigh
pm		10.29		SX	E	Liverpool Road Gds	Carnforth
pm	10.43	10.45			B	Manchester Exchange	Leigh
pm		10.59	379	SO	A News	Manchester Exchange	Carlisle
pm	11.08	11.09		SX	B	Manchester Exchange	Wigan NW
pm	11.10	11.12		SO	B Mails	Manchester Exchange	Wigan NW

SUNDAYS

am/pm	Time Arr.	Dept.	Train No.	Except	Class	From	To
am		1.22			A	Stalybridge	Wigan NW
am		1.41			H	Buxton	Springs Brance N/Sdgs
am		2.24	1		C PCLS	Manchester Exchange	Carnforth
am	8.49	8.52			B	Manchester Exchange	Wigan NW
am	9.01	9.52	431		B	Manchester Exchange	Liverpool Lime Street
am	9.54	9.56	448		B	Leeds City	Liverpool Lime Street
pm	3.00	3.02			B	Manchester Exchange	Wigan NW
pm	3.16	3.19	456		B	Manchester Exchange	Liverpool Lime Street
pm	6.49	6.52	387		B	Manchester Exchange	Liverpool Lime Street
pm	7.19	7.22			B	Manchester Exchange	Wigan NW
pm	9.04	9.06	389		B	Manchester Exchange	Liverpool Lime Street
pm		11.27	305		A	Manchester Exchange	Glasgow Central

Plate 88. Class '8F' No.48714 approaches Hough Lane c1965 with a coal train for Sanderson's Sidings, Worsley, from Speakman's Sidings Leigh. Tyldesley Station can just be made out at top left. The houses, middle right, since demolished and the area redeveloped, were known locally as the 'Jig' being built to the incline of the landscape or 'Banks' a derivative of which, 'Bongs,' became the colloquial name for Tyldesley. The shot is from Hough Lane box.

Great Boys Colliery, shown on the first O/S of 1849, was sited on the west side of Mort Lane, beyond the later (1930s) Pear Tree Estate. In 1855 it was sold by the executors of the late owner William Atkin, to John Fletcher and Samuel Scowcroft and from 1869, was in the sole possession of Fletcher. In the mid 1860s, a new pit, Pear Tree Colliery (sometimes also known as Great Boys) had been sunk by Fletcher & Scowcroft behind the *Colliers Arms* and *Red Lion* Public Houses on the north side of Sale Lane and the resultant dirt tips, although small in comparison to the larger mines, were a playground for us local kids in the 1940s & 50s. Now what's this got to do with railways you will be asking! Well, this is the interesting bit; to serve these pits, permission was given by the landowners, Bridgewater Estates, to construct a railway from a point near Hough Lane signal box, on the up side, for a private line which would tunnel under Sale Lane at its junction with Hough Lane and proceed north-east to connect with Pear Tree and Great Boys Collieries, a 20 year lease being signed in October 1868. If this railway was ever built is open to question as no further mention, or trace has been found. However, in the 1990s, house building commenced on the Great Boys site on Mort Lane the mine shafts of which proved troublesome, and not what the contractor expected. For a while construction ceased while further site investigations were carried out. You can learn a lot from the old O/S!

Author's Collection, (Jim Carter).

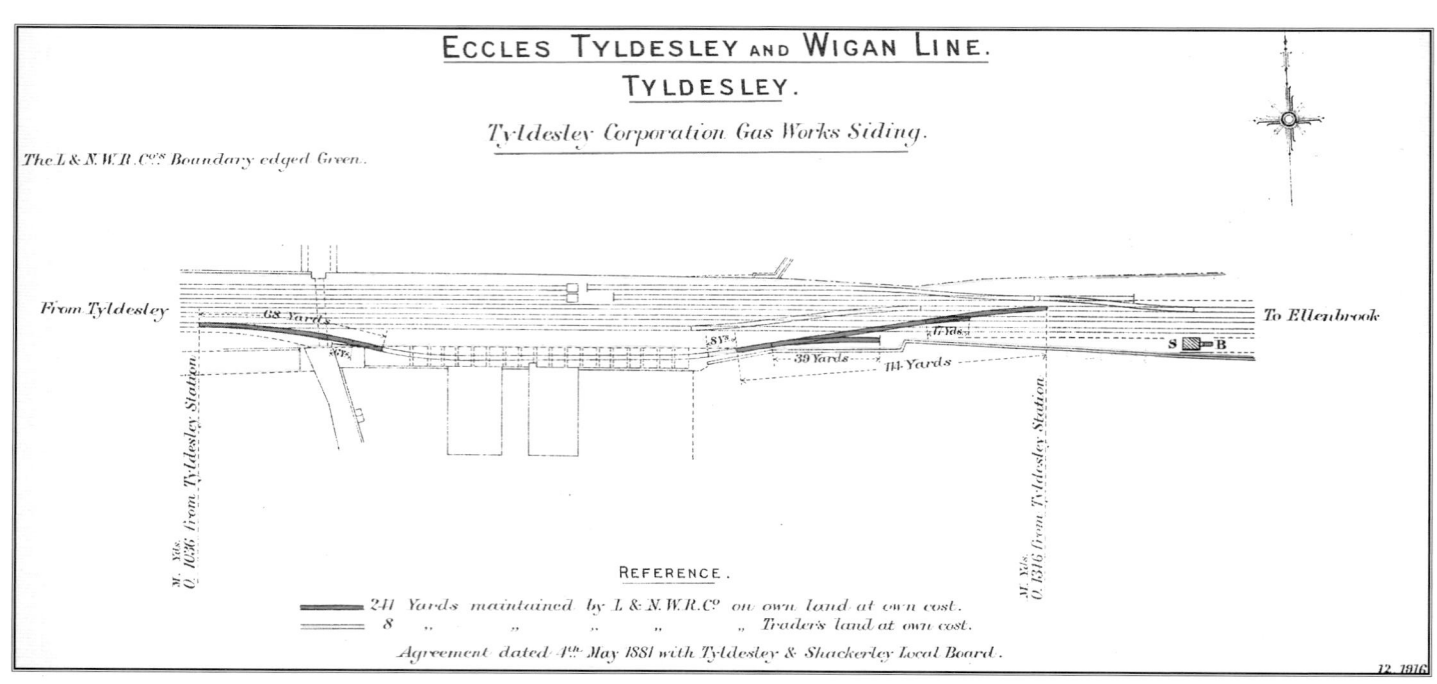

Fig 24. Tyldesley Gas Works Siding c1916 with Upton Lane underbridge, left, and the second Hough Lane signal box, right.
Courtesy, John Hall.

Plate 89. One of the Fairburn 2-6-4 Tank engines No.42297 approaches Hough Lane overbridge on 2nd May 1964 with a Manchester Exchange - Wigan North Western service. From here, the cutting was infilled in 1984 right up to Parr Brow, (A577) 'Bomb Bridge' in the background being demolished. It is where I spent many hours in my schooldays engine spotting, the bridge itself led from open farmland on the right, to Chester Road, the houses were built parallel with the railway in the mid 1920s. The houses, extreme left, are on Wardley Road and more property now occupies what was open ground between the latter and Hough Lane. *Peter Eckersley.*

Plate 90. B.R. Standard Class '9F' No.92016 is viewed from Parr Brow overbridge with Chester Road on the right and Bomb Bridge to the rear on 30th November 1966, with a coal train from Speakman's Sidings, Leigh. Here, the course of the railway had to be cut through an outcrop of the upper red sandstone, resulting in a cutting some 30 feet in depth on its north side. *Peter Eckersley.*

Plate 91. In 1984, infilling of the this cutting and removal of bridges and embankments began. In the background, Bomb Bridge has been demolished and it won't be long before most of this cutting is back to its pre 1860s level. Some of the Leigh railway arches were being demolished concomitantly and rubble from these, which included infill sandstone from this cutting when being built, was transported back here from whence it came. *Author.*

71

ELLENBROOK

The Bridgewater Collieries made connections here with the London & North Western in 1871 and their system of colliery railways hereabouts was extended to reach its zenith under the ownership of Manchester Collieries Ltd., in the 1930s. A volume in itself would be required to fully cover and give justice to the numerous lines and sidings, far beyond the scope of this book. Suffice to say that the Bridgewater Colliery Railways owe their beginnings to the horse drawn tramways and wagonways built to alleviate overcrowding on the unique underground canal system which emerged at Worsley Delph on the Bridgewater Canal first instituted by the third Duke of Bridgewater in 1765.

In this volume I will only deal with those standard gauge railways which had mainline connections.

The proposal for the London & North Western Railway's Eccles-Tyldesley-Wigan line in 1861 convinced the Bridgewater Estates Trustees of the need to work in association with the railways in order to effect a more rapid distribution of their increasing coal production. In this, they had been thwarted a number of times by the Lancashire & Yorkshire Railway whose plans for various incursions into the area had never been fulfilled. Therefore the impetus to construct or re-build their internal railways to standard gauge with various mainline connections and sidings, a process which had begun about ten years previously, now continued apace. Eventually these colliery lines were to become part of the Central Railways of Manchester Collieries Ltd in 1929, complete with their own locomotive repair and workshop facilities at Central Workshops, Walkden, which would become the main depot for such activities in NCB days*.

The proposed Eccles-Tyldesley-Wigan line also signalled a new phase of mining development by the Bridgewater Trustees, part of which was the sinking of the first shafts at Mosley Common in the 1860s, on a site previously mined for the Worsley Four Foot outcrop. Sinking was completed in late 1869, coal production beginning in 1870.

Mosley Common Colliery was situated south of the Eccles-Tyldesley-Wigan railway and eventually was to become the largest in the Manchester Coalfield. A new, standard gauge branch line, replacing an earlier tramway of 1835 was constructed to run from the new colliery to the Bridgewater Canal at Boothstown opening in 1873, together with an expansion of the sidings at Mosley Common. Two years previously a colliery railway from the Ellesmere Pit at Walkden had been built to Ellenbrook with spurs to the smaller City and Gatley pits. The Bridgewater Collieries standard gauge connection at Ellenbrook Sidings is concomitant with these works, opening in 1871.

*A complete map of the Central Railways system will be found on page 86

Plate 92. Stanier 2-6-4 tank No.2563 is seen between Ellenbrook and Parr Brow in May 1948 with a Wigan train. It is only five months since nationalisation of the railways and the new owners have yet to complete the renumbering of some 18,000 locomotives which came into Government hands on 1st January 1948. It would take some while to accomplish this and I can recall seeing coaching stock and locomotives still bearing the previous owner's initials into the mid 1950s.
W.D.Cooper,
(Cooperline).

Plate 93. Another '8F' No.48553, passes through Ellenbrook Station with a coal train from Speakman's Sidings, Leigh in mid 1965. The station here had closed in 1961 but today, with the chronic road congestion, would be booming. An all stations stopping train took 26 minutes from Ellenbrook to Manchester Exchange; try doing that today during the morning commute!

Author's Collection, (Jim Carter).

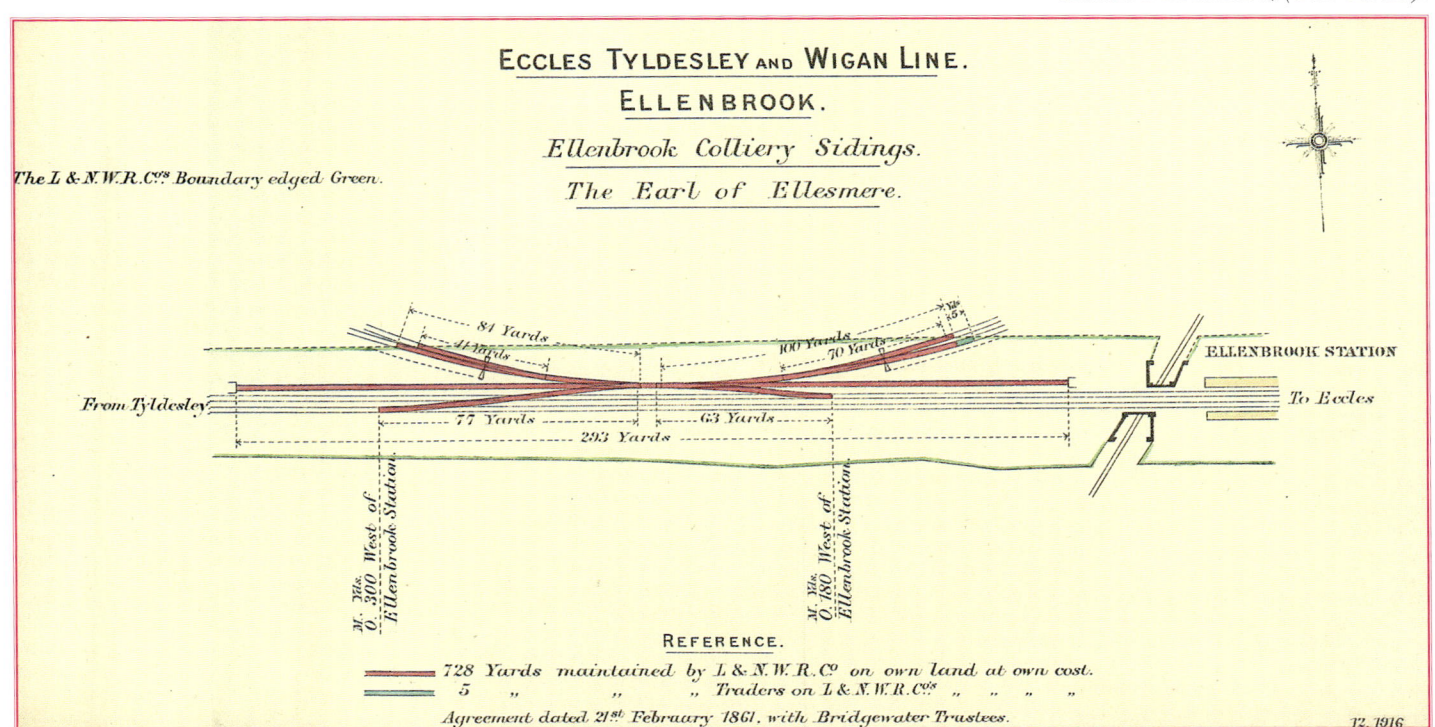

Fig 25. Ellenbrook Sidings at 1916. The colliery line running under the bridge is from Boothshall Bank, to Walkden and Ashton's Field.

Courtesy, John Hall.

73

Plate 94. BR Standard Class '4' No.75053 seen passing through Ellenbrook about 1958.
Stations U.K.

Plate 95. Parallel boilered 4-6-0 'Patriot' Class No.5502 *Royal Naval Division*, passes the Ellenbrook outer distant signal, which still has the London & North Western type lower quadrant arm, about 1946 with the 3.55pm Manchester - Windermere express through open country with Ladybridge in the background. The Broadway Estate would later be built on the left. The gradient here continued just beyond Ellenbrook Station and the plume of steam was visible at Parr Brow before the train came into view and each 'spotter' would try to be first to identify which class of engine it was. Such were the joys of a simple life!
W.D.Cooper, (Cooperline).

Plate 96. The 'Up' Manchester platform at Ellenbrook as viewed from its western end is pictured here on 31st December 1960, looking like it's been put together by some odd-jobber with a couple of vertical battens holding the gable end together and its pigeon-cote like roof appendage as an afterthought. There must be some explanation for this, somewhere!
John Ryan.

Plate 97. The Ellenbrook outer distant signal, left, is seen from the opposite direction to *Plate 95* as LMS 2-6-2T No.130 approaches Ladybrook Bridge with a Manchester Exchange service on 12th January 1946.
John Ryan Collection, (W.D.Cooper).

Plate 98. Seen near the same location as *Plate 95*, 'Jubliee' Class 4-6-0 No.45617 *Mauritius* passes with a Manchester Exchange - Glasgow express in the mid 1950s.
Author's Collection, (D.Evans).

Astley Green Colliery was situated on the northern bank of the Bridgewater Canal, to the south east of Tyldesley. Sinking of the shafts began here in 1908 by the Pilkington Coal Company, a subsidiary of the Clifton & Kearsley Coal Co. Ltd., on what was virtually a virgin coalfield stretching southward towards the Cheshire Plain. At the same time the colliery owners laid down a railway running 1½ miles south across Astley Moss to connect with the London & North Western's Liverpool to Manchester line at Astley. Similar methods of construction of this branch to those employed by George Stephenson during construction of the Liverpool & Manchester Railway were used, i.e. brushwood hurdles overlaid with ash and ballast.

In 1913 the Clifton & Kearsley Coal Company purchased the canal basin and facilities formerly used by George Green's Tyldesley Coal Company, the latter having ceased to use their railway south of the Eccles-Tyldesley main line by this period.

New installations were built alongside the Bridgewater Canal at Astley, replacing those originally built by the Tyldesley Coal Company.

Under the auspices of Manchester Collieries a new line of railway was built in 1931 from Astley Green Colliery to connect with the existing colliery railway at Boothshall Bank, allowing through running by colliery locomotives via Mosley Common and Walkden to Ashton's Field. In 1932 a modern washing plant was constructed and the sidings layout brought up to date.

In the early 1960s when in N.C.B. ownership, further updating of facilities brought Astley Green to the forefront as a coal producer in the Manchester coalfield and many local miners were transferred here as older collieries in the Wigan, Tyldesley and Atherton areas closed.

Closure of Astley Green was first proposed in April 1969 just as the colliery was increasing its production. Although a reprieve was announced in the following June, closure would eventually take place in 1970, the last coal being wound on 3rd April inst. Surface facilities continued in operation until October 1970 treating existing stocks and coal from other collieries that were rail connected and for a short while, the spectacle of heavily laden 0-6-0 colliery engines slogging up Boothshall and Walkden Banks to Ashton's Field presented railway photographers with a last opportunity to indulge their passion.

Plate 99. Somewhere amongst this crowd, Lady Pilkington cuts the first sod of No.1 pit at Astley Green on 7th May 1908. The sinking of this shaft though was not without its problems as the geology of the area contained a mixture of glacial drift, copious volumes of water and quicksand. The first seam at 772ft was the Worsley four-foot which outcropped at Tyldesley on the Shakerley Estate and had been mined since the 15th century. This gives some idea of the dip in coal seams as mining probed further south. *John Ryan Collection.*

Plate 100. One of the first locomotives at Astley Green was this 0-6-0 saddle tank built by Andrew Barclay in 1880 for Llanelly & Mynydd Mawr Railway, and purchased from J.F.Wake & Co, Darlington in 1914 and appropriately named *Astley Green* on arrival. It was sent to Walkden Yard in 1936 and sold as scrap to H.Stephenson & Sons Limited of Hindley.
John Ryan Collection.

Plate 101. Astley Green Colliery had triangular junctions with the Liverpool - Manchester main line on Astley Moss, east of Astley Station. On 29th November 1966, B.R. Standard class '5' No. 73157 is seen approaching the west connection with a coal train from Astley Green Sidings. In the distance is Astley signal box which controlled the level crossing. *Peter Eckersley.*

Plate 102. The eastern junction from Astley Green, its ground frame and connection with the Liverpool & Manchester line, are shown here as Stanier class '5' No.44681 gives an impressive display against a leaden sky on 29th November 1966 with a westbound freight.
Peter Eckersley.

77

Plate 103. 'Austerity' *Allen, HC/1777/1944,* had been stationed at Astley Green since 1950 and not withdrawn from service until 1968. It is seen here double heading with ex-Bridgwater Collieries 0-6-0 Side Tank of 1924 *Bridgewater,* shunting internal user wagons at Astley Green in 1966. Extreme left, on the horizon, is the housing estate which borders the L&NWR alongside Chester Road, where the deep cutting is, as in **Plate 90.** *Author's Collection, (Jim Carter).*

Plate 104. Having been transferred from Gin Pit in early 1966, 'Austerity' *Harry, HC/1776/1944,* underwent a complete overhaul at Walkden Yard before being sent to Astley Green where it is seen about to cross the Bridgewater Canal on a rising gradient, en-route to Astley Green Sidings on 7th March 1970. *John Ryan.*

Plate 105. Not long after overhaul *Harry* is seen again, this time in the sidings at the top of Boothshall Bank near Mosley Common Colliery, about to draw forward with a heavy load in 1966. *Author's Collection, (Jim Carter).*

Plate 106. With the A580 East Lancashire Road overbridge in the background, resplendent ex-North Staffordshire Railway 0-6-2 Side Tank No.2 waits to depart from Boothshall Bank sidings with a brake van tour of Central Railways on 3rd August 1964 which had begun at Worsley. On the other side of the bridge is Mosley Common Colliery. *John Ryan.*

Plate 107. Former No.2 of the North Staffordshire Railway, 0-6-2 Side Tank *Princess* is seen at Mosley Common Colliery about 1952. This is one of five purchased from the L.M.S. in 1937 by Manchester Collieries. On arrival at Walkden Yard it carried its L.M.S No.2271. In 1960, it was outshopped in its old North Staffordshire livery of Madder Lake with cream lining as No.2 and put on exhibit at Stoke-on-Trent Station for a while. It remained in that livery until withdrawn in 1965. *The Transport Treasury (G.Ellis)*.

Plate 108. At a point just south of Walkden Shed, 'Austerity' *Repulse*, HE/3698/1950, pauses en-route to Ashton's Field with a train from Astley Green on 2nd August 1967.

John Ryan.

Plate 109. A pair of 'Austerities' are seen at Walkden with a train for Ashton's Field on 4th April 1970. The banking engine is *Stanley, HE/3303/1945*.
P.Richardson.

Plate 110. A view of Walkden Shed on 27th December 1967 with, on the right, the old Ellesmere Colliery opened in 1870. The section of railway from Ellesmere Pit to the exchange sidings at Ellenbrook opened in October 1871. After closure in 1921, Ellesmere was used as a pumping station, the 'take' from the pit being allocated to Mosley Common Colliery. *John Ryan.*

Plate 111. Compared to the steep climbs up Boothshall and Walkden Banks the railway towards Ashton's Field and Brackley Collieries was relatively flat. On 14th March 1970 'Austerity' *Warrior, HE/3823/1954* appears to be making good headway with coal for the blending plant at Ashton Field. However, local housewives often complained that the locomotive's exhausts were staining their washing and a number of modifications were carried out to various engines without much success. *John Ryan.*

81

Ashton's Field pit began production in the late 1850s but was not connected to the standard gauge system, an extension of the route from Sandersons and Wardley, until 1865/6. The route to Ashton's Field from Walkden was built rather piecemeal, not completed until 1873/4.

Further north, Brackley Colliery, adjacent to the A6, opened in the late 1870s and the following year the Bridgewater Trustees purchased Wharton Hall Colliery which they operated as a working mine until 1927, thereafter it was retained as a pumping station. The headgear and winding house of this colliery was still in situ in the late 1950s when we kids would play on the smaller tip and I can remember being chased off by some irate bloke who came running out of the Winding House waving his arms about; complete nutter we thought! The headgear and outbuildings were demolished in 1964.

This colliery had actually been connected to a branch off the Little Hulton Extensions Railway by agreement between its previous owners and the L&NWR. Brackley Colliery was linked by a rather circuitous extension from Ashton's Field which passed under the L&NW Roe Green-Bolton branch near Plodder Lane, thence turning south, passing under the A6 to reach Wharton Hall and the tipping site at Cutacre by 1908. Cutacre Tip was reckoned to be the biggest in Western Europe and has only recently been removed. When, in 1888, the Lancashire & Yorkshire's Pendleton-Crow Nest, Hindley, line opened a sidings connection was laid to Wharton Hall.

Plate 112. Now how often did you have a steam locomotive passing over your street? Odd, today's readers might think so but actually it was quite common-place and had been since the progenitors of the industrial revolution realised that more horse power was needed to move all the necessities of industry. Now it so happens that this railway was here before the houses around it were built, and most of them are certainly post-war. 'Austerity' *Warrior* is working back towards Walkden on 14th March 1970 propelling empty wagons over the level crossing near Hill Top. These were the last workings, two per day, from Astley Green to Ashton's Field where the coal was blended with coal from Agecroft brought in by road transport to Ashton's Field, then transported by N.C.B. locos to Linnyshaw Moss Sidings for collection by B.R. and delivered to Kearsley Power Station. Traffic ceased on 2nd October 1970.

The track on the former L&NWR between Walkden and Little Hulton, and on the mineral branch, had been left in situ after the closure of the Roe Green-Bolton Great Moor St Branch in 1963 with the intention of effecting traffic movements between Mosley Common and Cutacre Tip as the M61 Motorway was about to carve a swathe through the Linnyshaw Branch towards its junction with the then M63 at Worsley. A proviso of this arrangement was that Mosley Common was to be kept open. However, Mosley Common Colliery closed on 10th February 1968 with Cutacre Tip closing at the same time, the last working from Cutacre had been the collection of empty wagons on 6th February. As Brackley Colliery had closed a couple of years earlier, the line from Cutacre to Ashton's Field was therefore taken out of use.

John Ryan.

ROE GREEN JUNCTION

Further London & North Western Acts of 1865-9 authorised a new branch line from a junction with the Wigan - Eccles route at Roe Green, to Bolton Great Moor Street where a new station was to be built on an adjacent site to the original station as opened in 1831. This had been almost totally demolished by a runaway goods train in 1858. Stations would also be provided at Walkden, Little Hulton and Plodder Lane. The line from Roe Green Junction to collieries at Little Hulton, as authorised in the 1865 Act, opened for freight Traffic on 1st July 1870. The 1869 Act authorised the extension of the Roe Green Branch to its junction with the Bolton & Leigh line at Fletcher Street and this opened on 16th November 1874. The new station at Great Moor Street had opened on 28th September 1874 with the passenger service to Hunts Bank (Manchester Victoria) via Roe Green beginning on 1st April 1875. Manchester Exchange sited west of Victoria was opened by the London & North Western in June 1884. Walkden became Walkden Low Level on 2nd June 1924, to distinguish it from the Lancashire & Yorkshire station. The Manchester Exchange-Great Moor Street passenger service was withdrawn on 29th March 1954 and the stations closed, the same date as those on the Great Moor Street-Kenyon Junction line except for Kenyon Junction itself which remained open for passenger services from Lime Street to Manchester Exchange via Leigh and Tyldesley until 2nd January 1961. Goods facilities remained at Plodder Lane until 30th January 1965.

Plodder Lane's four road engine shed was authorised in 1874 but soon became overcrowded, enlargements taking place in the 1890s. As a sub-shed of Patricroft, Plodder Lane worked the local passenger services to Manchester, Bolton and Kenyon along with freights from the local collieries on the Roe Green Branch. Before closure of the shed took place in 1954 many of the turns on the Bolton & Leigh line were worked by Plodder Lane crews.

In the mid 1930s plans were drawn up by the LMS for a station at Roe Green Junction with platforms serving both the Bolton and Wigan lines. It is probable that the outbreak of W.W.II curtailed this scheme and consequently the station was never built.

Plate 113. LMS Class '5' No.5075 is seen west of Roe Green, just beyond Greenleach Lane overbridge, working a Manchester Exchange - Wigan North Western local train on 19th April 1948. The stock appears to be all LMS 'Period II'. *W.D.Cooper, (Cooperline).*

Plate 114. Parallel boilered 'Royal Scot' Class No.46107 *Argyll and Sutherland Highlander* passes under Greenleach Lane bridge not long after nationalisation on the Down line with what is thought to be a holiday special off the Central Division lines, complete with luggage van behind the engine. Note the absence of any smokebox number plate! *W.D.Cooper, (Cooperline).*

Plate 115. Soon after closure of the Roe Green Branch, a Manchester bound DMU passes with a Liverpool Lime Street via Kenyon and Pennington Junctions to Manchester Exchange train. *Author's Collection, (Alan Palmer).*

ROE GREEN JUNCTION

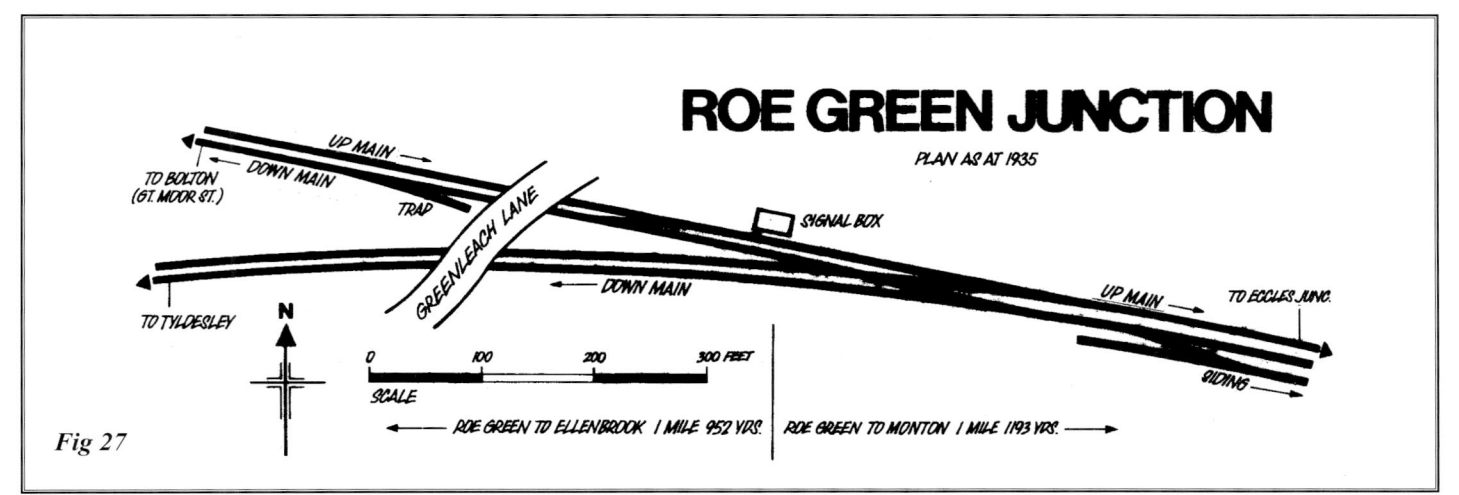

PLAN AS AT 1935

Fig 27

TO BOLTON (GT. MOOR ST.) — UP MAIN — DOWN MAIN — TRAP — GREENLEACH LANE — SIGNAL BOX — DOWN MAIN — UP MAIN — TO ECCLES JUNC. — SIDINGS — TO TYLDESLEY

N

SCALE 0 100 200 300 FEET

← ROE GREEN TO ELLENBROOK 1 MILE 952 YDS. | ROE GREEN TO MONTON 1 MILE 1193 YDS. →

Plate 116. Stanier 2 cylinder 2-6-4 tank No.42610 approaches Roe Green Junction on 14th April 1949 and is seen west of Sanderson's Sidings with a Manchester Exchange - Wigan North Western local train. *W.D.Cooper, (Cooperline).*

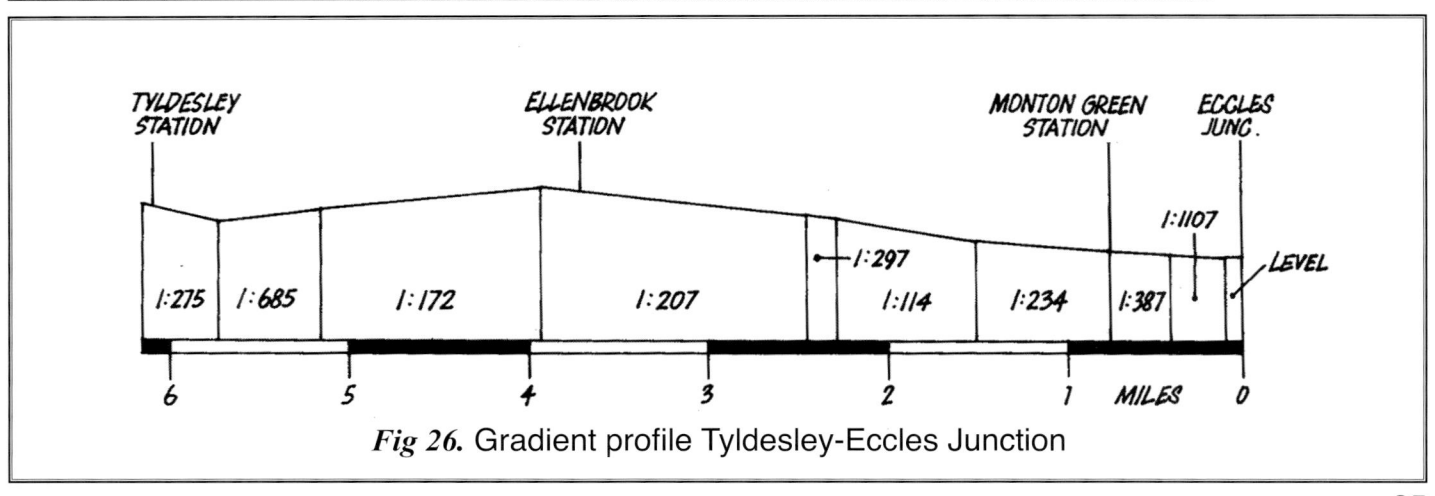

Fig 26. Gradient profile Tyldesley-Eccles Junction

TYLDESLEY STATION — ELLENBROOK STATION — MONTON GREEN STATION — ECCLES JUNC.

1:275 | 1:685 | 1:172 | 1:207 | 1:297 | 1:114 | 1:234 | 1:387 | 1:1107 | LEVEL

6   5   4   3   2   1   0   MILES

85

Fig 28.

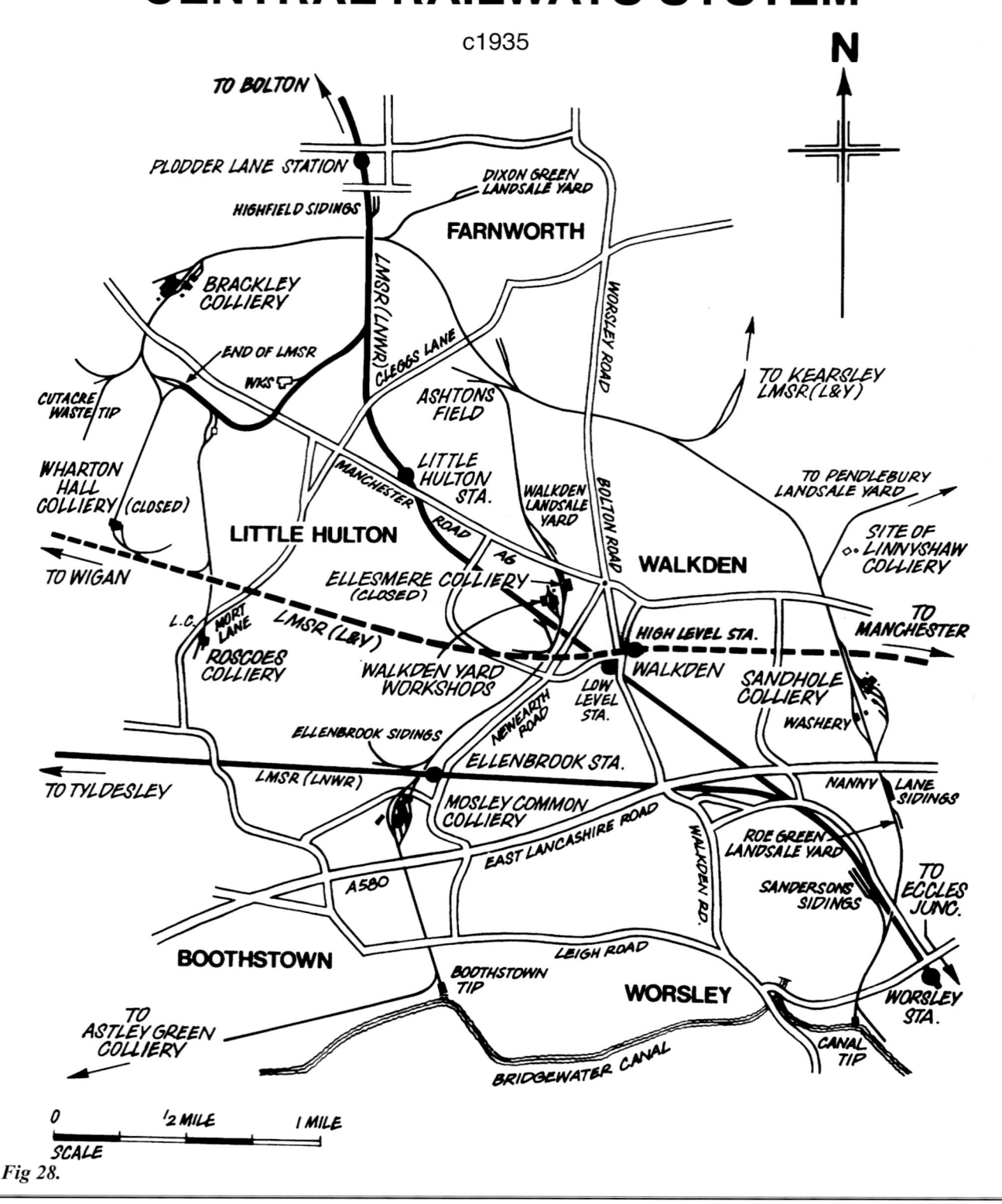

SANDERSON'S SIDINGS

Sanderson's Sidings, located between Roe Green and Worsley, was the first main-line connection for the dispatch of coal traffic originating on the Bridgewater Collieries system and dates from the opening of the Eccles-Tyldesley-Wigan line.

Sanderson's Pit had been sunk about 1835 using a horse drawn narrow gauge line to connect with the Bridgewater Canal at Worsley. The 1847 proposal for the Manchester & Southport Railway which, had it been built, would have passed to the north of Sanderson's Pit, had the effect of persuading the Bridgewater Trustees to convert their Sandersons tramway to standard gauge and this was completed in 1852.

Mining developments moved on apace and Bridgewater Colliery was sunk to the north of Sanderson's Pit in the 1860s and the railway system extended to serve it. In later years it would be further extended to Ashton's Field Colliery at Walkden. and by 1908 had reached Cutacre Tip, south-west of Brackley Colliery.

Access to the sidings was effected by a short north to west curve, involving reversal by colliery locomotives when descending from Sandhole, (the later name for Bridgewater Colliery). The main London & North Western lines passed beneath the colliery lines at this location.

Sandhole Shed was home to a number of locomotives for working the traffic north to Ashton Field, Linnyshaw Moss Sidings and Pendlebury Landsale Yard; or south to Sanderson's Sidings, Roe Green Landsale Yard and Worsley Canal Wharf. Nanney Lane Sidings, situated between Sandhole and Sanderson's Sidings, was the location of the stocking roads for traffic being transferred from Sanderson's for points north, or traffic working south.

Sandhole Colliery had closed in 1962 but the washery remained open to receive coal traffic from other collieries, which included slack from Bedford Colliery, Leigh, worked to Sanderson's by British Railways from Speakman's Sidings. The re-opening of Nook washery in 1966 made this arrangement redundant and as a consequence the connection at Sanderson's Sidings with British Railways was out of use by late 1966.

Plate 117. Ex-London & North Western Coal Tank No.7803 leaves the environs of Roe Green behind and is seen on the approach to Sanderson's Sidings on 10th June 1947, working the 5.45p.m. Bolton Great Moor Street - Manchester Exchange service. These Plodder Lane engines had been the mainstay of local passenger services for years until the arrival of the Ex-LMS Ivatt 2-6-2 tanks in 1948.
W.D.Cooper, (Cooperline).

Plate 118. A murky day in December 1965 as BR Standard No.73039 arrives at Sanderson's Sidings with a train of slack from Speakman's Sidings, Leigh for washing at Sandhole Colliery. The train will reverse and deposit its load in the sidings and a colliery locomotive will take the wagons to Sandhole over the bridge from where the photographer has taken his shot. *Tony Oldfield.*

Plate 119. 'Patriot' Class No.5513 passes Sanderson's Sidings with the afternoon Manchester Exchange - Barrow express on 22nd March 1948. Greenleach Lane runs parallel to the railway at this location. *W.D.Cooper, (Cooperline).*

Plate 120. In the mid 1960s Stanier Class '5' No 44832 passes Sanderson's Sidings with a mixed freight for Patricroft North Yard.
Author's Collection (Jim Carter).

Plate 121. 'Austerity' 0-6-0ST *Repulse, HE/3698/1950,* is seen at Nanney Lane Sidings on 27th January 1965 working to Sandhole Colliery with a train of internal user wagons. In the top left hand corner are the houses on Glenn Avenue and Mulgrave Road. There were four stocking roads here, plus the Up and Down lines.

The normal load from Sandhole to Linnyshaw Moss was sixteen, thirty two with a banker. On approaching the loop at Linyshaw the banker dropped off and returned to Sandhole. All the dirt from Sandhole was worked to Cutacre Tip
Tony Oldfield.

89

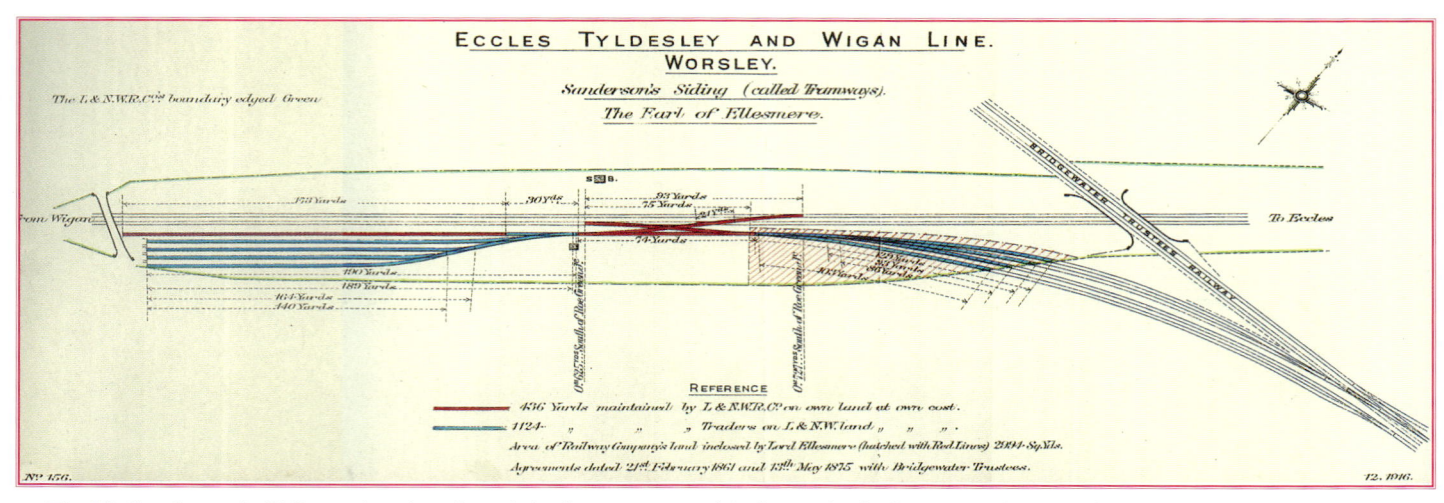

Fig 29. Sanderson's Sidings showing the original agreement with the Earl of Ellesmere of 21st February 1861 and the later agreement with the Bridgewater Trustees of 13th May 1875. A mistake by the cartographer has imposed a misaligned north orientation. It needs to be rotated about 45 degrees anticlockwise to be correct. *Courtesy, John Hall.*

Plate 122. Atkinson, Walker & Co. of Preston had developed an unusual design of shunter with a vertical boiler and a high speed steam engine operating a four wheel drive. This was sent for trial on the Bridgewater Collieries system in 1928, spending a few days shunting in the vicinity of Sandhole and Sanderson's Sidings where it is seen between duties. The gent in the cab is obviously of some importance, definitely not the engine's driver! *John Ryan Collection.*

Plate 123. Track relaying is in progress at Sanderson's Sidings in April 1950. The ex-LMS Class '5' No.5199, still not having received its new numbering; in fact, on the cabside there is no number at all! *W.D.Cooper, (Cooperline).*

Plate 124. The view at Sandhole Colliery on 27th December 1967 as the crew of 'Austerity' *Wizard, HE/3843/1956,* pause for a moment's conversation. *John Ryan.*

Plate 125. Ex-North Staffordshire *Sir Robert* passes Linnyshaw Moss Sidings, the curvature of the line towards the exchange sidings is visible far left, where traffic was transferred to B.R.

Sir Robert is en-route to the blending plant at Ashton's Field on 2nd August 1967. *John Ryan.*

Sandhole Colliery closed in September 1968, inward traffic from Sanderson's Sidings having ceased in 1966 and by December, the connections with B.R. at Sanderson's had been taken out. The line northwards from Sandhole to Linnyshaw Moss was also taken out of use in 1968, only Linnyshaw to Ashton's Field remained to carry traffic to the exchange sidings at Kearsley which was then worked on the western section of colliery railway between Astley Green and Ashton's Field for blending, then by reversal towards the exchange sidings. About forty wagons per day were worked in two trips at this period.

Coal traffic ceased on the Bridgewater Collieries system on 2nd October 1970 when the last wagons were exchanged with B.R at Linnyshaw Moss, the 'last' movement being that of an 0-6-0 diesel shunter on 12th October inst. which had undergone overhaul at Walkden Yard and under its own power moved to Agecroft Colliery.

In late April 1971 some 200 steel wagons were dispatched from Walkden, after repairs, to Astley Green Sidings and collected by B.R. destined for Bold and Bickershaw Collieries. The line between Astley Green and Walkden remained open for a while to enable locomotives sent to

91

Plate 126. Warrior takes water at Ashton's Field on 2nd August 1967. The engine is one of a number fitted with a Giesl ejector in place of the original chimney, the first of which was *Charles,* HC/1778/1944, in 1961
John Ryan.

Plate 127. Ex-North Staffordshire *Sir Robert* is seen crossing the embankment which, when built, cut Black Leach Reservoir in two during construction of the line to Ashton's Field in 1865/6. The date is also 2nd August 1967.
John Ryan.

Astley Green by road for overhaul at Walkden until facilities for such operations were provided there, as locomotives from far and wide were now being dispatched to Walkden Yard for servicing and overhaul. By mid-1971, all the track on the Bridgewater system had been lifted, except that is, for a short section at Walkden, between Manchester Road and the bridge under the L&Y line for testing locomotives after repairs which continued until early 1980, the last being *Joseph* from Bold Colliery.

Thereafter, the works concentrated on the repair of diesel and narrow gauge underground locomotives until 1983. The works finally closed in 1986. Part of the trackbed at Walkden was used as an access road to the Ellesmere shopping centre and a housing estate occupies the site of Walkden Workshops. When the M61 first opened it was possible to see part of the Linnyshaw Moss trackbed alongside the motorway but with the passing years all has been overtaken by vegetative growth.

WORSLEY

Worsley Station was built of white brick and the heads of the windows and doors arched over in white, red and black bricks. The accommodation provided comprised two first and two second class waiting rooms and a booking office. The waiting room on the Down (Wigan) side was said to be 'spacious' and in the same style as the main buildings. The platforms of over 300 feet in length, were paved with blue tiles with stone borders and roofed over in glass giving some protection to the passengers. A less elaborate canopy projected, at eaves level in cantilevered fashion, from the Down platform waiting rooms.

In its early years, Worsley Station, surrounded in rural tranquillity, was a shining jewel in the crown of the London & North Western Railway.

This was the only station on the route to be of brick construction, all the others were of timber.

Roads to the station were quickly opened out and house building in the area increased as those who were able to afford to commute settled in the vicinity.

A hundred years after Brindley had constructed his canal to Manchester, the arrival of the railways had spurred on the deep mining activity around Worsley and for the next century the steam locomotive provided the power required to move the vast tonnages of coal produced.

Worsley had been the venue for the inaugural sod cutting ceremony on 'Old Factory' site, about half a mile from Worsley Village, in September 1861. The invited guests had assembled at the *Grapes Inn,* Worsley, which occupied the present M60 (formerly M63) junction adjacent to *Worsley Court House,* before processing, headed by the Earl of Ellesmere's Band to the appointed place.

The first 'sod' was to be cut by the Earl of Ellesmere and there is little doubt that on his insistence, Worsley had a station worthy of his position. It also had a horse dock and siding, another concession to the Earl by the railway company.

A 'select' company of Navvies, those stalwart representatives of that hardy race of labourers, included one of their number bearing aloft a spade of burnished steel which was to be used in the inaugural ceremony, followed by another with an ornamental wheelbarrow, all of the group dressed in immaculate smocks. Then came the Directors and Chairman of the London & North Western, Gentlemen of the district, Engineers and contractors.

The chosen site, a picturesque nook known at Old Factory had been fitted with stages for the accommodation of the guests and a projecting platform erected from which the first barrowful would be tipped.

Plate 128. An Edwardian view of Worsley Station looking eastwards in the Manchester direction. The photograph is taken from the footbridge over the lines. It looks positively idyllic, redolent of an age long past.

Stations U.K.

Plate 129. Another Edwarian view at Worsley in the snow on the approach from Worsley Road. Note the horse box in the head shunt. This really was as picturesque a little station ever constructed by the London & North Western, but greatly influenced by the landowner. *Author's Collection.*

Plate 130. It's springtime at Worsley, and noticable even in a monotone photograph. Stanier 2-6-4 tank No.42660 gets away from Worsley Station on 9th April 1964 with a Wigan North Western train. *Peter Eckersley.*

After the customary speeches, The Earl proceeded to use the spade, the handle of which was made of spanish mahogany, putting several rounds into the wheelbarrow and wheeling it to the end of the platform tipping it in a workmanlike manner into a deep hollow to the cheers of the gathered assembly. Mr Moon, Chairman of the railway company, did likewise as did a number of others. The procession then returned to Worsley Court House which had been suitably adorned with banners and decorations. At 3p.m. a sumptuous dinner was served to about 200 guests. The list of guests is a who's-who of local trade and commerce including:- John and Ralph Fletcher, Richard Guest, Caleb Wright, George Green, John Holland, T.T.Hayes, James Diggle, H.Jackson, W.Ramsden, J&E.Burton, the Mayors of Manchester, Oldham and Warrington, the M.P. for Wigan, H.Woods and representatives for St.Helens.

Plate 131. Worsley station has lost its canopy some time ago and a cheap and nasty felted substitute erected over the doorway. Class '5' No.45005 passes through with a Liverpool Lime Street - Manchester Exchange train on 24th October 1964. *Peter Eckersley.*

Plate 132. A two car Class '108' DMU arrives at Worsley about 1962 with a Manchester Exchange service, looking very smart with its 'whiskers'.
Author's Collection.
(Alan Palmer.)

In his speech, Thomas Part of Wigan, refers to the Lancashire & Yorkshire plan to build a railway in the same vicinity in 1847, the powers of which had been allowed to lapse. W.F.Hulton for his part, remembers his introduction, by his father, to George Stephenson, and to the latter being persuaded to leave Newcastle in order to *concoct that scheme of railway, the Bolton & Leigh* (to cheers) which had preceded the Liverpool & Manchester.

Mr. Treadwell, the contractor, stated he could almost positively fix the opening date as 1st May 1863. His enthusiasm for the project would later be undone by the British climate as prolonged, excessive wet weather in the summer of 1862 caused delays, resulting in a much later opening date than anticipated. For now though all were pleased that at last a new line of railway, the advent of which had been so long, was finally to materialise.

95

Plate 133. Stanier tank No.42574 arrives at Worsley on 25th April 1964 with a local train for Wigan. Just look at the decrepit state of the station buildings; was this a deliberate attempt to undermine patronage by allowing the rot to continue?
Peter Eckersley.

Plate 134. On the last day of service 3rd May 1969, Mr James Hinson of Salford is pictured on the Up (Manchester) platform at Worsley against the half demolished station buildings.
David Norman.

MONTON GREEN

Monton Green was an all timber station built on an embankment and supported by cross braced wooden piles. The platforms themselves spanned Parrin Lane, but were reached by enclosed stairways from the adjacent Green Lane at the Manchester end of the station. Opening in November 1887, the station catered for the increasing suburban commuter traffic into Manchester at a time when the railways were consolidating their transport monopoly by expanding their services and improving line capacity generally.

The beginning of the scenic footpath, westward along the route of the railway trackbed to Worsley and Roe Green, begins at Monton Green, where canal and railway ran side by side.

Patricroft crews boarded passenger trains at Monton Green when 'working the cushions', that is, relieving another crew who were at the end of their shift. A good example of this was trip workings over the Bolton & Leigh Railway from Bag Lane. The engine would be worked light to Tyldesley awaiting the relieving crew and there might even have been time for a couple of 'scoops' to wash down the dust!

Plate 135. Monton Green Signal Cabin was sited alongside the Up line again at the Manchester end, having 18 levers and worked three turns, opening at 5am Monday until 1.45pm Sunday in the LMS period. It is seen here about 1966. *Peter Hampson.*

Plate 136. 'Jinty' 47378, having been on duty as pilot engine at Bolton Great Moor Street is seen returning to shed at Patricroft in the company of a Class '8F' and brake van off a trip working to Speakman's Sidings, Leigh, running coupled from Tyldesley to 'save the block' in October 1964. *Tony Oldfield.*

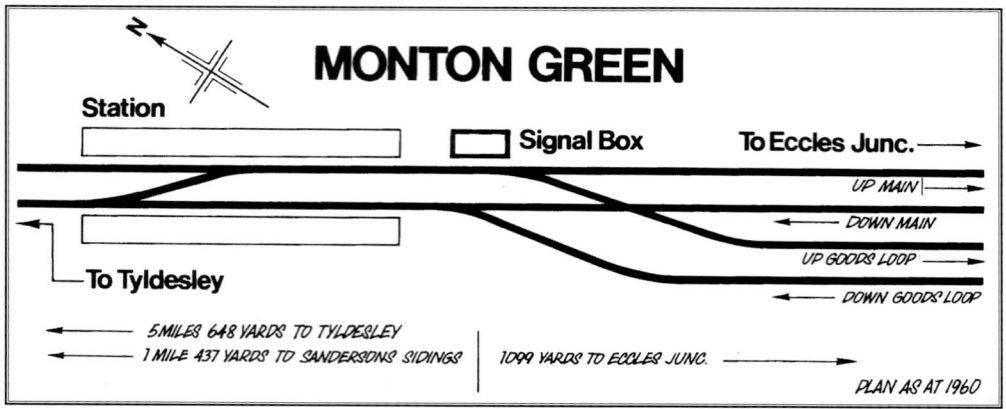

Fig 30. General arrangement at Monton Green c1960.

Plate 137. Monton Green Station looking eastwards to Patricroft in late L.M.S. days, c1946. Out of sight on the right were the Monton Green Up and Down Loop lines. In the distance is the bridge which carried the Patricroft to Molyneux Junction, or 'Black Harry' line as it was known, over the Eccles-Tyldesley lines.
Author's Collection.

Plate 138, below. On the approach to Monton Green, 'Clan' Pacific No.72001 *Clan Cameron* is seen passing Patricroft North Yard in the summer of 1963 with the 4.15pm Manchester Exchange to Glasgow train. St. Andrews Parish Church is prominent top left with Wellington Road and the Engineer's Sidings of the same name mostly hidden by the locomotive's exhaust also on the left. To the rear of train is Patricroft North Sidings signal box. The photograph is taken from the 'Black Harry' line overbridge, more of which is to follow.

This class of locomotives, ten in all, were almost identical to the 'Britannia' class but with a smaller boiler and being around eight tons lighter were originally intended for use on the Scottish Highland lines. However, things didn't work out as planned and the class spent most of their lives working the Manchester/Liverpool expresses to Windermere or Glasgow and as such became frequent visitors, and favourites amongst the spotters, along the Tyldesley route.
Author's Collection,
(Jim Carter).

Plate 139. Monton Green Station is seen here viewed from the west and is probably from the Edwardian period, platform access is at the Manchester end of the station.
John Ryan Collection.

Plate 140. Monton Green Station on 3rd April 1969. The working is the 17.22 Manchester Exchange to Leigh and not a special as it says on the indicator blind.
John Ryan.

THE BLACK HARRY LINE

Plate 141. In May 1952, ex L.M.S, Fowler designed 0-8-0 No.49667, begins the climb over the Eccles-Tyldesley lines with the 8.15pm Patricroft-Radcliffe return empties all of which appear to be the older wooden bodied type. *W.D.Cooper, (Cooperline).*

Plate 142. Garages now occupy the sites of Nos 22-26 Temple Drive as seen in this recent view. See text, page 101.
Tom Pike.

Plate 143. In 1964 the bridge which carried the Patricroft-Molyneux line over Monton Road was demolished to allow the road to be widened. On the left is the *Princess Cinema* and in the distance, Quaker Bridge. See also **Plates 144 & 147**.
Tom Pike.

Plate 144. On 16th March 1963, a brakevan railtour of Central Railways and other local lines traversed the then extent of the Patricroft - Clifton Branch, otherwise known as the Black Harry Line. The locomotive used on this tour was Patricroft's Class '3F' 0-6-0 No.47378. The ensemble is seen at the then extent of the line at Quaker Bridge which had been built by John Scott, ironfounders of Stockport, connecting Monton Green with Ellesmere Park. The bridge is named after Quaker James King, who, together with John Lancaster had mining interests here at Patricroft and also at Lower Ince, Wigan.

*Author's Collection,
(Brian Hilton).*

On 2nd February 1850, a new 3½ mile branch line opened from Patricroft, by a junction with the Liverpool & Manchester Railway, to Molyneux Junction at Clifton, on the East Lancashire's line to Bury. Principally built for the carriage of coal from the mines around Agecroft, Pendlebury and Clifton, for a short period of four months a passenger service between Liverpool, Bury and Rossendale was in operation until June, thereafter the route saw only the occasional passenger excursion traffic until 1939.

The most notable feature along the route was the 1,298 yard long Clifton Hall Tunnel which began north of Swinton Golf Course on the approach to much higher ground. To ease the difficult work during its construction, eight shafts were sunk from the surface to track level, not only providing ventilation but enabling debris to be lifted clear. Upon completion of the tunnel the shafts were bricked up at roof level and infilled from the top. It was later to become known as the "Black Harry" line. The name, it is said, derived from the construction foreman, a man of dark appearance with stubble to match.

When the Eccles Junction - Wigan route opened in 1864, a level crossing was in operation at Patricroft until 1884 when an overbridge was built necessitating a slight deviation. At the same time, a curve from Eccles Junction to the Clifton Branch opened on 26th May 1884. This did not last long, closing on 31st May 1891, although some of the track remained in use as Engineer's Sidings.

The line was closed for the duration of World War II, and used for the storage of chlorine tank wagons. It re-opened for through mineral traffic on 6th October 1947, although lightly used by 1951, only three scheduled workings daily with one extra on Thursdays and Saturdays.

Although the tunnel was inspected on a regular basis, latterly by Ganger E.Nash on 13th April 1953, who reported to his superiors a partial fall of the brick lining on the tracks resulting in the immediate closure of the line. Drawings were prepared for emergency repairs and ribs ordered from Gorton Works. Disaster was to strike however at 5.35a.m. on 28th April 1953, when this section of the tunnel roof collapsed, the infill pouring into the tunnel taking with it two houses, Nos. 22, & 24 Temple Drive, Swinton, and part of No.26. Five sleeping occupants plunged to their deaths amongst the rubble in the abyss. The subsidence left a 20ft deep crater. The civil authorities were alerted by a police inspector, and the railway authorities by Mr. T.Jones, both residing in Temple Drive.

The houses in Temple Drive had been built in 1909, the developers apparently unaware of the existence of these filled in shafts. The Inspectors report into the collapse found that it had occurred above No.3 shaft. During the line's construction it appears that timber shoring was used to support the shafts, and in due course, replaced by timber frames supporting longitudinal bearers which were then built into the brick lining of the tunnel. It was found that the timber bearers had rotted to such an extent that the brick arch ring of the tunnel could no longer withstand the pressure of tons of loose wet sand and earth imposed upon it and, combined with stresses from unstable ground, gave way.

Plate 145. A view from the northern end of Clifton Hall Sidings, March 1958. *John Ryan.*

It appears that some sections of the tunnel had, at various periods, been reinforced with steel ribs made from redundant rails but not at this particular section, although schedules were in hand to carry out this work.

It was now necessary to determine the exact positions of the other seven shafts, and all but one, No.4 shaft, were under parts of the tunnel already strengthened but some additional ribs were, nevertheless, inserted. No.4 shaft was strengthened by the insertion of eleven pairs of steel ribs and the inspector was satisfied that no further problems would occur.

The inquest returned a verdict of "accidental death" but not until March the following year were the findings of a public inquiry into the disaster made known.

At the inquiry, Brigadier C.A.Langley of the Ministry of Transport and Civil Aviation, stated that the disaster was:- *due entirely to an inherent weakness in the construction of the tunnel* and, that the loss of vitally important records relating to the construction of the Black Harry Tunnel *contributed materially to the disaster.* *

There are various dates given for the permanent closure of the line as a through route, although it would not have been a difficult decision for B.R. to take in closing it. The most likely date is 13th April 1953 when inspection of the tunnel took place. What is certain is that the tunnel was infilled in 1959 from the south, Patricroft end, and thereafter, the truncated branch from Quaker Bridge to Patricroft was used for wagon storage until tracklifting began in 1962.

Today, part of the railway trackbed of the line is walkable from Monton Green to Swinton Golf Course.

* *Swinton & Pendlebury Journal.*

Plate 146. The view looking northwards at Swinton towards 'Black Harry' tunnel in May 1959 during the process of in-filling. A 2ft narrow gauge railway has been laid using one of the rails of the existing standard gauge track with a second rail laid inside. On the right, a passing loop facilitated wagon movements. *Harry Townley.*

Plate 147. The view looking from Quaker Bridge towards Patricroft as the participants gather for an impromptu conference. The use of brake vans on tours such as this was a common occurrence in those days and even if these brake vans were still around in sufficient numbers it still wouldn't happen on today's railway. *John Ryan.*

The mining activity along this branch was concentrated at is northern end by Messrs Andrew Knowles & Sons who opened their first mine in the Clifton area about 1814. The Clifton Hall Colliery is believed to date from the 1820s and initially was served by a horse drawn tramway to the Manchester, Bolton & Bury Canal. Two more shafts were sunk here in 1838 and with the opening of the L&NW's Clifton Hall Branch in 1850 which ran past the colliery on its west side to Molyneux Junction, it is believed a siding was put in to serve the Clifton Hall pits. In 1873, a new screening plant and washery were built on the west side of the L&NW line and by an agreement of 15th March 1873 a new bank of sidings was built and the original removed.

Wheatsheaf Colliery, also referred to as Pendlebury Colliery, had opened about 1825 to the north west of Clifton Hall Colliery and in 1846 new shafts were sunk at Wheatsheaf which eventually, in the late 1880s, were connected to the screening plant at Clifton Hall by a tubway about 1/2 long, part of which was tunnelled under higher ground. About the same period the tramway to the canal was replaced by a tubway. Wheatsheaf Colliery was modernised in the 1890s and further screening facilities were built at Clifton Hall Colliery to cope with the increasing production and the sidings at the latter extended under an agreements with the L&NW of 31st December 1892 and 1st July 1914, to cater for increasing rail haulage, much of it to Weaste Wharf for shipment on the Manchester Ship Canal worked to Patricroft Sidings and then tripped down the branch at Stott Lane. The full extent of the sidings are shown in *Fig 31*.

Clifton Hall Colliery, which had also become a part of Manchester Collieries in 1929, ceased production the same year, one of the shafts being retained for the ventilation of

Plate 148. This view at Clifton Hall c1957 is taken from above the tunnel portal looking in a northerly direction. Clifton Hall No.1 signalbox is right of centre and the curvature of the track and sidings arrangements disappear out of shot to the left. The former Lancashire & Yorkshire lines are seen in the distance.
Author's Collection, (Harry Townley).

103

Plate 149. Returning to Patricroft from Quaker Bridge, 47378 crosses over the London & North Western's Eccles-Tyldesley route between Monton Green and Eccles Junction. *John Ryan.*

Wheatsheaf Colliery which itself was modernised in the 1930s as an increasing amount of small coal was being sent to Outwood Colliery, Ratcliffe, by rail for washing and processing, the plant at Clifton Hall being out of use.

Outwood Colliery, sited on the east side of the East Lancashire Railway (Lancashire & Yorkshire Railway from 13th August 1859) had come into the possession of the Clifton & Kersley* Coal Co. Ltd. in 1909 becoming a constituent part of Manchester Collieries in 1929.

A serious fire at Outwood led to production being abandoned in 1931 but the washing plant continued in operation processing coal from Wheatsheaf and other local mines and also from Astley Green. Outwood was taken over by the N.C.B. in 1947 at nationalisation and continued in operation until closure in 1956, the sidings agreement with B.R. being terminated on 22nd April 1957. *Contemporary spelling.

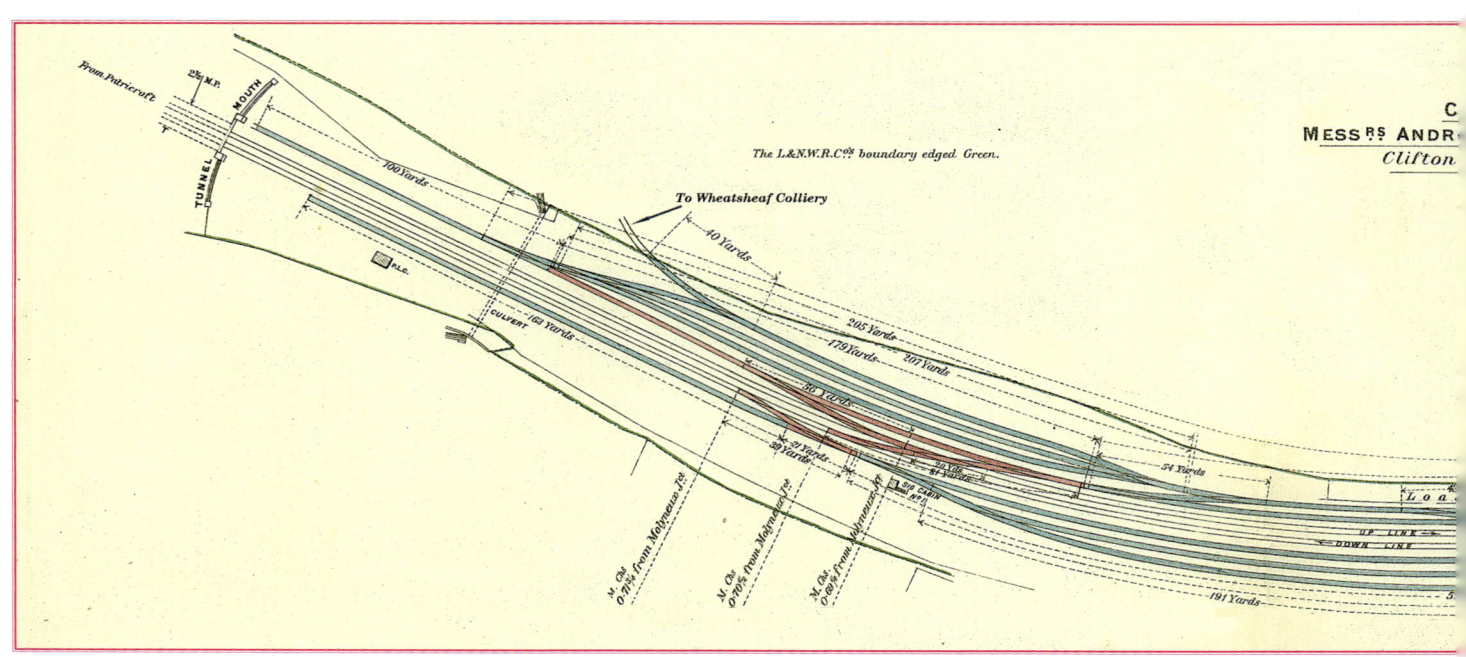

Plate 150. Clifton Hall No.1 signalbox almost at the end of its working life in March 1958. A small box, having only 9 working levers. *John Ryan.*

Plate 151. BR Standard 2-6-2 No.82009 is seen in Monton Green Loop about 1962. To the rear of the picture engineer's wagons are stored on the former connecting line to the 'Black Harry' route which still has track in situ. *Author's Collection (Jim Carter)*

Fig 31, Below. The sidings and general layout at Andrew Knowles Clifton Hall Colliery Sidings c1918. The main lines emerge from the northern portal of Clifton Hall Tunnel, far left, continuing to Molyneux Junction, right, where the East Lancashire Railway's route to Bury is met. Clifton Hall No.2 signalbox was located at the northern end, far right. Wheatsheaf Colliery closed in June 1961 allowing closure of the Clifton Hall Sidings - Molyneux Junction section on 16th June. *Courtesy, John Ryan.*

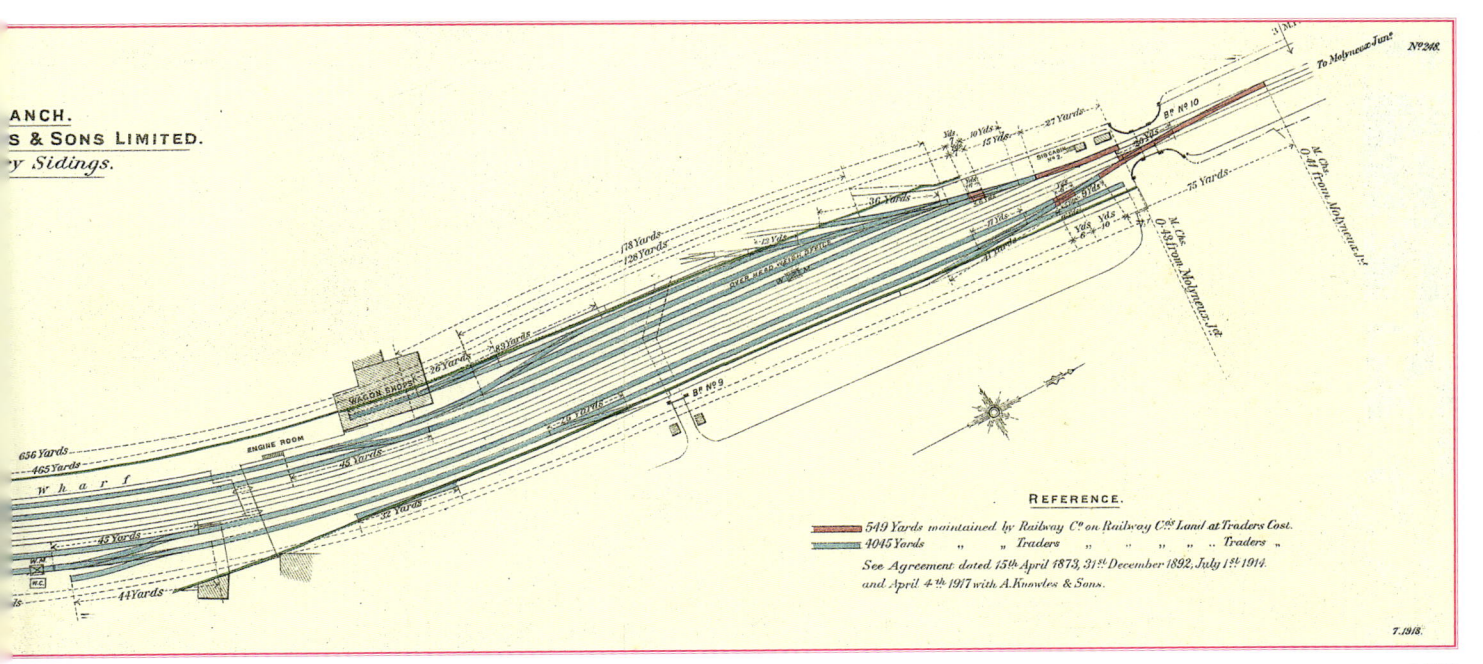

105

PATRICROFT

Construction of an engine shed at Patricroft began on a greenfield site to the west of Manchester in the triangle between the Eccles Junction to Wigan, Liverpool & Manchester lines and the Clifton Branch in April 1884. It was built originally to accommodate locomotives from the overcrowded shed at Ordsall Lane and had eight roads. In 1905, Patricroft 'New' shed, as it came to be known, was opened. This had ten roads and was approached from the east, that is from Manchester as opposed to the 1884 shed which was approached from the opposite direction. During the mid 1930s the LMS carried out improvements, including a 70ft turntable to replace the earlier L&NW installation. 'New' shed also received a new pitched roof replacing the original northlight pattern, but the 1884 shed had to wait until the BR era for attention, being almost completely re-built with the corrugated sheet style roof favoured by the new owners.

From an allocation of some thirty locomotives in 1885, rising to one hundred and twenty plus in the 1920s, the figure dropped to around seventy in the 1950s and early 1960s.

Patricroft shed closed at the end of the steam era and in fact provided many of the locomotives for the end of steam specials. Its most famous personality was undoubtedly railwayman Jim Carter who had begun his railway career at Sutton Oak Shed, St. Helens. After a short spell at Widnes, and National Service, Jim transferred to Patricroft and was never to be seen without his camera, on or off the footplate and the images he captured on film few can equal.

He became friendly with W.D.Cooper who often visited Patricroft Shed. Jim always referred to him as 'Wilf' and to make sure he got a good shot would position the engines for him. The two of them got on well together and accompanied each other on photographic jaunts further afield.

On closure of Patricroft Shed in 1968, Jim was transferred to Newton Heath where further opportunities through the lens presented themselves. Now though, it was the turn of the diesels to be captured on film.

W.D.Cooper passed away in 1998 after a short illness. Jim, whose health had not been good over a number of years, died in 2011. They have left us with some wonderful images of the steam engine in its working environment. I feel it a privilege to have known them both.

Plate 152. An L.C.G.B Special leaves the environs of Eccles Junction behind and runs alongside the Engineer's Sidings at Patricroft on 6th April 1968 with the Lancastrian Railtour. Four bridges is to the rear of the train. *Author's Collection, (Jim Carter)*

Plate 153. The Line Inspectors coach hauled by Ivatt Class '2' No. 46437 is seen near Four Bridges which straddle the railway at Eccles Junction. The date is July 1965 at which period the engine was at Newton Heath and this working a Newton Heath turn.
Tony Oldfield.

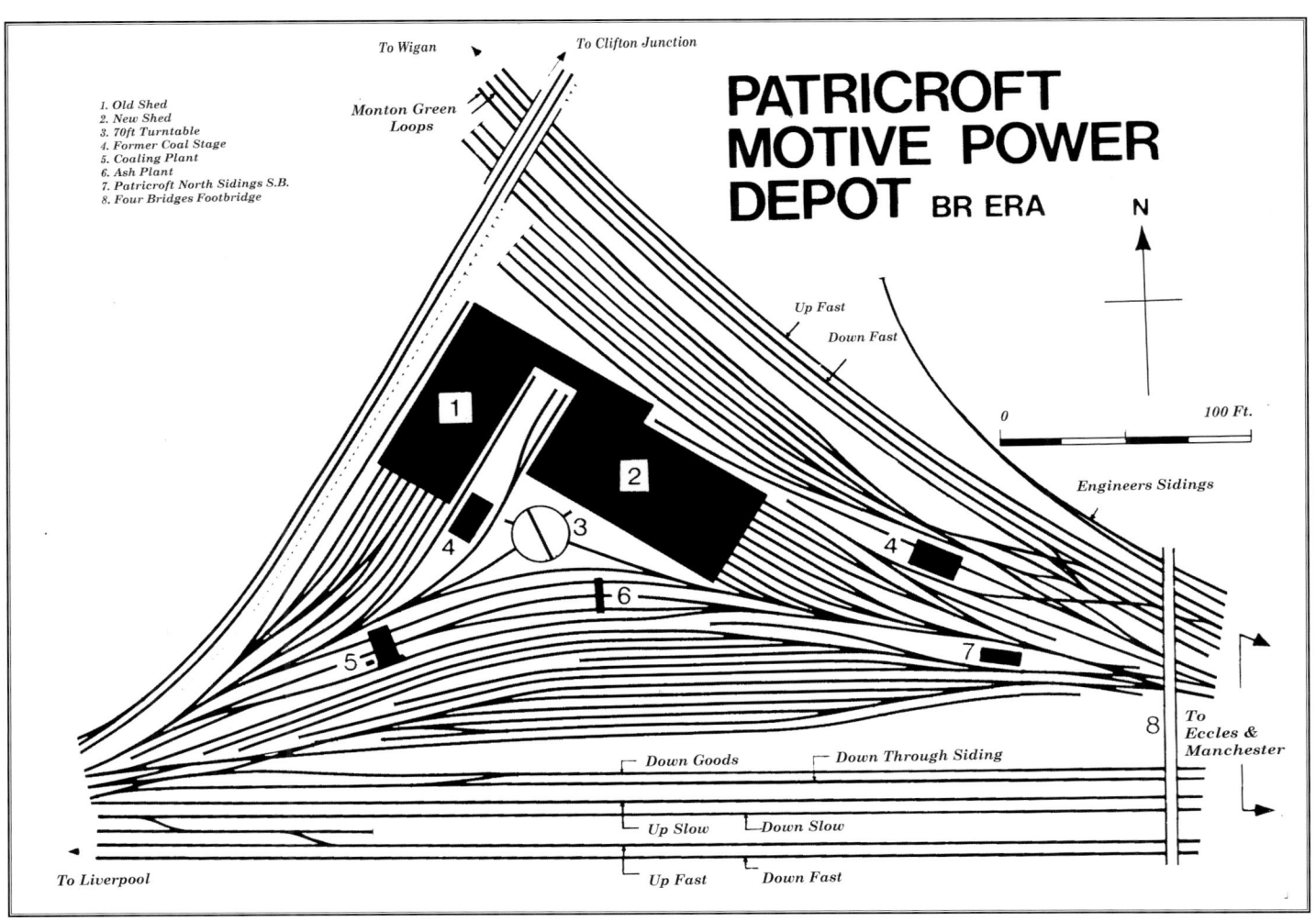

PATRICROFT MOTIVE POWER DEPOT BR ERA

1. Old Shed
2. New Shed
3. 70ft Turntable
4. Former Coal Stage
5. Coaling Plant
6. Ash Plant
7. Patricroft North Sidings S.B.
8. Four Bridges Footbridge

107

Plate 154. 'Royal Scot' Class No.46155 *The Lancer* is all coaled up with a good head of steam ready to depart Patricroft Shed to work the 4.15 Manchester Exchange - Glasgow Central express in the early 1960s.

By the mid 1920s the L.M.S. were in dire need of an express engine capable of hauling 500 tons at 55/60 mph. The then Chief Mechanical Engineer Sir Henry Fowler was at pains to build a 4-6-2 'Pacific'. However, the L.M.S hierarchy had other ideas and subsequently borrowed a G.W.R. 'Castle' class 4-6-0 for trials and were suitably impressed. A request to the G.W.R. to borrow 'Castle' class drawings was rebuffed, and as a consequence, the L.M.S. turned to Maunsell of the S.R. who was more forthcoming and a set of drawings for the 'Lord Nelson' class 4-6-0 were sent to Derby. At this time it was impossible for the L.M.S. to construct a new locomotive in time for the 1927 timetable. Therefore, a request was made to the North British Locomotive Company to construct, in double-quick-time, 50 locomotives based on the 'Lord Nelson' but with three cylinders instead of two and Horwich valve configuration which had proved so successful on their 2-6-0s. The result was the 'Royal Scot' class, generally regarded as the best 4-6-0 ever produced in Great Britain.
Author's Collection, (Jim Carter).

Plate 156, opposite. Who said engines were never clean? An absolutely sparkling '8F' No. 48375 glistenes in the sunshine at Patricroft about 1965, the driver no doubt admiring Jim's technique.
Author's Collection (Jim Carter).

Plate 155. A rare visitor to Patricroft in the shape of 'Coronation' Class 4-6-2 No.46256 *Sir William A.Stanier F.R.S.* seen coming off the Liverpool & Manchester lines on 14th April 1964. The penultimate member of its class, and designed by its namesake with detail alterations instituted by Ivatt, these fine locomotives met an untimely end due to the headlong rush towards dieselisation in the 1960s. The first of their numbers to be withdrawn were 46227, 46231 & 46232 in 1962. However, the following year a futher thirteen engines succumbed and three more in early 1964. The biggest shock was to come in September 1964 when no less than eighteen of the class were withdrawn *en-bloc*, leaving 46256 to carry the flag for another month. *W.D.Cooper. (Cooperline).*

Plate 157. This Stanier class '5' No.45282, very nicely lined out complete with boiler bands, doesn't look in bad nick either 'when seen outside No.2 shed in the mid 1960s. As regards 'spotting' here, Sunday was the best day as it was quieter, and far less chance of being told to 'Hop it', or other phrases to that effect! *Author's Collection, (Jim Carter).*

Plate 158. This view towards Eccles may well be on a Sunday as all seems quiet. 'Britannia' class 4-6-2 No.70009 is positioned in front of the coaling plant minus its *Alfred the Great* nameplates which probably dates it to 1966 when many of the named engines had their plates removed for safekeeping. The locomotive was withdrawn in January 1967. *Author's Collection, (Jim Carter).*

Plate 159. The L.M.S. 4-4-0, 3 cylinder compound engines as seen here, were a Post-grouping development of the Johnson designed Midland compound, with modified dimensions. No.41098 is captured at Patricroft Shed Sidings on 16th April 1949 and whilst it has received its new number (40,000 was added to L.M.S. engines) and emblazoned with the lettering of its new owners, it is without the first B.R. emblem.
W.D.Cooper (Cooperline).

Plate 160. Positioned perfectly, for photography that is, Britannia No.70051 *Firth of Forth* on the turntable at Patricroft and, in all probability, being turned to work an evening express. The engine carries a '5A', Crewe North shedplate. Its nameplates were removed by April 1966, being withdrawn in December 1967.
Author's Collection, (Jim Carter).

111

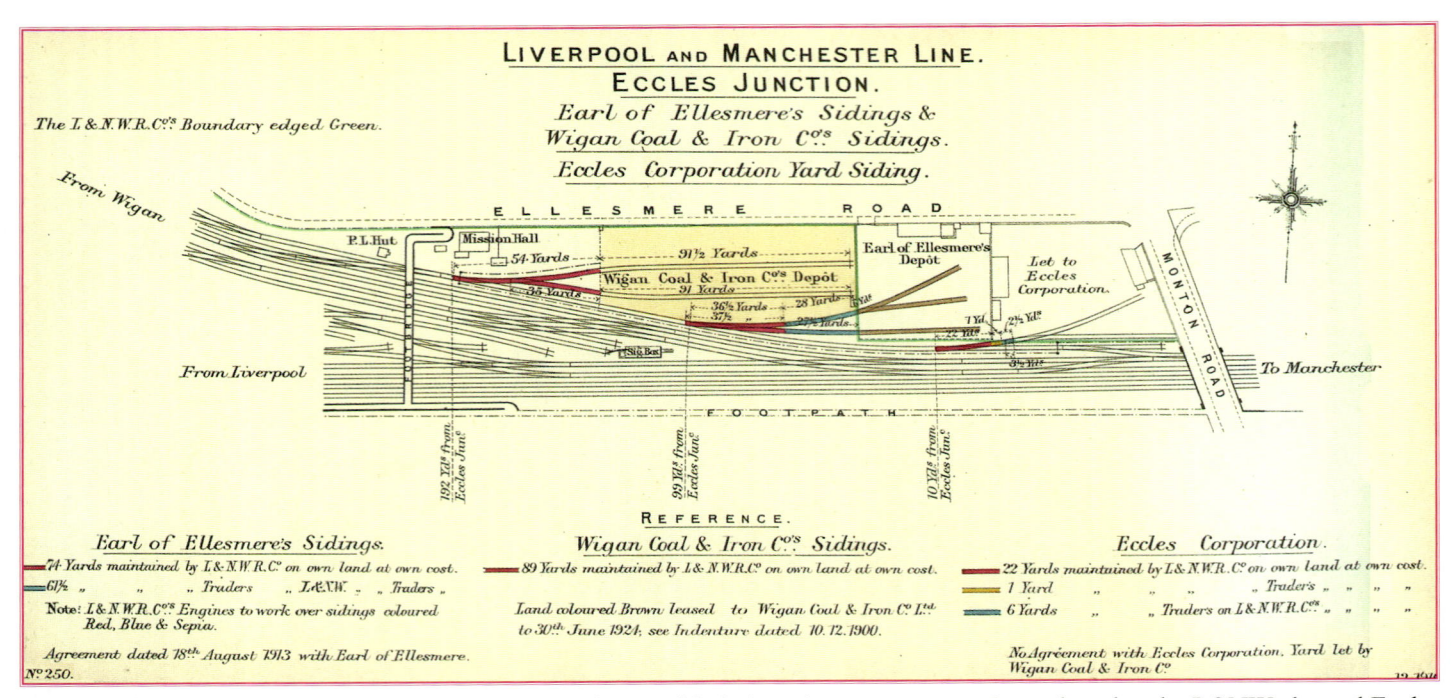

Fig 33. The sidings alongside Ellesmere Road are shown with their various agreements. I wonder what the L&NW charged Eccles Corporation for maintaining 1 yard of track?
Courtesy, John Hall.

Plate 161. Towards the end of steam, many of the specials commemorating the event were worked by Patricroft locomotives and crews. Stanier Class '5' 4-6-0 No.45156 *Ayrshire Yeomanry* was one of the engines to participate and is seen here in April 1968. Driver Jim Carter is leaning out of the cab window, the fireman is unidentified. The houses on Wellington Road and the Engineer's Sidings are on the extreme right with the Black Harry overbridge, centre.
Tony Oldfield

ECCLES TO MANCHESTER

Eccles Station was the scene of a serious accident at 8,18a.m. on 30th December 1941 in which 23 people were killed an a further 56 seriously injured.

Two passenger trains were involved, the 6.53am Rochdale-Pennington with 2-6-4T No. 2406 in charge, and the 6.53am Kenyon–Manchester Exchange (via Leigh and Tyldesley) hauled by 2-6-2T No. 207. Each train consisted of eight non-corridor coaches.

The accident occurred in dense fog which had persisted for over 21 hours previously, with visibility down to ten yards in places and when fogsignalling arrangements were in operation. It was still dark and some 37 minutes before the end of blackout regulations. The temperature was 0° C (32° F).

Traffic patterns had been disrupted by the prolonged period of fog and both trains were running late, the Pennington bound train by 27 minutes and the Manchester train by 49 minutes. Arrival of the Manchester train at Eccles Station, on the Up Slow, was at 8.15am. Because of congestion ahead, the train was crossed, by the Signalman at Eccles Station Cabin having received acceptance from the next cabin at Cross Lane Junction, from the Up Slow to the Up Fast. This manoeuvre necessitated crossing the Down Slow, upon which the Pennington train was travelling at approximately 35mph, having passed the Eccles Outer Home Signal at 'Danger'.

The engine of the Pennington train struck the first coach of the crossing Manchester train amidships and was derailed. Slewing to the right, the locomotive ripped through the second and third coaches completely demolishing them and came to rest 70 yards from the initial impact, embedded in the fourth coach and resting in the Up Slow Line cess.

The leading coach of the Pennington train was also completely destroyed and the second and third coaches partially crushed. All lines were blocked by the debris except the Down Fast and this, together with the Up Fast, were utilised to clear the wreckage with the assistance of the breakdown cranes. Normal working was not resumed until 37 hours later.

Plate 162. 'Britannia' Class 4-6-2 No.70050 *Firth of Clyde* takes the Tyldesley route at Eccles Junction in August 1956 with a morning train from Manchester Exchange.
W.D.Cooper, (Cooperline).

Many local people still recall this terrible accident, although it happened over seventy years ago. Some were on the Manchester bound train at the time, having boarded at local stations. Others had near misses, fate on that particular day showing its guiding hand. In the latter class was Mr. W. D. Cooper, one of the photographic contributors to these volumes, who had walked to Worsley Station that morning, a few minutes earlier than he normally would have done in clearer weather. Because of the fog, trains were running out of sequence and as he arrived at Worsley, a train pulled into the station. This was probably a late running Ex-Bolton Great Moor Street-Manchester local, which Mr. Cooper duly boarded. Here we are talking about just a few seconds, and yet, those few moments which, in a lifetime are immeasurable, did on this occasion, make all the difference between life and death.

Having stopped at Monton Green and Eccles, the Bolton-Manchester train continued on the Up Slow towards Weaste at a sedate pace as a train flashed by in the opposite direction. The memory of it was with W.D. Cooper all his life, for this was non other than the ill fated Rochdale-Pennington, which in a couple of minutes would collide with the Kenyon-Manchester train that had called at Worsley shortly after the Ex-Bolton.

At the subsequent inquiry, the reporting Inspector, Major G. R. S. Wilson, held that the Signalman at Eccles Station was "primarily responsible", but also that the Driver of the Pennington train "must accept a considerable share of the responsibility". However, the real culprit was undeniably the fog and the implications for the working of the railway in such circumstances.

Today, the Liverpool & Manchester route has recently been electrified and many of the older DMUs replaced by more modern, but not new, electric traction in the form of class '319' units. As we went to press, it was announced, on 30th September 2015, that the electrification of the Manchester Victoria - Leeds route would now go ahead after being put on the backburner the previous June which made a mockery of the much vaunted 'Northern Powerhouse' idea of which this electrification project was seen as vital to its success. However, it won't be operative until 2020; better late than never though!

Plate 163. Rebuilt 'Patriot' class No.45526 *Morecambe and Heysham,* slows for the junction at Eccles to take the Tyldesley line working the 7.05p.m. Liverpool Road - Carlisle Viaduct Yard, due through Tyldesley at 7.35p.m. *W.D.Cooper, (Cooperline).*

Plate 164. Eccles Station is seen here in the Edwardian period and is a typical London & North Western timbered construction with mock Elizabethan brick chimney stacks and Dutch barn style gables. It presents a picture of the railways in maturity, the people milling around and a tram waiting for the 'off' to Deansgate; a far cry from the present Eccles Station. *Tom Pike.*

Plate 165. Fairburn 2-6-4T passes through Eccles Station with *The Wirral & Mersey Special* on 22nd October 1966, a railtour of South Lancashire and North Cheshire railways which began at Liverpool Riverside at 9.00a.m. and terminated at 18.05p.m. at Liverpool Central. *Peter Eckersley.*

Plate 166. 'Royal Scot' No.46144 *Honourable Artillery Company*, heads west towards Eccles Station on 5th June 1962 as a BR Standard passes the water softening plant heading towards Manchester.
W.D.Cooper, (Cooperline).

Plate 167. Their tender runneth over. Seen working a Liverpool - Hull service c1945/6 is 'Jubilee' class No.5704 *Leviathan* with a Fowler tender on the up fast coming to the end of Eccles Troughs. It is to be hoped that the coach windows are closed and that the fireman lifts the scoop quickly. Post World War II, the area on the left would be cleared to make way for the Ladywell Flats but whether the new properties enhanced the environment and provided a better life for those within is a matter for debate!
Author's Collection, (D.Evans).

Plate 168. Approximately 20 years separate this view at the same location from the one opposite, also showing the recent reconstruction of the area. The troughs are still in place but look to be dry as B.R.Standard Class '5' No.73127 passes on 25th June 1966. On the right is the Ship Canal Branch and Stott Lane Sidings.
Peter Eckersley.

Plate 169. Stott Lane Sidings are shown here about 1945/6 and seem to be overflowing with traffic the wagons nearest all loaded with timber. A light engine descends down the Ship Canal Branch, which passed under the Liverpool-Manchester lines east of Weaste Station, to Weaste Junction Sidings.
Author's Collection (D.Evans).

Plate 170. Weaste Station is viewed here c1947 and there appears to be some remedial work in progress to the platform edge with all the rubble stacked on the platform. Just as well then that the station closed to passengers in October 1942. Originally Weaste Lane, renamed in July 1856.
Author's Collection.

117

Plate 171. The railtour which traversed the Black Harry line on 16th March 1963 also had a little jaunt down the Ship Canal Sidings Branch and is seen here taking water at Weaste before its descent to the sidings, another opportunity for a photo shoot.
John Ryan.

Plate 172. In 1962 Railwayman Jim Carter booked on at Patricroft and was told to proceed to Wigan North Western to act as pilotman for a Manchester bound freight. Now it had always been Jim's ambition to drive one of the 'Coronation' class 4-6-2s to 'get amongst the big green uns' as he put it.

Well on this day Jim was about to get his wish, for as the freight rolled into North Western and came to a stand at the end of platform 4, *I couldn't believe it,* he said. He knew his pilot job was to take the Tyldesley route to Eccles Junction but never expected the engine to be 46257 *City of Salford*, the last of its class, built in 1947 and, appropriately named for this Ordsall Lane freight. It was not uncommon for these locomotives to work the Eccles-Tyldesley-Wigan line as there are a number of occasions when, due to accidents on the W.C.M.L., traffic was diverted via London Road, Castlefield Junction and Ordsall, plus more regular diversions due to P.W.Works.

As far as I know, this is the only photo Jim took from the cab of 46257. The view shows the train approaching Weaste Station, and Jim was a happy man, getting his hands on the controls of *a big green un*, for a short while at least!

Author's Collection,
(Jim Carter).

Plate 173. Cross Lane Station looking west as shot from a passing train c1955. The station was to close in July 1959. Cross Lane Junction is on the left beyond the bridge and the signal box on the right controlled the cattle dock.
Author's Collection.

Plate 174. Stanier '8F' No.48065, is seen at Ordsall Lane, Salford, crossing from Down Fast to Down Slow heading west with a rake of empty stone hoppers ; empty that is, except for the one next to the engine which would suggest it's either short weight or the discharge doors won't work! Just look though at the railway here compared to the present day; it really makes you wonder what on earth happened to scrap all this, and not just here, but nationwide. Ordsall Lane No.4 box is prominent, centre with Duncan Street far right.
Author's Collection, (Jim Carter).

Plate 175. A Trans-Pennine unit has a 2 car DMU in tow as it passes Ordsall Lane No.2 box. This particular box was the second at this location opening in 1885 with an 80 lever frame. It was to close on 22nd October 1978.
Tom Sutch.

Plate 176. On approaching Manchester Exchange Station the former London & North Western lines ran parallel with those of the Lancashire & Yorkshire Railway. About 1962, 'Jubilee' Class No45661 *Vernon* passes Deal Street signal box on the approach to Manchester Victoria as seen from Exchange Station. *Vernon* was a regular engine on the 3.55pm Manchester Exchange- Barrow/Windermere express in the 1950s. At the time it was shedded at Newton Heath. *Author's Collection, (Jim Carter).*

120

Plate 177. Beneath the dark shadows of Manchester Exchange Station, 'Patriot' Class No.45549, one of the un-named, un-rebuilt members of its class, rests between duties c1960. The engine carries an '8B' Warrington, Dallam shedplate.

Author's Collection, (Jim Carter).

Through workings from Manchester to Carlisle and Glasgow via Eccles Junction and Tyldesley, operated from the opening of this route. The fastest train to Glasgow was the 2.35 pm departure from Hunts Bank, calling at Worsley at 2.48, Tyldesley 2.55, Wigan 3.08 and Preston 3.37, to arrive Glasgow at 9.30pm, a journey time of 6 hours 55 minutes, quite a creditable time in the 1864-70 period. The Up working took some twenty minutes longer, departing Glasgow at 9.45am, reaching Tyldesley at 4.35pm and arriving in Manchester on the hour at 5.00pm.

During the 1880s a departure at 2.00 pm from Manchester stopped only at Tyldesley, 2.17 pm, before reaching Wigan where connections were made with the 1.45 pm departure from Liverpool to depart Wigan at 2.38 pm, reaching Preston at 3.00 pm and Glasgow at 8.00 pm, giving an even 6 hours journey. This in fact was five minutes faster than the 'Scotch Mail' which left Manchester at 1.00 am, ran non-stop to Wigan arriving at 1.30 am and reached Glasgow at 7.05 am. A fast return train left Glasgow at 10.00 am, stopped at Wigan, 3.46 pm, Tyldesley, 3.59 pm, reaching Manchester at 4.20 pm, again twenty minutes longer on the return.

In the early 1890s a direct Manchester Exchange to Windermere service departed Exchange at 4.15 pm, stopped at Tyldesley at 4.31 pm and arrived in Wigan North Western at 4.43 pm to combine with the 3.55 pm from Liverpool which reached Wigan at 4.37 pm. Departure from Wigan was at 4.49 pm, arriving Preston at 5.10 pm and Windermere at 6.50 pm. Additionally, on Tuesdays only, this train called at Cross Lane, 4.19 pm, to pick up passengers for the north of Preston only. The return working departed Windermere at 8.10 am, arrived Wigan, 10.00 am, Tyldesley, 10.14 am and Manchester Exchange at 10.31am.

121

LEIGH CHRONICLE RAILWAY TIME TABLES

17th SEPTEMBER, 1864

OBSERVE.—*Passengers for Bolton, Bedford, Leigh, Bradshaw Leach, Kenyon, and Stations on the Bolton Branch change Carriages at Tyldesley.*

NEW LINE

The class of trains refers to the Manchester, Eccles, Leigh, and Wigan line only.
From Manchester, Tyldesley, Leigh to Wigan, Preston, and the North.
WEEK DAYS ONLY.

	1,2,3.	1,2,3.	1 & 2.	1,2,3.	1 & 2.	1,2,3.	1 & 2.	1 & 2.	1,2,3.	1,2,3.	1 & 2.	1,2,3.	1,2,3.	1 & 2.
Manchester ...	6 5	8 0	9 30	10 0	11 20	1 05	1 30	2 35	3 40	4 30	5 15	5 50	7 20	7 40
Cross Lane	6 13	8 8	...	10 8	...	1 13	...	...	3 48	...	...	5 58	7 28	...
Eccles	6 20	8 15	...	10 15	...	1 20	...	...	3 55	4 42	...	6 5	7 37	...
Worsley	6 25	8 20	9 45	10 20	...	1 25	...	2 48	4 0	4 46	...	6 10	7 45	7 55
Ellenbrook	6 30	8 25	...	10 25	...	1 30	...	...	4 5	4 50	...	6 15	7 47	8 0
Tyldesley ... arr.	6 35	8 30	9 55	10 30	11 40	1 35	1 50	2 55	4 10	4 55	5 33	6 20	7 53	8 5
Tyldesley .. lves .	7 10	8 40	10 15	...	11 50	...	1 55	3 0	...	5 10	...	6 25	...	8 5
Bedford, Leigh, arr.	7 15	8 45	10 20	...	11 55	...	2 0	3 5	...	5 15	...	6 30	...	8 10
Bedford, Leigh .lv	...	8 5	9 15	10 0	11 15	...	1 28	2 35	...	4 20	...	...	...	7 25
Tyldesley, ... arr.	...	8 10	9 20	10 5	11 20	...	1 33	2 45	...	4 20	...	...	...	7 30
Tyldesley.. .dep.	6 35	8 30	9 55	10 30	11 45	...	1 50	2 55	...	4 55	5 33	...	...	8 5
Chowbent	6 39	8 34	9 59	...	10 34	...	1 54	...	...	4 59	...	...	...	8 9
Hindley Green	6 43	8 38	...	10 38	...	...	...	...	...	5 3	...	...	...	8 13
Platt Bridge	6 48	8 43	...	10 43	...	...	...	...	...	5 8	...	...	...	8 19
Wigan	6 55	8 50	10 10	10 50	11 58	...	2 7	3 8	...	5 15	5 45	...	...	8 25
Preston	7 55	...	10 48	...	12 30	...	2 40	3 37	...	5 50	6 28	...	...	9 5
Fleetwood	9 4	...	12 0	...	1 40	...	4 35	4 35	...	7 18	...	...	...	...
Lancaster	9 0	...	11 32	...	1 40	...	3 18	...	...	6 42	...	...	...	10 5
Carlisle	2 15	...	1 55	...	4 40	...	5 45	6 10	...	9 10	...	...	...	...
Edinburgh	5 40	...	5 40	...	...	...	...	9 10	...	12 25	...	...	...	...
Glasgow ..... arr.	6 15	...	6 15	...	...	...	...	9 30	...	12 35	...	...	...	...

From Preston, Wigan, the North, and Tyldesley and Leigh, to Manchester.
WEEK DAYS ONLY.

	1,2,3.	1,2,3.	1 & 2.	1,2,3.	1 & 2.	1,2,3.	1 & 2.	1 & 2.	1,2,3.	1,2,3.	1 & 2.	1,2,3.	1,2,3.	1 & 2.
Glasgow	...	...	...	...	...	...	...	...	9 45	...	...	7 30	...	1 0
Edinburgh	...	...	...	...	...	...	...	...	10 0	...	...	7 45	...	1 0
Carlisle	...	...	...	8 10	7 45	...	...	...	1 5	...	...	1 45	...	5 0
Lancaster	...	7 15	9 7	10 26	11 12	...	...	...	3 9	...	...	5 0	...	7 23
Fleetwood	...	7 5	8 5	10 0	11 30	...	...	...	2 55	...	...	5 15	...	7 0
Preston	6 15	8 20	10 0	11 15	12 25	...	...	...	3 50	...	...	6 20	...	8 15
Wigan	7 5	9 5	11 0	11 50	1 15	...	2 35	...	4 20	5 50	...	7 15	...	8 50
Platt Bridge	7 10	9 10	11 5	...	1 20	...	2 40	...	...	5 55	...	7 20	...	...
Hindley Green	7 15	9 15	11 10	...	1 25	...	2 45	...	...	6 0	...	7 25	...	...
Chowbent	7 19	9 19	11 14	12 0	1 29	...	2 49	...	...	6 5	...	7 29	...	...
Tyldesley	7 23	9 23	11 18	12 5	1 33	...	2 56	...	4 35	6 10	...	7 33	...	9 5
Tyldesley .. leaves	8 40	9 25	11 50	...	1 55	...	3 0	...	5 10	6 25	...	8 5	...	...
Bedford, Leigh, arr.	8 45	9 30	11 55	...	2 0	...	3 5	...	5 15	6 30	...	8 10	...	...
Bedford, Leigh . .lv	...	9 15	11 15	...	1 28	...	2 40	...	4 20	6 2	...	7 25	...	8 50
Tyldesley, ... arr.	... 9 21	11 20	...	1 33	...	2 45	...	4 25	6 7	...	7 30	...	8 55	...
Tyldesley	7 23	9 23	11 22	12 5	1 33	1 50	2 55	4 20	4 35	6 10	6 45	7 33	8 46	9 5
Ellenbrook	7 28	9 28	11 27	...	...	1 55	2 58	4 25	...	6 15	6 50	7 38	8 50	...
Worsley	7 33	9 33	11 32	12 15	...	2 0	3 3	4 30	4 45	6 20	6 55	7 43	8 56	9 13
Eccles	7 38	9 38	...	...	...	2 5	3 8	4 35	...	6 25	7 0	7 48	8 58	...
Cross Lane	7 45	9 45	...	...	...	...	3 15	...	...	...	7 7	...	...	...
Manchester	7 55	9 55	11 50	12 30	1 55	2 22	3 25	4 50	5 0	6 40	7 15	8 0	9 15	9 25

Manchester, Tyldesley, Leigh, to Wigan, Preston, and the North.
SUNDAYS ONLY.

	1,2,3.	1 & 2.	1,2,3.	1,2,3.	1,2,3.
Manchester ...	8 40	9 10	2 0	3 0	6 30
Cross Lane	8 48	...	2 8	3 38	6 38
Eccles	8 55	...	2 15	3 45	6 45
Worsley	9 0	9 25	2 20	3 50	6 50
Ellenbrook	9 5	9 30	2 25	3 55	6 55
Tyldesley, ... arr.	9 10	9 35	2 30	4 0	7 0
Tyldesley, ..leaves	9 10	9 36	...	...	7 80
Bedford, Leigh arr.	9 15	9 40	...	...	7 35
Bedford, Leigh, lvs.	...	9 43	...	...	6 45
Tyldesley, ..arrives	...	9 48	...	...	6 50
Tyldesley, ..dep.	9 10	9 56	...	...	7 0
Chowbent	9 14	9 59	...	...	7 4
Hindley Green	9 18	...	...	...	7 8
Platt Bridge	9 23	...	...	...	7 13
Wigan	9 30	...	...	...	7 20
Preston	10 35	...	...	...	8 40
Fleetwood	...	...	...	...	...
Lancaster	...	...	...	...	...
Carlisle	...	...	...	...	...
Edinburgh	...	...	...	...	...
Glasgow	...	...	...	...	...

Preston, Wigan, and the North, and from Tyldesley and Leigh, to Manchester.
SUNDAYS ONLY.

	1,2,3.	1,2,3.	1,2,3.	1,2,3.	1,2,3.
Glasgow	...	...	...	...	...
Edinburgh	...	...	...	...	...
Carlisle	...	...	...	...	...
Lancaster	...	...	...	...	...
Fleetwood	...	...	...	...	...
Preston	8 30	...	...	...	...
Wigan	10 0	...	...	...	...
Platt Bridge	10 5	...	...	...	...
Hindley Green	10 10	...	...	...	...
Chowbent	10 14	...	...	...	...
Tyldesley	10 18	...	...	...	...
Tyldesley, ..leaves	10 25	...	...	...	...
Bedford, Leigh, ..	10 30	...	...	...	...
Bedford, Leigh, lvs.	10 10	...	...	6 45	8 5
Tyldesley	10 15	...	...	6 50	8 10
Tyldesley	10 18	2 40	5 0	7 0	8 20
Ellenbrook	10 23	2 45	5 5	7 5	8 25
Worsley	10 28	2 50	5 10	7 10	8 30
Eccles	10 33	2 55	5 13	7 13	8 35
Cross Lane	10 40	3 3	5 22	7 22	8 42
Manchester ...	10 50	3 12	5 30	7 39	8 50

From Tyldesley and Leigh, to Liverpool and the South.

WEEK DAYS.   SUNDAYS.

Manchester	6 5	8 0	... ...	9 30	11 20	1 30	2 35	4 30	5 50	7 40	8 40	9 10	... ...	6 30
Tyldesley	7 10	8 40	9 25	10 15	11 50	1 55	3 0	5 10	6 25	8 5	9 10	9 36	10 25	6 30	7 30
Bedford, Lgh...	7 15	8 45	9 30	10 20	11 55	2 0	3 5	5 15	6 30	8 10	9 15	9 40	10 30	6 35	7 35
Bradshaw Leach	7 20	8 50	9 35	... ...	12 0	2 5	3 10	5 20	6 35	8 15	9 20	9 45	10 35	6 40	7 40
Kenyon	7 36	9 6	9 40	10 35	1 10	2 10	3 28	5 55	7 24	8 17	9 25	10 0	10 40	6 51	7 45
Newton	7 50	9 16	... ...	10 42	1 18	... ...	3 35	6 0	7 31	8 22	... ...	10 7	... ...	7 5
St. Helens	7 35	9 15	... ...	11 15	... ...	... ...	3 30	6 0	8 0	... ...	... ...	9 40	... ...	7 0
Liverpool	8 55	10 0	... ...	11 25	... ...	... ...	4 20	6 40	8 20	9 10	10 0	10 45	... ...	7 50
Warrington	8 20	9 37	... ...	10 50	1 34	... ...	... ...	6 45	... ...	9 20	... ...	... ...	... ...	7 50
Chester	... ...	10 15	... ...	11 45	2 10	... ...	... ...	7 50	... ...	10 0	... ...	... ...	... ...	8 45

From Liverpool and the South, to Leigh and Tyldesley.

WEEK DAYS   SUNDAYS.

Chester	... ...	... ...	8 15	... ...	... ...	2 40	4 25	... ...	... ...	... ...	... ...	... ...	5 50
Warrington	... ...	... ...	9 6	... ...	... ...	3 30	5 15	... ...	... ...	... ...	... ...	... ...	6 40
Liverpool	6 30	... ...	9 5	10 0	12 0	3 0	4 40	... ...	7 30	... ...	8 40	... ...	7 10
St. Helens	7 5	... ...	9 15	10 15	12 30	3 30	5 0	... ...	8 0	... ...	9 10	... ...	7 0
Newton	7 32	... ...	9 40	10 39	12 52	3 55	5 23	... ...	8 23	... ...	9 33	... ...	7 40
Kenyon	7 55	9 5	9 50	11 5	1 10	2 30	4 10	5 55	7 15	8 40	9 35	10 0	6 5	7 55
Bradshaw Leach	8 0	9 10	9 55	11 10	... ...	2 35	4 15	... ...	7 20	8 45	9 38	10 5	6 10	8 0
Bedford, Lgh...	8 5	9 15	10 0	11 15	1 28	2 40	4 20	6 2	7 25	8 50	9 43	10 10	6 15	8 5
Tyldesley	8 10	9 20	10 5	11 20	1 33	2 45	4 25	6 7	7 30	8 55	9 48	10 15	6 20	8 10
Manchester	... ...	9 55	... ...	11 50	1 5	3 25	5 0	6 40	8 5	9 20	... ...	10 50	7 50	8 50

From Bolton, to Manchester, via Tyldesley.

WEEK DAYS   SUNDAYS.
1, 2, 3. 1, 2, 3. 1, 2, 3. 1, 2, 3. 1, 2, 3. 1, 2, 3. 1, 2, 3. 1, 2, 3. 1, 2, 3.

Bolton	7 45	9 20	10 50	1 0	2 25	4 0	7 5	8 40	6 0	7 0
Daubhill	7 49	9 24	10 54	1 4	2 29	4 4	7 9	8 44	6 4	7 4
Chequerbent	7 55	9 30	11 0	1 10	2 35	4 10	7 15	8 50	6 10	7 10
Atherton	8 1	9 36	11 6	1 16	2 41	4 16	7 21	8 56	6 16	7 16
Chowbent	8 5	9 40	11 10	1 21	2 45	4 21	7 26	9 1	6 21	7 21
Tyldesley	8 10	9 45	11 15	1 25	2 50	4 25	7 30	9 5	6 25	7 25
Bedford, Leigh, arr.	8 45	10 20	11 55	2 0	3 5	5 15	8 10	9 15	6 35	7 35
Manchester	9 55	... ...	11 50	1 55	3 25	5 0	8 0	10 50	7 30	8 50

From Manchester, to Bolton, via Tyldesley.

WEEK DAYS   SUNDAYS.
1, 2, 3. 1, 2, 3. 1, 2, 3. 1, 2, 3. 1, 2, 3. 1, 2, 3. 1, 2, 3. 1, 2, 3. 1, 2, 3.

Manchester, depart	8 0	9 30	11 20	*1 30	2 35	5 15	7 40	9 10	6 30
Bedford, Leigh, depart...	8 5	10 0	11 15	1 18	2 40	... ...	7 25	9 43	8 5
Tyldesley	8 35	10 10	11 50	1 50	3 0	5 40	8 10	9 56	8 15
Chowbent	8 40	10 14	11 54	1 55	3 4	5 44	8 14	9 58	8 19
Atherton	8 45	10 19	11 59	2 0	3 9	5 49	8 19	10 4	8 24
Chequerbent	8 55	10 25	12 3	2 6	3 13	5 53	8 23	10 8	8 8
Daubhill...........	9 0	10 32	12 10	2 12	3 20	6 0	8 30	10 15	8 35
Bolton	9 5	10 30	12 15	2 17	3 26	6 6	8 36	10 20	8 40

Passengers to and from Bolton, change at Chowbent by this train. All other change at Tyldesley.

OLD LINE

From Bolton, Atherton, and Leigh, to Manchester, Liverpool, and London.

WEEK DAYS   SUNDAYS.
1,2,3. 1 & 2* 1 & 2. 1 & 2.† 1 & 2.‡ 1 & 2§ 1 & 2.‖ 1,2,3** 1,2,3. 1,2,3.¶ 1,2,3.¶

Bolton	7 0	8 35	... ...	10 0	12 40	3 30	4 30	6 50	8 15	8 40	6 0	7 0
Daubhill	7 4	8 39	... ...	10 3	12 44	3 34	4 34	6 54	8 19	8 44	6 4	7 4
Chequerbent	7 10	8 44	... ...	10 8	12 49	3 40	4 40	7 0	8 25	8 50	6 10	7 10
Atherton	7 16	8 49	9 23	10 13	12 54	3 46	4 45	7 5	8 31	8 56	6 16	7 16
Leigh	7 22	8 54	9 28	10 19	12 59	3 52	4 50	7 12	8 37	... ...	... ...	... ...
Bradshaw Leach	7 26	8 58	9 31	... ...	1 3	3 56	4 53	7 17	8 40	9 20	6 40	7 40
Kenyon	7 30	9 4	9 35	10 25	1 7	4 0	4 56	7 22	8 45	9 25	6 45	7 45
Manchester, arr.	8 30	10 15	10 15	11 30	1 45	4 45	5 20	8 29	9 35	10 25	... ...	8 32
Newton	7 50	9 5	... ...	10 44	1 45	4 15	6 0	7 35	... ...	9 40	7 5	... ...
St. Helens, arr.	8 20	10 0	... ...	... ...	2 55	4 45	6 30	8 42	... ...	10 20	7 40	... ...
Liverpool	8 55	10 0	... ...	11 25	2 55	5 3	6 40	8 20	... ...	10 55	7 50	... ...
Wigan	... ...	10 13	... ...	12 0	2 11	5 20	... ...	9 29	... ...	9 53	7 30	... ...
Preston	... ...	10 43	... ...	12 30	2 40	5 50	... ...	9 5	... ...	10 35	8 40	... ...
Warrington .	8 20	9 37	... ...	11 31	1 34	4 48	6 42	8 0	... ...	10 20	7 40	... ...
Chester	... ...	10 45	10 45	11 45	2 10	5 20	7 50	... ...	... ...	10 55	8 35	... ...
Birmingham	1 30	12 30	... ...	3 0	5 45	7 20	10 55	... ...	... ...	1 40	... ...	... ...
London	5 55	2 30	... ...	5 45	9 15	9 50	... ...	5 50a.m.	... ...	... ...	5 0	... ...

* 3rd to Wigan. † 3rd to Manchester, Liverpool, Birmingham, Wigan, Chester, and London, arriving at 7-5 p.m.
‡ 3rd to St. Helens and Wigan. § 3rd to Manchester and Wigan. ‖ 3rd to Birmingham and Chester. ** 1,2, 3 to all except London. ¶ By Tyldesley.

From London, Liverpool and Manchester, to Leigh, Atherton, and Bolton.

London	9 0p.m.	... ...	... ...	... ...	6 15	10 0	... ...	11 20	... ...	... ...	... ...	10 0
Birmingham	10 30 „	... ...	... ...	6 0	8 45	11 15	... ...	12 20	... ...	... ...	... ...	1 5
Chester	... ...	... ...	8 15	9 0	12 5	1 50	... ...	4 25	... ...	7 10	... ...	5 50
Warrington .	7 1	8 30	9 6	9 20	12 50	2 28	... ...	5 15	7 0	8 0	... ...	6 40
Preston	6 15	... ...	8 20	... ...	11 10	3 5	... ...	... ...	6 20	... ...	... ...	6 5
Wigan	7 0	... ...	8 54	... ...	11 45	3 40	... ...	4 20	7 4	... ...	... ...	6 42
Liverpool	6 30	7 40	9 5	10 0	12 0	3 0	4 20	4 40	6 45	... ...	7 45	7 0
St. Helens	7 5	... ...	9 15	10 15	12 30	3 30	4 10	5 0	7 0	... ...	8 15	7 0
Newton	7 32	8 45	9 40	10 39	12 52	3 55	4 50	5 23	7 16	... ...	8 38	7 40
Manchester ...	7 0	... ...	9 10	... ...	12 40	3 30	... ...	A	6 45	... ...	8 40	6 15
Kenyon	7 45	9 10	9 55	11 0	1 15	4 15	5 15	5 48	7 40	... ...	8 55	9 30	6 33	7 53
Bradshaw Leach	7 48	... ...	9 58	11 3	1 18	4 18	5 18	... ...	7 43	... ...	8 58	9 38	6 56	8 0
Leigh	7 51	9 16	10 3	11 6	1 21	4 21	5 21	5 54	7 46	... ...	9 1	... ...	6 59	... ...
Atherton	7 57	9 22	10 10	11 12	1 27	4 27	5 27	6 1	7 53	... ...	9 7	10 4	7 5	8 24
Chequerbent	8 3	9 28	10 20	11 18	1 33	4 33	5 33	6 9	8 0	... ...	9 17	10 8	7 11	8 29
Daubhill...........	8 9	9 34	10 26	11 24	1 39	4 45	5 39	6 23	8 7	... ...	9 23	10 15	7 17	8 35
Bolton, arr.	8 15	9 40	10 30	11 30	1 45	4 50	5 45	6 30	8 15	... ...	9 30	10 20	7 25	8 40

The late l9th century was a period of change regarding passenger services from Manchester to the north; many ceased to operate or were superseded by improved or new services and facilities to cater for increasing demand, including the opening of Manchester Exchange Station in 1884 and in the 1890s the first of the exclusive 'Club' trains made their appearance, available for use by season ticket holders only.

Early in the 20th century the 4.15 pm to Windermere also called at Hindley Green on Tuesdays and Thursdays, giving a three minutes later arrival in Windermere.

The Fridays only express 'Club' train for Windermere departed Manchester Exchange at 5.07 pm and working via Bickershaw and Amberswood East Junctions traversed the former Lancashire Union Railways Whelley route to arrive in Preston at 5.58 pm and Windermere at 7.12 pm. The Mondays only return train departed Windermere at 8.30 am but worked via Wigan North Western arriving at 10.00 am, thence running non-stop via Tyldesley to arrive Manchester Exchange at 10.26 am.

In the same period a 'Corridor Express' left Manchester Exchange at 5.45 pm, running non-stop to arrive in Preston at 6.31 pm and connected with the 5.50 pm from Liverpool Exchange which contained a through dining car. Departure from Preston was at 6.40 pm, arriving in Glasgow Central at 11.00 pm, thereby reducing the fastest journey time to five hours fifteen minutes. The timing of this train, 46 minutes to Preston from Manchester, suggest it also worked via the Whelley route. However, the return working which had left Glasgow at 4.30 pm went via Wigan, 9.26 pm, to arrive in Manchester Exchange at 9.55 pm.

From 1911, the 5.07 pm to Windermere worked daily, Saturdays and Sundays excepted, with the same timing, 51 minutes to Preston with the Down service. The Up train from Windermere again went via Wigan North Western, arriving at 10.00 am with an additional stop being made at Tyldesley upon notification being given to the guard before leaving Oxenholme.

Timing of the 5.45 pm to Glasgow remained the same for the Down train but an additional 12 minutes had been added to the Up working, arrival in Manchester at 10.07 pm. Slight timing changes affected the 4.15 pm to Windermere from Manchester Exchange. An additional stop at Eccles was made, if, on booking, passengers gave notification at the station. Arrival at Tyldesley was now at 4.34 pm, Wigan 4.49 pm, Preston 5.17 pm and Windermere 6.56 pm, six minutes later than the 1890's timing.

Between the two world wars the principal p.m. departures from Manchester Exchange were firstly the 4.10 to Windermere & Barrow, calling at Eccles, 4.18, Tyldesley 4.29, Wigan 4.43. and Preston at 5.10 to arrive in Windermere at 6.45 pm. A Direct Up express departed Windermere at 4.05 pm, reaching Preston at 5.57, Wigan 6.20, Tyldesley 6.32, Eccles 6.45 and Manchester Exchange at 6.54 pm. This train also carried through coaches to/from Morecambe which were detached/attached at Lancaster.

Next away was the 5.00pm. 'Restaurant Car Express' to Glasgow running non-stop to arrive Wigan at 5.30 and Preston at 6.05. In the late 1930s the timing of this train had been brought forward to 4.45pm, but an additional departure from Exchange at 5.05 pm also contained through coaches for Glasgow and Edinburgh, the 4.45 taking 5hrs 10minutes to reach Glasgow and the 5.05 taking 5hrs 36 minutes. An equivalent Up working made an extra stop at Tyldesley at 7.10 pm, to arrive in Manchester at 7.31 pm. As established in London & North Western days these workings combined and split at Wigan or Preston with Ex-Liverpool workings.

Finally from Exchange the 5.10pm 'Club' train to Windermere, which from London & North Western days included exclusive saloons for the commuting businessman. This train ran non-stop via Tyldesley, Bickershaw Junction and Hindley & Platt Bridge to join the Whelley route at Amberswood East Junction, taking 44 minutes to reach Preston at 5.54 and arriving in Windermere at 7.07 pm. This was now the only regular, ex-Manchester Exchange passenger train, diagrammed to work over the Great Central Railway. The morning 'Club' train departed Windermere at 8.30am, reached Preston at 9.40am and here again worked via Wigan North Western to arrive there at 10.03am and then ran non-stop to Manchester Exchange in 27 minutes.

Post W.W.II. the Windermere & Barrow train consistently departed from Manchester Exchange at 3.55 pm, calling at Eccles, Tyldesley and Wigan, arrived Preston at 5.03 pm to reach Barrow at 7.05 pm. and Windermere at 7.11 pm. The 4.15 pm to Glasgow, complete with through restaurant car, ran non-stop to Preston arriving at 5.14 pm, only 11 minutes behind the Barrow train. Connections were made with the 4.25 pm from Liverpool Exchange departing Preston at 5.30 pm. A much later arrival in Glasgow was at 10.40 pm as the railways struggled with the effects of a run down and neglected system in post war Britain.

Throughout the intervening years the successor of the 1880's 'Scotch Mail' continued to run from Manchester Exchange, including sleeping coaches and in the 1950s a through coach from York, which had departed at 9.50 pm, was attached at Manchester. Departure for Glasgow was at 1.10am and arrival at 7.45 am.

The former Club train, departing still at 5.10 pm from Manchester Exchange, continued to use the Whelley route, but now worked over ex-Lancashire & Yorkshire metals via the Walkden High Level lines, Hindley No. 2 and De Trafford Junctions, arriving Preston at 6.02 pm and Windermere at 7.32 pm. It is probable that this change of route was instituted slightly before W.W.II, after the introduction of new power boxes at Deal Street and Victoria West, Manchester, along with track modifications completed in March 1929 which provided new connections from the 'A' Slow, or Ordsall Lane Lines, to the 'B' Slow, or Pendleton Lines. Departing from Windermere at 8.10 am, the corresponding Up train reached Preston at 9.29 am and Wigan at 9.56 am, then ran non-stop via Tyldesley to Eccles, arriving at 10.24 am and Exchange at 10.33 am, some 20 minutes longer than the pre-war working.

By 1955 the Barrow train departed Exchange at 3.53 pm, stopped at Tyldesley at 4.17 pm, Wigan at 4.36 pm and Preston at 5.03 pm, arriving in Barrow at 7.11 pm. Coaches to/from Morecambe continued to be attached/detached at Lancaster.

It appears considerable effort had been made to improve the timing of the 4.15 pm Manchester Exchange to Glasgow train which now arrived at its destination at 10.10 pm, an improvement of 30 minutes over the immediate post-war timing.

A two minute later arrival in Windermere was the only timing change to 5.10 pm departure from Manchester Exchange and this train continued using Walkden high level lines, Hindley No. 2 and De Trafford Junctions to gain access to the Whelley line.

In the early 1960s timetable, departure time from Manchester for the Glasgow train was the same at 4.15 pm. It again stopped at Wigan North Western, departing at 4.53 pm to arrive Preston at 5.20 pm connecting with the 4.35 pm from Liverpool Exchange which contained through coaches for Glasgow and Edinburgh. Arrival time in Glasgow had been improved by a further half hour to 9.40 pm.

The Barrow train now departed from Manchester Victoria at 4.03 pm and travelled via the former Lancashire & Yorkshire lines to Preston, arriving at 5.10 pm, and Barrow at 7.00 pm.

The 5.10 pm Manchester Exchange-Windermere had continued to use the Walkden high level-Whelley route running non-stop to reach Preston at 6.02 pm, and as it had throughout the post war years, making connections with the Ex 5.00 pm Liverpool Exchange-Windermere, arriving in Windermere at 7.35 pm. The Whelley route ceased to be used by regular passenger diagrams from September 1965.

Elimination of the Barrow service via Tyldesley was countered by a stop at Tyldesley, from June 1964, of the 4.15pm to Glasgow; this the first stoppage of a direct Glasgow train here since the 1880s but it was merely a prelude to the withdrawal of local passenger services from Manchester Exchange via Tyldesley to Wigan North Western. This service withdrawal was first proposed in September of 1963 which, in the event was reprieved due to public objections. However, any satisfaction gained from this by the objectors was short lived, closure eventually occurring in November 1964.

Consequently the Glasgow service departed from Victoria, working to Preston via Lancashire & Yorkshire metals and an era of exactly 100 years of fast passenger express trains to the North via Tyldesley had come to an end.

British Railways Board

PUBLIC NOTICE

Withdrawal of Railway Passenger Services

(Transport Act, 1962)

The London Midland Area Board hereby give notice in accordance with Section 56 (7) of the Transport Act, 1962, that on and from Monday, 9th September, 1963, they propose to discontinue the stopping passenger services between

MANCHESTER (Exchange) & WIGAN (North Western)

It appears to the Board that the following alternative services will be available to and from Wigan :—

BY RAIL
From and to Manchester (Victoria), Swinton, Atherton (Central) and Wigan (Wallgate).

BY ROAD
By Lancashire United Transport, Salford City Transport, Leigh and Wigan Corporation Services.

Area	Bus Route Number
Eccles	No through service
Monton Green	No through service
Worsley	32
Tyldesley	32
Leigh	54, 58

OBJECTIONS

Any user of the rail service it is proposed to withdraw and any body representing such users desirous of objecting to the proposed withdrawal of services may lodge objections within six weeks of 19th July, 1963, i.e., not later than 30th August, 1963, addressing any objections to the Secretary of the Transport Users' Consultative Committee for the North Western Area, Peter House, 2, Oxford Street, Manchester, 1.

Note: If any objections are lodged within the period specified above, the closure cannot be proceeded with until The Transport Users' Consultative Committee has reported to the Minister and the Minister has given his consent (Section 56 (8) of the Transport Act, 1962).

Plate 178. A Trans-Pennine unit approaching Manchester Exchange Station with the 10.40 from Liverpool Lime Street in September 1961. These units were introduced over the Liverpool-Manchester-Trans-Pennine route in March 1961 and although they principally worked over the Chat Moss route, they were no strangers to the Eccles -Tyldesley - Leigh - Pennington - Kenyon Junction lines when diverted at weekends. *B.R.*

The next attempt at closure of passenger services was to be even more dramatic with an intended closure notification to take place in October 1968. Much more, however was at stake, for this was to be a complete closure of the railway. It may well be that mining closures and the resultant loss of income from a route which, from its very beginning, had transported millions of tons of coal from local collieries along its length had a dramatic effect on BR's balance sheet, but behind this smokescreen was a much more controversial reason for closure.

In the event, a stay of execution was obtained on account of the many objections and the Minister of Transport reconsidered closure in the light of concerted opposition by hundreds of users and local politicians alike and the closure date of 7th October was postponed.

However, rather like many planning applications which get any number of repulses, if you ask the same question often enough you will eventually get the answer you're looking for. Thus in February 1969 the final proposal for closure was announced.

The then Minister of Transport, one Richard Marsh, when considering his decision whether or not to implement the proposed withdrawal of passenger services: *has, however, had to take into account the very heavy expenditure which would be incurred in constructing a rail bridge over the line of the proposed M64* (M602) *Motorway near Monton Green if the highway authority were to be prevented from breaking the formation of the loop line.* Thus in one sentence, services over the Eccles-Tyldesley-Leigh loop were condemned. It was allright to spend the required millions on constructing a new motorway but not a few tens of thousands on preserving the existing railway operations. What was good for the goose certainly wasn't good for the gander!

The closure report also stated that:- *He, the minister therefore requests the Board* (B.R.Board) *to preserve intact the formation, track and station sites except for that part of the formation which crosses the line of the M64 at Monton Green on the understanding that if it were to be decided in due course that a rail service should be restored this would be physically possible by constructing a rail bridge over the road. The minister will give further consideration to the rest of the formation when the PTA have had an opportunity to consider the matter and to give him* their views. And finally:- *Accordingly, the minister, in exercise of his powers under section 56 of the Transport Act of 1962 and under section 54 of the Transport Act of 1968 gives his consent to the closure subject to the following conditions.*

In effect, the *conditions* consisted of an Annex in two parts listing existing, Part 1, and revised, Part 2, of bus services and the requirement of the bus operators to give the minister notice of any proposed alterations to these services and that:- *the National Bus Company and the British Railways Board shall take reasonable steps to keep themselves informed of any such proposals or alterations as are mentioned.*

In due course, closure notices were posted at all stations to take effect from Monday 5th May 1969. In fact the last trains ran over the route on the evening of 3rd inst, on the return of BICC specials from Leigh to Blackpool.

The whole episode of repeated closure attempts and the revised bus services, were a complete nonsense, finally borne out by the M64 land requirement. It mattered not one jot that this line was a vital requirement to a co-ordinated transport policy and the seemingly intransigent attitude of those in authority when a major part of South Lancashire would be denied rail access. The situation since closure has been one of chronic congestion on the roads generally, and endless tailbacks on the A580; and what have we now had imposed upon us, a *mis*guided busway which the vast majority oppose and which will only add to the congestion. So much for freedom of choice!

British Railways Board
PUBLIC NOTICE — TRANSPORT ACT, 1962

PASSENGER SERVICES

In connection with the London Midland Region's proposal to withdraw the existing weekday stopping passenger train services between:—

MANCHESTER EXCHANGE & LIVERPOOL LIME ST.
(via Tyldesley and via Patricroft)
MANCHESTER EXCHANGE and LEIGH

And introduce a revised service between:—

MANCHESTER EXCHANGE & LIVERPOOL LIME ST.
(via Patricroft)

involving the discontinuance of all passenger train services on the following section of line:—

ECCLES JUNCTION and KENYON JUNCTION
(via Tyldesley)

and from the following stations:—

LEIGH	MONTON GREEN
TYLDESLEY	WORSLEY

"Subject to the authorisation of the additional and revised bus services, by road service licences issued by the Traffic Commissioners under the Road Traffic Acts." The Minister of Transport's decision regarding the above withdrawal and revision of services, and closure of stations, will be implemented with effect from May 5, 1969.

ANNEX
PART 1
Existing bus services provided under road service licences granted under the Road Traffic Acts 1960-62

Services provided by Lancashire United Transport Limited
 Service 11 Clifton — Monton Green — Eccles
  17 Pendlebury — Monton Green — Eccles
  83 Atherton — Tyldesley — Worsley — Farnworth.
Services provided jointly by Lancashire United Transport Limited and Salford City Transport
 Service 9 Walkden — Worsley — Monton Green — Eccles — Manchester
  20 Farnworth — Monton Green — Eccles — Cadishead — Glazebrook.
  23 Worsley — Manchester.
Service provided jointly by Lancashire United Transport Limited, Salford City Transport and Bolton Corporation
 Service 12 Bolton — Worsley — Manchester.
Service provided jointly by Lancashire United Transport Limited, Salford City and Leigh Corporation
 Service 26 Leigh — Worsley — Manchester
Services provided jointly by Lancashire United Transport Limited, Salford City Transport and Wigan Corporation
 Service 32 Wigan — Tyldesley — Worsley — Manchester
Service provided jointly by Lancashire United Transport Limited, Salford City Transport, Ribble Motor Services Limited, and Leigh and St Helens Corporations
 Service 39 Liverpool — St Helens — Newton — Leigh — Tyldesley — Manchester
Service provided jointly by Lancashire United Transport Limited and Bolton Corporation
 Service 41 Bolton — Worsley — Eccles.
Services provided jointly by Lancashire United Transport Limited and Bolton and Leigh Corporations
 Service 50 Leigh — Newton — Warrington
  82 Leigh — Atherton — Bolton (connectional service)
Services provided jointly by Lancashire United Transport Limited and Leigh Corporation
 Service 51 Leigh — Newton — Warrington
  52 Leigh — Newton — Earlestown — Ashton
  84 Leigh — Atherton — Tyldesley — Mosley Common
Service provided jointly by Salford City Transport and Bury Corporation
 Service 6 Eccles — Monton Green — Radcliffe
Services provided by Salford City Transport
 Service 19/21 Manchester — Swinton — Pendlebury (connectional service)
  27/28 Monton Green — Eccles — Manchester
  66 Peel Green — Monton Green — Eccles — Manchester.
Services provided jointly by Salford City Transport and Manchester Corporation
 Service 15 Worsley — Monton Green — Eccles — Manchester.
  57/77 Swinton — Manchester — Reddish (connectional service).

PART II
Additional and Revised Bus Services

1. A non-stop service taking approximately 8 minutes between Tyldesley Square and Atherton Railway Station, Monday — Friday at the following approximate starting times:—
 ex Tyldesley — Atherton Railway Station
  0648 0742 0802
 to make a reasonable connection in each case with a train to Manchester Victoria Station.
 ex Atherton Railway Station — Tyldesley
  1715 1741 1815 1843
 to make reasonable connections in each case with a train from Manchester Victoria Station.
2. A non-stop service taking approximately 10 minutes between Leigh (Spinning Jenny Street) and Atherton Railway Station, Monday — Friday at the following approximate starting times:—
 ex Leigh — Atherton Railway Station
  0646 0740 0800
 to make reasonable connections in each case with a train to Manchester Victoria Station.
 ex Atherton Railway Station — Leigh
  1715 1741 1815 1843
 to make reasonable connections in each case with a train from Manchester Victoria Station.
3. The existing 0650 bus ex Leigh to St Helens on Lancashire United Transport Ltd. service 39 (specified in Part I of the Annex) to be extended back to Atherton (Punch Bowl) to depart from there at approximately 0642 providing a connection at Atherton with the bus on Lancashire United Transport Ltd. service 83 leaving Tyldesley at 0628, and to make a reasonable connection at Newton-le-Willows with a train to Liverpool.
NOTE: In this Annex the expression "approximately" in relation to a time specified for any service includes any reasonable variation of the time so specified having regard to the class or classes of passengers likely to be carried by the service at the specified time.

In view of the Minister's decision, the London Midland Region will withdraw the stopping passenger train services and close the stations concerned on a date shortly to be announced.
R. L. E. LAWRENCE,
Euston Station, General Manager,
London N.W.1. London Midland Region.

Annex to the closure proposal February 1969 above and left, the closure notice.

Plate 179. Horwich built 'Crab' No.2858 rests alongside Platform 1 at Manchester Exchange c1935. *Author's Collection.*

Plate 180. Albeit that we are a little outside our prescribed area with this picture of a London & North Western 0-6-0 climbing Miles Platting Bank, the first wagon behind the engine is of interest being that it is one of Astley & Tyldesley Collieries, a major coal producer on the Leigh Branch. It is unfortunately undated. My best guess is late 1920s or early 1930s.
Author's Collection.

TYLDESLEY & JACKSON'S SIDINGS

The Tyldesley-Leigh-Pennington line with installations at Jackson's Sidings, Speakman's Sidings and Leigh Goods, in addition to the Pennington Loop lines taking in Pennington East & West, the small box at Bickershaw Colliery, the larger signal box at Abram North adjacent to Bolton House Road, and Hindley Field Junction box were all the lot of Tyldesley S&T gangs.

With the run down in traffic via the Pennington Loop and Pennington South Junction to Bickershaw lines in the 1950s the signalling at Pennington South for Bickershaw was reduced in status to "calling on" operation controlled from Pennington South, the ancient London & North Western pattern lower quadrant signals removed, London Midland upper quadrant arms being installed there about 1955.

Pennington West Junction box had closed on 25th August 1951 and post World War II was a Porter/Signalman's job open as and when required. Pennington East Junction box closed on 28th October 1953.

Like the Eccles-Wigan line, the branch from Tyldesley through Leigh to Pennington where a junction was made with the Bolton-Kenyon Junction line, was also opened on 1st September 1864 with just one intermediate station on the branch at Bedford/Leigh. This was to become Leigh & Bedford on 1st August 1876, and finally, on 1st July 1914 Leigh, as by then the town had considerably outgrown the previous township boundaries and Leigh was regarded as more appropriate.

The Parish of Leigh was formed of six separate townships namely, Atherton, Astley, Bedford, Pennington, Westleigh and Tyldesley-with-Shakerley. The latter had, when the railway was built, the largest population and was the centre-piece of the Wigan-Eccles route, acknowledged by the London & North Western Railway as having the greatest potential for mining development and expected to contribute greatly to the revenue derived from the new lines. In 1875, the Local Boards of Bedford, Westleigh and Pennington were amalgamated, hence the station name change, and in the early years of the twentieth century the population passed the 50,000 mark.

Previously, the nearest station had been at Astley on Stephenson's Liverpool-Manchester line of 1830 at a distance of some 4½ miles, an arduous trek through the bleak landscape of Chat Moss and although now very much drained can still be an inhospitable place through an unfettered landscape.

Plate 181. Tyldesley Station is seen here looking east in the Edwardian period with Tyldesley No.1 signalbox just visible. No. 2 box was nearer the junction with the Leigh lines. Both of these boxes were made redundant when the new B.R. Type '15' box opened in 1963.   *Author's Collection.*

Plate 182. On a murky 13th February 1966, Class '8F' No.48213, crosses over the junction of the Wigan and Leigh lines at Tyldesley with a coal train from Speakman's Sidings for the washery at Sandhole Colliery via Sanderson's Sidings Worsley.
Peter Eckersley.

Plate 183. The view from the cab of a Manchester bound DMU as it approaches Tyldesley Station. Note the subsidence to the Down Siding on the far right. Alongside this would have been the platform 4 road which was lifted a short time after withdrawal of the Manchester - Wigan services in 1964.
Eddie Bellass.

Plate 184. On the last day of passenger services over the Eccles-Tyldesley-Leigh route, a two car DMU, the 17.40 Manchester Exchange-Liverpool Lime Street calls at Tyldesley. *John Ryan.*

Plate 185. A look inside Tyldesley Signal Box probably taken whilst Jim Carter was awaiting passage back to Patricroft 'on the cushions' after working trip freights over the old Bolton & Leigh line. Their charge would have been left on the Up line near the box awaiting a relief crew from Patricroft who would also arrive 'on the cushions', in other words, by a regular passenger train. There might have even been time for a 'couple of scoops' in the *Railway* on Wareing Street, the station approach road. Red levers are home signals, yellows are distant signals and white are spares. The chevron levers are detonator placers, blue are facing point lock levers and red with white bands are line clear indicators (locked by block). The chap with hand on bell is believed to be Ron Ainsley whose job it was to assess footplate crews and had been sent from Patricroft for this purpose.
Author's Collection, (Jim Carter).

131

Plate 186. The view on the outside of Tyldesley signal box seen about the time of closure. This box, built on the wagon turntable site abutting Lemon Street bridge, was opened in 1963, replacing the older Tyldesley Nos.1 & 2 boxes of L&NW vintage. It was a B.R. Type '15' with a brick base, timber frame upper storey and flat roof. *Peter Hampson.*

Plate 187. In May 1967 some permanent way work seems to be going on near Jackson's Sidings signal box, possibly the lifting of the connection into the sidings as the last departures from Jacksons were in 1966. Class '8F' No.48714 appears to be running around its train parked on the Down line. *Peter Eckersley.*

Plate 188. From Jackson's Sidings to Tyldesley the official gradient was 1:100. However, mining subsidence had made this much worse, particularly from 1960 onwards as the late Tom Yates, of Tyldesley S&T Dept., remembered having constantly to attend the signalling apparatus when the track was packed up with ash ballast.

In the mid 1960s, a heavy coal train from Jacksons gets to grip with the incline on the approach to Tyldesley Station in this dramatic view from the footplate of the banking Stanier '8F'. The distant signal is at caution, in all probability to allow a Leigh - Manchester Exchange passenger train to clear the station.

In the following pages, a series of photographs that were taken by Patricroft engineman Jim Carter in the mid 1960s are shown when working from Jackson's Sidings.

Author's Collection, (Jim Carter).

Plate 189, Below. The stopblocks at Jackson's Sidings can be seen, extreme right, just below Tyldesley Parish Church, as a coal train from Speakman's Sidings, Leigh approaches c1967. These stopblocks were left in situ after the sidings had been lifted.

Both the distant and home signals are cleared for its passage through Tyldesley.

Peter Eckersley.

133

134

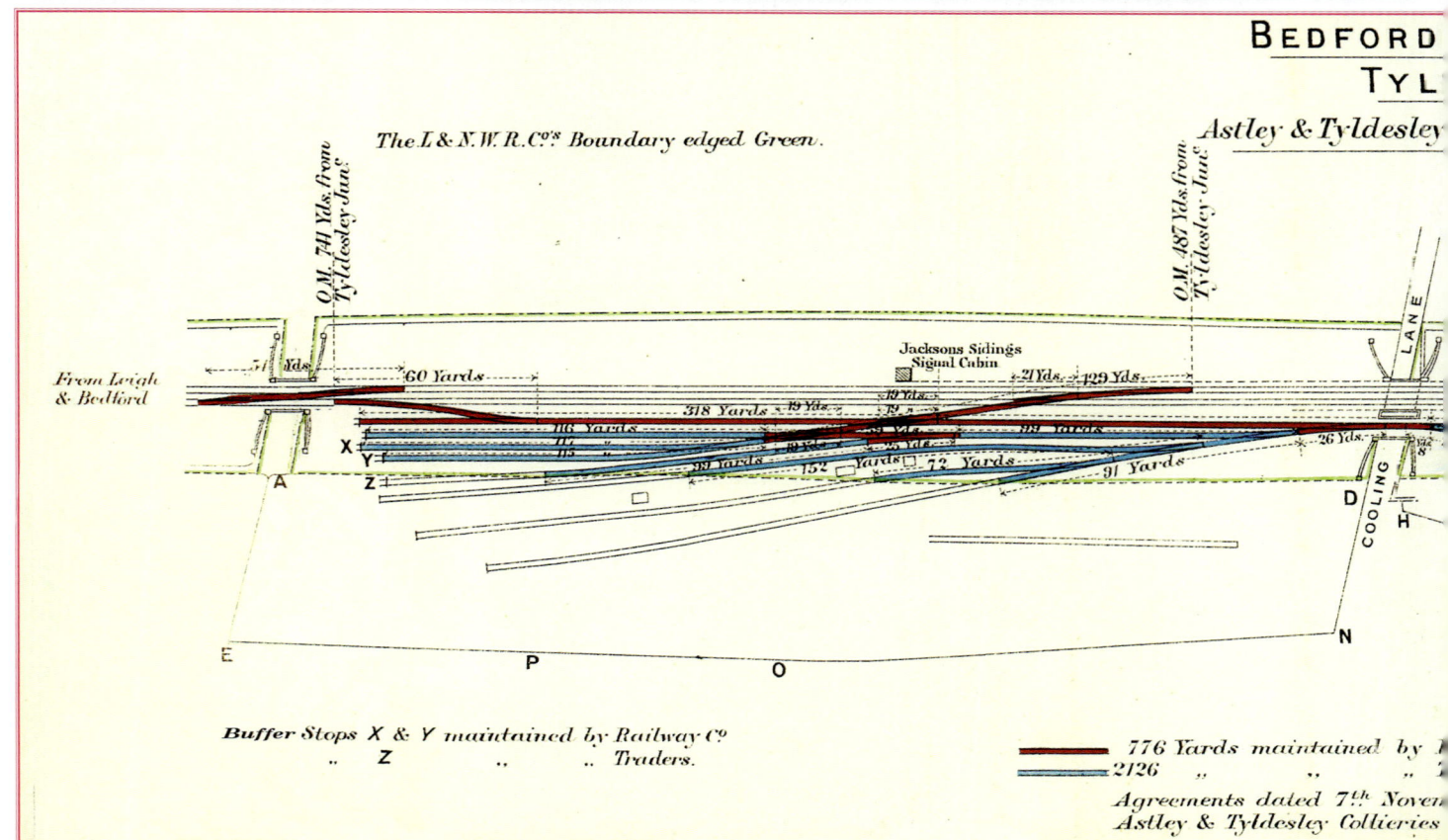

Plate 191. This, I feel, is the appropriate place to include a shot of Jim Carter, pictured on the left wih an unknown fireman, probably at Patricroft on night shift. Jim's superb eye for a shot has preserved for ever these timeless scenes at Tyldesley of an age long gone; an age in which the railway enthusiasts whose yearning for the steam locomotive never leaves them, regard as pure nostalgia.
Author's Collection, (Jim Carter).

Plate 190, left. Class '8F' No.48491, passes Jackson's Sidings with a coal train from Speakman's Sidings, Leigh. In the background is the Tyldesley-Wigan line carried over Squire's Lane by the overbridge and behind that Caleb Wright's Barnfield Mill at Tyldesley.
Author's Collection, (Jim Carter).

Fig 34. Astley & Tyldesley Collieries/Jackson's Sidings c1916 and the later agreements with the L&NW. *Courtesy, John Hall.*

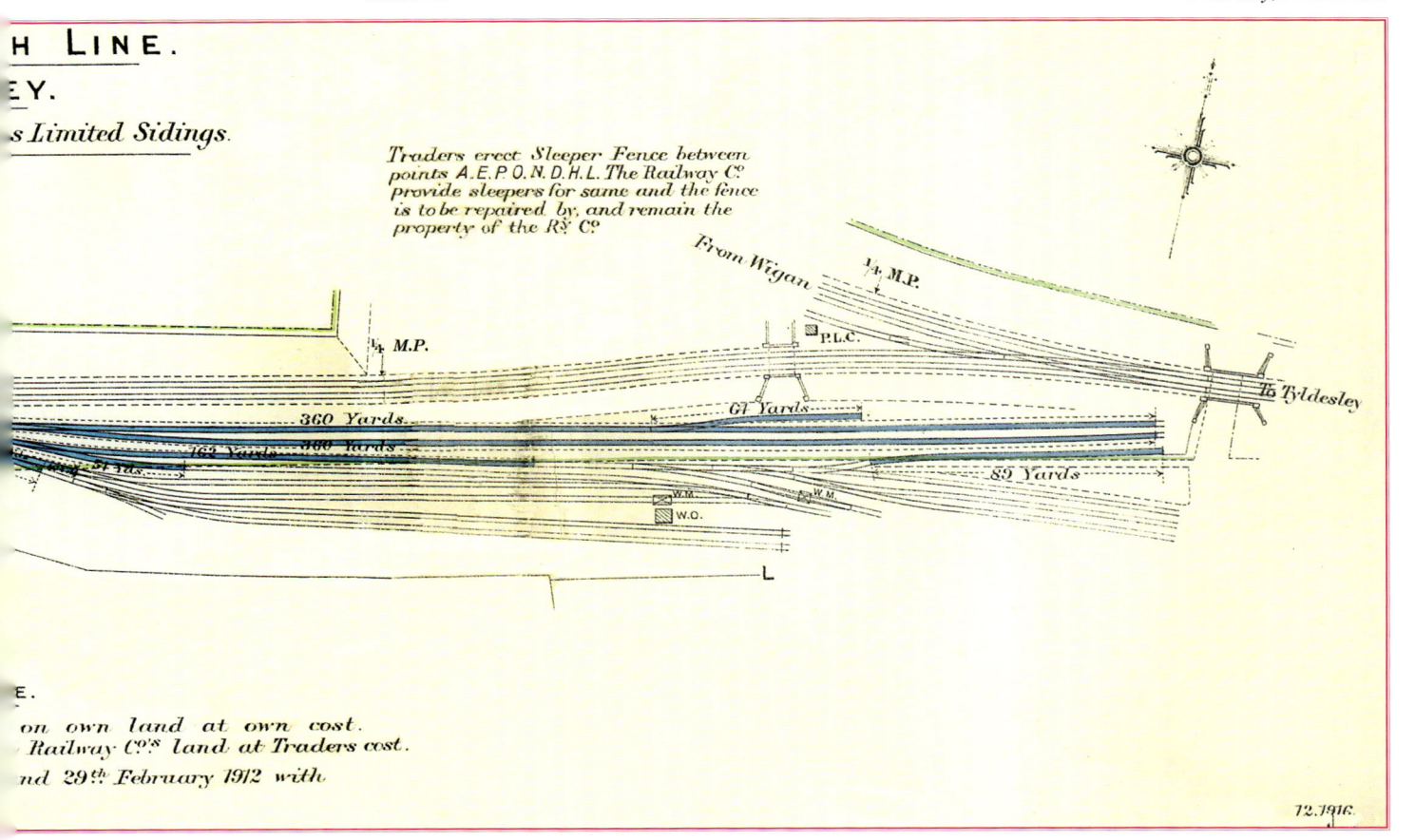

Plate 192. Another superb view of 92019 as she begins to creep forward to the mainline junction. For the period, when often as not, many steam locomotives were in poor condition, this engine shows little sign of steam leakage.

Plate 193. As the '9F' approaches Jackson's Sidings box, a coal train from Speakman's Sidings, Leigh, passes, worked by an unidentified '8F' up front and 48636 banking.
Both, Author's Collection, (Jim Carter).

Plate 194. In the early years after nationalisation of the railways 'Patriot' Class No. 45519 *Lady Godiva*, passes Jackson's Sidings.
Peter Hampson Collection.

Plate 195. A forward facing view towards Jackson's Sidings signal box of '9F' No.92019 as the driver, Cliff Davis, keeps an eye towards the rear of his train as Jim Carter attends to the camera work having stoked up the firebox for effect. The train is bound for Garston Docks for export. In the background, an engine and van pass on the main lines eastbound. As can be seen, the track ballast is pure ash of which there was quite a ready supply available to deal with the constant problems caused by mining subsidence not only in the sidings but also on the main lines. Ideal also for the grass to colonise! *Author's Collection, (Jim Carter).*

Plate 196. '8F' No.48636 is doing its share of the work as the coal train from Speakman's Sidings passes Jacksons and below, *Plate 197,* the same train from Speakman's Sidings climbs the bank towards Tyldesley as 92019 arrives at Jackson's Sidings box. A panoramic view of the town is seen here with Squire's Lane bridge and Barnfield Mills to the left, and St. George's Colliery, far right.

Both, Author's Collection, (Jim Carter).

Plate 198. A BR Standard Class '5', banked by an '8F' approaches Jackson's Sidings with an early morning coal train from Speakman's Sidings. Through the mist, Lilford Woods can be discerned.
Author's Collection, (Jim Carter).

The origin of the name Jackson's Sidings is from George and Samuel Jackson who were the commercial brains of Astley & Tyldesley Collieries who mined the area south of the railway at Tyldesley.

One of the first on the scene though was one John Darlington who obtained a lease from Malcolm Ross of Astley Hall in 1845, to mine the Worsley Four Foot seam on land east of Bedford Lodge. This was, unfortunately, a couple of years before the first Ordnance Survey was carried out so there is no trace of this, or the 2ft tramroads or railroads constructed to serve it until later editions. Instead, one has to consult the Astley tithe map for that year to find evidence of these early workings and railways.

About the same period, a Bedford Colliery, not to be confused with John Speakman's colliery of the same name of later years, came into the ownership of W.E.Milner in 1845, having previously worked by Milner and two associates from 1841. The leases for this particular Bedford Colliery were under *Hampson's on the Fold,* on land owned by one Joseph Eckersley. In 1853, the colliery is advertised to let, the leases being *under the Folds Estate.* A further advert in the Leigh Chronicle in February gives reference to a railway from Bedford Colliery to the Duke of Bridgewater's canal at Leigh, the take being under the Folds Estate with a railway some *¾ mile in length, now in use.* Although the 1840s survey, or the Bedford (Leigh) tithe map of 1846, give no clues as to the whereabouts of this line, it is reasonable to assume, therefore, that Bedford Collieries owners were using Darlington's line, or a connecting branch to it, to gain canal access at Marsland Green. This was far from unusual and there are other local examples of line sharing between colliery owners.

In 1853 Darlington's and Milner's collieries were taken over by George and Samuel Jackson, Salt Merchants, James Lord, Joseph Wood and Samuel Wild, coal proprietor; thus we have the Astley & Tyldesley Coal and Salt Company formed in 1864, to become a limited concern about 1875.

Bedford Colliery was closed in 1864, Messrs Jackson & Company now concentrating their mining efforts in the Astley and Tyldesley areas. They had already begun to sink St. George's Colliery in May 1860 and by September of 1861 had reached the Crombourke seam at 185 yards and a second mine sunk to a depth of 90 yards. They were confidently expecting the London & North Western's new railway to be open in late 1862.

In the event, this was not to be, due entirely to the unpredictable nature of the British climate. Nevertheless, they constructed their colliery railways towards Jackson's Sidings to the standard gauge from their existing collieries, output being around 500 tons per day which they were expecting to double once the main line came on stream.

The first deep mines at Nook Colliery were sunk in 1866 and eventually comprised five shafts. No.4 shaft at 944 yards worked the Arley seam, passing through no less than 18 other workable seams on the way down and I can remember my father, who started working at Nook in 1930, saying how hot it was at that depth. Yet other mines were, he said, *much colder.* Gin Pit Colliery was operating c1850, on the site of earlier mining activity.

Connections at Jackson's Siding therefore, existed from the outset, possibly even before the railway was officially opened. By the mid 1880s, the narrow gauge railway of earlier years to the canal wharf at Marsland Green had been converted to standard gauge, allowing Astley & Tyldesley Collieries to get the best of both worlds either dispatching via the canal or railway, transported by their own locomotives.

Gin:- A contrivance, a machine, especially for hoisting in engineering or mining. Often worked by horse power to turn a winding apparatus by means of a capstan, the horse going around affixed to a spar, in a never decreasing circle.

There seems little doubt that this is how Gin Pit, and the village it spawned, got their name and much has been written of this association between the two in various books, magazines and newspapers over the years.

From the 1830s, or even earlier, Gin Pit became the centre of a mining complex, complete with its own engineering workshops, sawmill, timber yard and all the other necessary requirements of a working colliery, serviced by a large internal railway system, upon which generations of families lived, worked and died.

With the sinking of the deep mines the system was rapidly expanding and the first housing was built at Gin Pit by the colliery owners in 1874, the streets being named after the directors of the company. Intermittent building continued until about 1909, yet still isolated from the nearby town. In more recent times new housing developments have taken place, encroaching on the former colliery sites and reclamation of former mining areas has taken place.

The first known standard gauge locomotive to work on the Gin Pit railway is believed to be *Tyldesley,* an 0-6-0 saddle tank supplied in 1868 to the Astley & Tyldesley Coal and Salt Co. This was renamed *Jackson* in early 1872, surviving on the system until 1895 when it was sold on.

In 1874, a 2-2-0 well tank arrived having been purchased by George Peace from the Lancashire & Yorkshire Railway having originally been built for the Preston & Wyre Railway. This was scrapped around 1900. Two 0-6-0s were purchased new in in 1875 and 1886; *Maden* from Manning Wardle of Leeds, and *Astley* from Sharp Stewart of Manchester respectively. *Maden* was scrapped in 1910, *Astley* being sold on in 1920.

A second *Tyldesley* arrived in 1894, an 0-6-0 from Peckett & Sons of Bristol. *Jackson*, the 0-6-0 of 1868 was taken in part exchange.

There now followed three locomotives from Lowca Engineering at Whitehaven, all 0-6-0 side tanks; *T.B. Wood* in 1899, *James Lord* in 1903 and *George Peace* in 1906. These, together with another *Maden* of 1910 and *Emanuel Clegg* of 1924, both of which were 0-8-0 side tanks, an unusual wheel arrangement for colliery locomotives, both with outside cylinders and designed specially for Gin Pit by Nasmyth-Wilson & Co. of Patricroft. These five locomotives provided the bulk of the motive power over the system until the late 1940s.

After the formation of Manchester Collieries in 1929, other locomotives worked on the system as replacements when one of the regular engines needed overhauling, including *Chowbent* from Chanters Colliery in the early 1940s, *Violet* from Bridgewater Colliery and *Colonel* from Howe Bridge. With nationalisation of the mines in 1947, movement of engines between collieries became more commonplace and some of Gin Pit's regulars spent short spells at other collieries. *James Lord* had already gone to Bedford Colliery prior to nationalisation and never returned.

Plate 199. The first of the 0-6-0 'Austerities' to arrive on the Gin Pit system was *W.H.R.* RSH/7174/1944, which is seen at Gin Pit in 1958. It had been purchased second hand from the War Department being delivered to Walkden Yard on 18th June 1947, arriving at Gin Pit on the 30th inst.

Before mine closures began to take effect in the early 1960s, it is worth noting that some 67% of the working male population of Tyldesley worked in the mining industry, either on the surface or below ground. A percentage this large was by no means unusual for mining towns.

Author's Collection.

As an aside, colliery locomotives were allowed to travel under their own steam between Fletcher Burrows Atherton Collieries and Jackson's Sidings for a payment of £1.00 per annum by an agreement of 14th December 1933 with the L.M.S. A pilot driver was provided by the railway company, paid for by the colliery company. It is likely that this replaced much older working arrangements between the collieries and London & North Western.

The first of the 0-6-0 'Austerities' to arrive at Gin Pit was *W.H.R.* in September 1947, followed by *Gordon* from Chanters in 1950. The latter was replaced by *Renown* in in August 1951 from Parsonage Colliery, Leigh. This was said to have "three good legs and a bad'un" so was put on the easiest task which was working to Marsland Green.

With the closure of the last Nook mine on 6th August 1965, the 'Austerities' *Renown* and *Weasel* were retained to move coal stocks and deal with coal from Chanters Colliery as their washing plant had broken down. As closure of Chanters was also imminent, it was decided to use Nook washery rather than carry out repairs at Chanters. The railway from Nook to the canal wharf at Marsland Green had ceased being used in 1964.

Jackson's Sidings were in a terrible state by this period but was the only exit point for the coal from Chanters, the pointwork having to be levered over to get the trains out onto the main lines. *Renown* and *Weasel* had been sent to Walkden and 'Austerity' *Harry* was engaged for a while at the latter end to work the traffic from Nook to Jackson's Sidings for onward transportation to Garston Dock, Liverpool, via Kenyon Junction until February 1966. *Harry* was reported back at Walkden Yard in March 1966.

Again in April 1966, Nook washery was brought back into operation to wash slack from Bedford Colliery which had necessitated the colliery railway from Bedford to Gin Pit being re-levelled as it was also in a bad state. 'Austerity' *Humphrey* arrived from Chanters under its own steam and was later joined by *Renown*. Jackson's Sidings, however, had been closed and the washed slack had to be worked back to Bedford and despatched via Speakman's Sidings.

Plate 200*. Nasmyth-Wilson built 0-8-0 *Maden* of 1910, is about to pass under Ley Road bridge at Gin Pit c1962 in its final year of service. It is seen working from Nook Colliery with empty internal user wagons.* *Author's Collection, (F.D. Smith).*

Plate 201*. The other Nasmyth-Wilson built 0-8-0, *Emanuel Clegg,* is seen withdrawn outside Gin Pit works in 1958 minus its nameplates. It never worked again and was broken up in June 1965.* *Author's Collection.*

Plate 202. Austerity 0-6-0ST *Humphrey* passes through Gin Pit village with what looks like a train of slack from Bedford Colliery on 10th October 1965 for Nook Washery, the one at Bedford Colliery being out of commission. *Mike Taylor.*

From Nook & Gin Pit Collieries post W.W.II., three trips per day would be made by colliery locomotives to the wharf on the Bridgewater Canal at Marsland Green on almost level track. These trips consisted of about 25 wagons in consignments known as 'boats', 'landsales' or 'bunkers' usually worked by a locomotive considered the weakest of a stud of five engines allocated to the Gin Pit system. On the morning trip the 'boats', containing slack for the power stations at Barton or Westwood, Wigan, usually went straight into their road for discharge into the barges, each barge holding three wagon loads. After the boats had been shunted the landsales were knocked off into their sidings. 'Bunkers' were special red banded Manchester Colliery wagons to go up the ramp for loading into road transport and when pushed onto the gantry the lorry would come underneath and by a wheel and chain apparatus worked by the lorry driver, discharged.

The mid-day trip usually brought only 'boats' for Runcorn Gas Works and occasionally, 2 or 3 'bunkers' tripped with these if requested. The next job on returning to Nook would be to collect 21 wagons of slack and propel these to Marsland Green about 3p.m. and clear any empties from the sidings.

Even in the 1940s, a shire horse was still employed at Marsland Green to haul the wagons from the boat road to be tipped into the barges. Although there was a slight fall towards the canal the older wagons with grease axle boxes needed some effort to induce movement. There was also a turntable here used to turn the wagons if the open end was facing the wrong way.

I can recall seeing these trains crossing Manchester Road in the late 1950s, Marsland Green Wharf last being used in 1964.

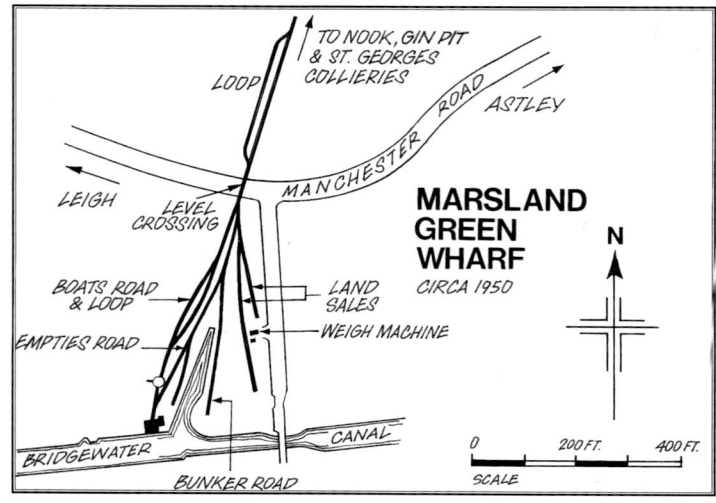

Fig 35. Details at Marsland Green Wharf c1950.

142

Plate 203. Austerity 0-6-0 *Humphrey* is seen again, this time en-route from Bedford Colliery across the dirt fields towards Nook Colliery with a slack train 13th September 1967. *John Ryan.*

Plate 204. An elevated view of the colliery railway from Bedford with Nook Colliery in the background also on 13th September 1967. This is the sort of landscape that was once a familiar sight all over the coalfields of Britain when coal was king. *John Ryan.*

Plate 205. The colliery railway from Bedford Colliery to Nook and Gin Pits crossed Green Lane and Queensway on the level. Here, the crossing at Queensway is seen looking east on 13th September 1967. In the background are the dirt tips seen in *Plates 203 & 204*, and beyond, on the horizon is Nook Colliery.

John Ryan.

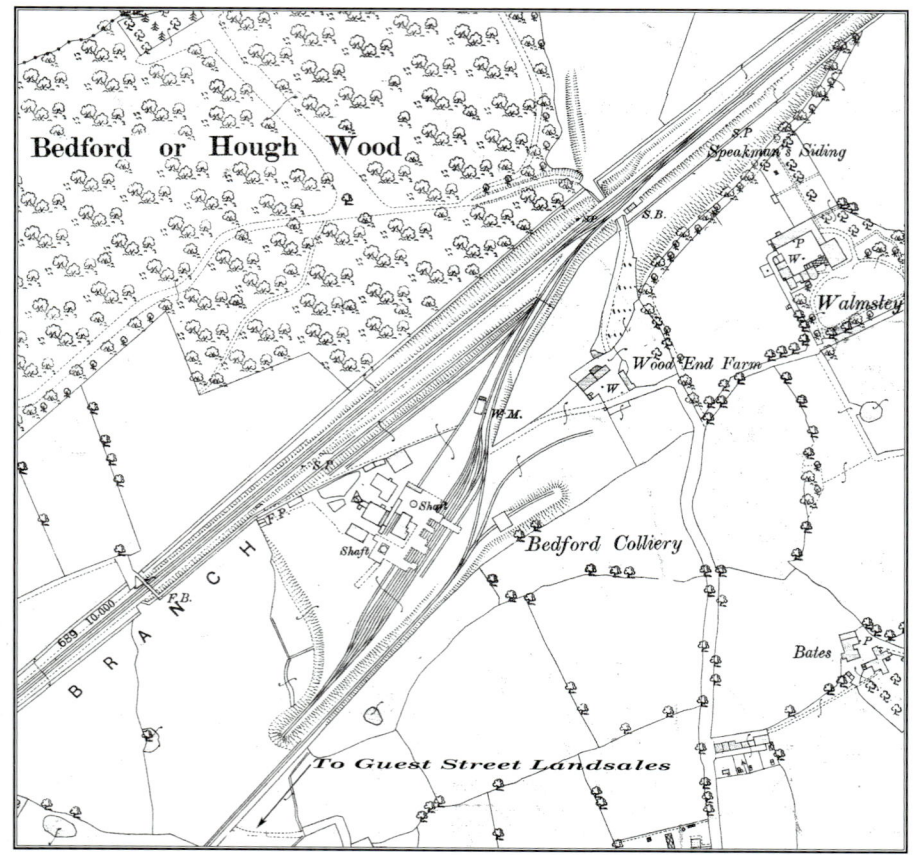

Fig 36. The 1892/3 Ordnance Survey shows the then layout of Speakman's Sidings and Bedford Colliery. Rail connections to the colliery were authorised by Crewe in June 1882 and this necessitated the establishment of a new block post to cope with the extra traffic. Deepening of the mines here had taken place in the mid-1880s. Note also 'Wood End Farm', in all probability the source of local name for the colliery. The Mineral Railway going out of picture, bottom left, goes to the landsale yard on Guest Street on the south side of Holden Road. *See also* **Fig 38**.

SPEAKMAN'S SIDINGS

Sinking of Bedford, 'Wood End' Colliery was begun in 1874 by John Speakman whose father, also John, had owned collieries in the Westleigh area including the idyllically named Hearts-o-th-Meadows Colliery, later known as Priestners. John Speakman senior had died in 1873. Bedford Colliery began winding coal in 1876. In the early years of the colliery the coal was for local consumption only, transported by horse and cart.

Between 1883 and 1886 the shafts at Bedford were deepened and mainline and sidings connections built under an agreement with the London & North Western of 31st July 1882, which was authorised by the Railways and Signalling Department at Crewe in June 1882. The plan included provision of a new block post and signalling at an estimated cost of £510 with a 20 lever signal box alongside the Up line near the level crossing.

John Speakman of Bedford Colliery died on 3rd June 1893 and the colliery was taken over by his sons, Harry and Fred, becoming John Speakman & Sons, and from 1st August 1914, a Limited Company.

A private line of railway about ½ mile in length to Guest Street Landsale Yard is almost certainly concomitant with the new works and is shown on the second series Ordnance Survey of 1888/92. In later years this line also served a brickworks and a patent fuel plant built around the time of the first world war. It is believed to have closed in the 1930s but the outbuildings remained in situ for many years.

It is not thought that Bedford Colliery had any locomotives of their own prior to the 1882 works being carried out. After that date a second hand engine of unknown origin was purchased and in 1897 a new locomotive was ordered from Vulcan Foundry of Newton-le-Willows. It was given the name *The Sirdar* and remained in use for many years. There was also an 0-6-0 built for the Potteries, Shrewsbury & North Wales Railway by Manning Wardle of Leeds, purchased by Bedford Colliery and named *Bedford* on acquisition in 1910.

In 1929 Bedford Colliery became a part of Manchester Collieries Ltd, set up to counter the effects of recession in

Plate 206. Class '8F' No.48224 departs the environs of Speakman's Sidings with a coal train for Patricroft on 18th October 1966 assisted by another '8F' banking.. Note the dip in the track to the rear caused by mining subsidence. *Peter Eckersley.*

145

Plate 207. On 11th May 1967 '8F' No.48671 and the banker, sister '8F' No.48636, raise the echoes as they climb the gradient from Speakman's Sidings working to Patricroft with a heavy coal train. Again, the railway here has suffered from mining subsidence.

Peter Eckersley.

the coal industry by a more efficient pooling of resources. Some much needed investment was then carried out at Bedford including a new screening plant, new headgear to No.2 shaft and a new line of railway from Bedford to the Astley & Tyldesley railway system at Gin Pit, construction of which began in 1930 allowing Bedford coal to reach Marsland Green Wharf on the Bridgewater Canal.

About 1930, *The Sirdar* was sent from Bedford to Robin Hood Sidings, Clifton, and *Bedford* went to Astley Green Colliery until withdrawn in 1947. Throughout the 1930s and early 1940s the regular locomotive at Bedford was *Gower*, an 0-6-0 saddle tank built for Bridgewater Trustees in 1882. In April 1945, this was broken up at Gin Pit and replaced by former Astley & Tyldesley Collieries *James Lord,* an 0-6-0 side tank built in 1903 by Lowca engineering of Whitehaven.

The colliery became a part of the No.1 Manchester Area, North West Division at Nationalisation on 1st January 1947. Around the 1949/50 period the screening plant at Bedford was closed, coal being sent to Nook via the 1930s built line across Green Lane for screening.

On 1st January 1952, Bedford was transferred to the No.2.Wigan Area and former Wigan Coal & Iron locomotive *Kirkless* was noted here in 1955 when *James Lord* was out of service. The latter was subsequently broken up at Bedford in 1960. Meanwhile, *Atlas*, a former Fletcher Burrows engine, had arrived at Bedford from Chanters Colliery, firstly in 1953, for a short spell and again in 1959 to replace *James Lord.* When *Atlas* went to Walkden Yard in 1962 for overhaul, it was replaced in January the same year by *Colonel,* an 0-6-0 saddle tank from Wheatsheaf Colliery which proved itself unsuitable and was laid up. The replacement for *Colonel* was *Renown,* HE/3697/1950 one of the 0-6-0 'Austerity' saddle tanks from Gin Pit.

From January 1961, the Wigan area had been divided between the Manchester and St. Helens areas and Bedford Colliery was back under Walkden as part of the East Lancashire Area.

Atlas returned to Bedford in December 1962 outshopped in maroon livery but was not steamed until February 1963 because of the extreme cold of the 1962/3 winter, the authorities baulked at the idea of putting water in its boiler.

Plate 208. The view from the rear of the same train with '8F' No.48636 giving banking assistance to the train engine, sister '8F' No.48671 which has almost reached the top of the bank. The slow movement of these trains from Speakmans gave the photographer ample time to walk down a few yards for the shot.
Peter Eckersley.

Plate 209. 0-6-0 saddle tank *Colonel* shunts an internal user wagon at Bedford Colliery on 22nd April 1962.
Peter Eckersley.

It must be remembered that this was the most severe winter since 1947, not equalled in its severity until the two consecutive winters of 2009 and 2010.

Atlas remained at Bedford until November 1966 when it was sent to Walkden Yard for boiler repairs which, in the event, were not carried out and the locomotive was laid up until late 1968 when it was scrapped.

With the departure of *Atlas*, another 'Austerity' direct from overhaul at Walkden, namely *Rodney*, arrived at Bedford and promptly blotted its copy book by demolishing part of the engine shed. Rodney stayed on until March 1967, being replaced by *Renown* until late October 1967 when the colliery was closed. In December 1967, *Rodney* was coupled to *Humphrey*, the last engine at Gin Pit, and, under their own steam, made their way from Jackson's Sidings to Walkden Yard. So ended the mining industry in Tyldesley.

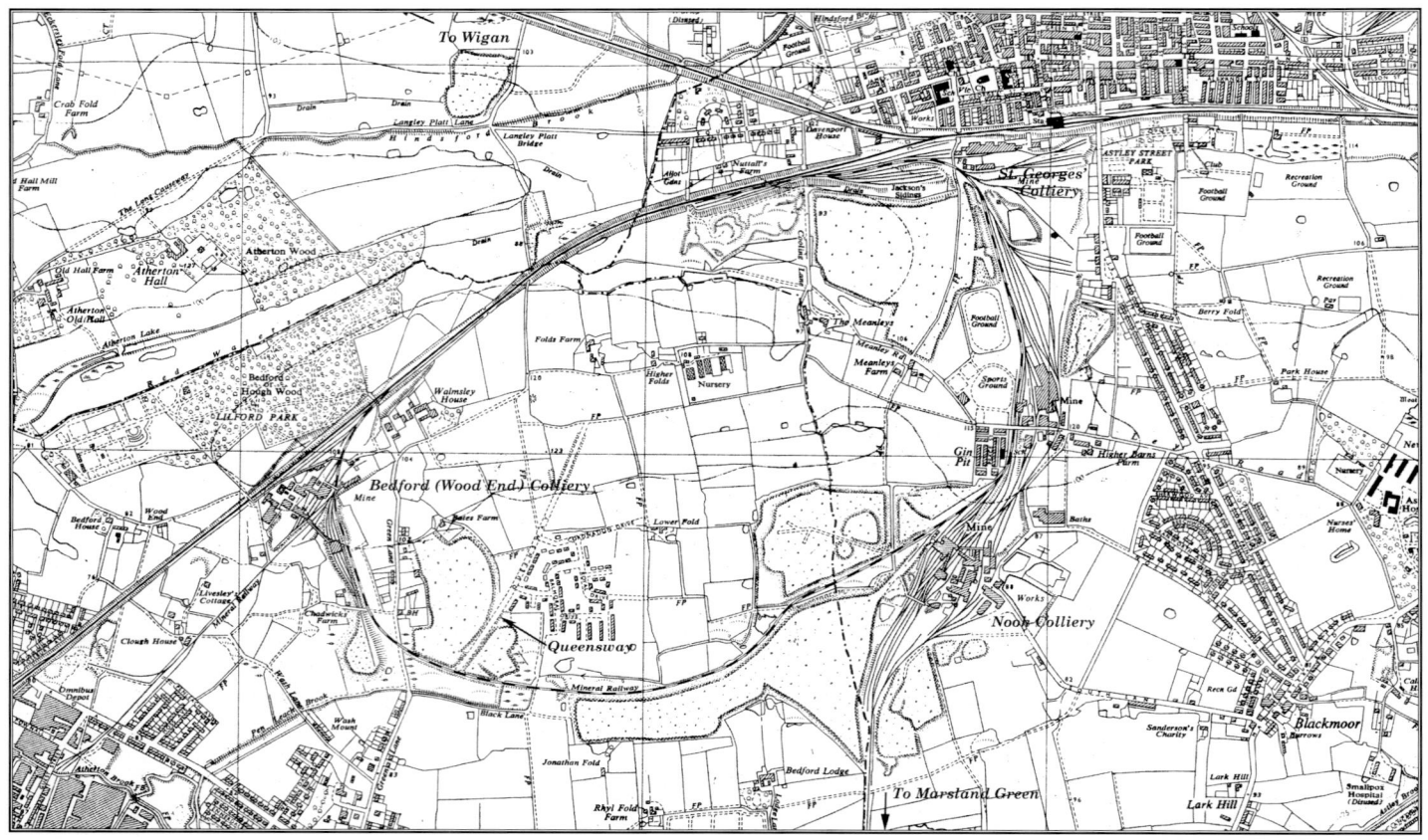

Fig 37. The Astley & Tyldesley Collieries rail system, together with St. Georges', Nook and Gin Pits, Jackson's Sidings, Speakman's Sidings and Bedford Colliery are all shown on this 1950s Ordnance Survey. The mineral line from Bedford to Gin Pit and Nook was built after the formation of Manchester Collieries in 1929. Note how Gin Pit Village is sandwiched between Gin and Nook Pits. The colliery line crosses only Green Lane at this juncture as Queensway is still under construction in preparation for the new housing estate at Higher Folds. Note also the the dotted lines on one of the dirt tips, indicating a temporary railway which was moved from time to time allowing even dispersal of the pit waste.

Plate 210. Fletcher Burrows 0-6-0 locomotive *Atlas* with a couple of 'white banders' at Bedford Colliery c1958. After the formation of Manchester Collieries in 1929, engines which beforehand would only have been found at their owner's colliery, were moved around as requirements and servicing schedules dictated, *Atlas,* for example, previously employed at one of the Atherton Collieries locations.

Author's Collection

Plate 211. A view of the screens at Bedford Colliery, which were very distinctive in their roof shape, seen not long before closure in October 1967. *John Ryan.*

Plate 212. An unusual view of Bedford Colliery on 13th September 1967 with 'Austerity' *Renown* shunting empties. This is No.3 shaft which was sunk to a depth of 880 yards. *John Ryan.*

Plate 213. The view towards the main lines from Bedford Colliery on 13th September 1967. You might just be able to see the Lancashire United Transport Depot at Howe Bridge on the horizon right of centre, with Atherton in the background. Again the 'Austerity' is *Renown*. The weighbridge is left of centre, having a speed limit over it of 2mph. *John Ryan.*

Plate 214. One of the Capprotti fitted B.R. Standard Class '5s' No.73143, propells a rake of empties into Speakman's Sidings in March 1964, the brake van can be seen on the main line to the rear. *John Chalcroft Collection, (Jim Carter).*

Plate 215. The view towards Leigh on 28th September 1963 as a two car DMU works a Manchester Exchange - Liverpool Lime Street service. The photo is taken from the occupation bridge known locally as 'Iron Bridge'. George Shaw's Brewery is in the centre of picture and the mills of Leigh, prominent in the Bedford area. *Peter Eckersley.*

Plate 216. Stanier Class '5' No.45046 passes Speakman's Sidings and Bedford Colliery on 25th June 1966 with a holiday excursion special as this would be the first of the local two weeks holidays. In the background the undulations of the track due to mining subsidence are visible On the left are Lilford Woods.
Peter Eckersley.

Plate 217. An unusual view at Speakman's Sidings taken from the rear of a passing, Liverpool bound DMU with colliery locomotive *Atlas* engaged on shunting duties in 1966. There are empties and a guards van in the reception sidings. The signal box seen here replaced the earlier original which had been situated along the Up line. *Tony Oldfield.*

Plate 218. A two car DMU Nos. M50776 & M50811 approach 'Iron Bridge' west of Speakman's Sidings on 30th October 1968 with a Manchester Exchange service. At the time of writing the 'misguided' busway is under construction here and follows the railway trackbed from Leigh to Ellenbrook where it then diverges to join the A580.
Ian Isherwood.

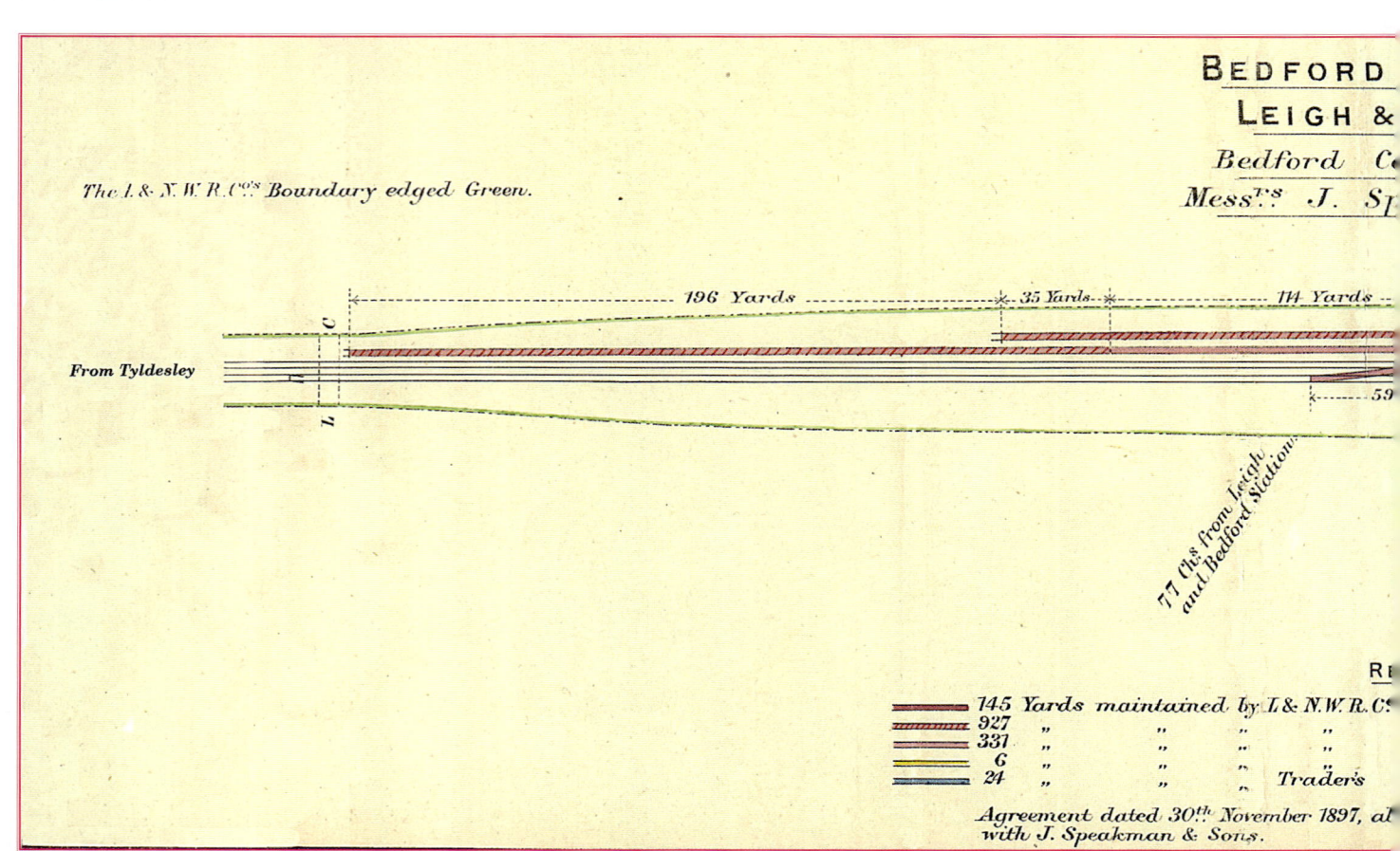

Plate 219. Holden Road and its bridge, sited west of Speakman's Sidings was so named after the mill owner Sir John Holden. It was built about 1905 to give an alternative road in and out of Leigh on an east to west axis and was paid for by the London & North Western Railway. The bridge is seen here in 1971 when removal of the ironwork was about to commence. It was a good time to be in the scrap metal business.

Alf Yates.

Fig38. Speakman's Colliery Sidings. This is the final arrangement here which superseded the earlier arrangements instituted in 1882 when a new block post was provided. *Courtesy, John Hall.*

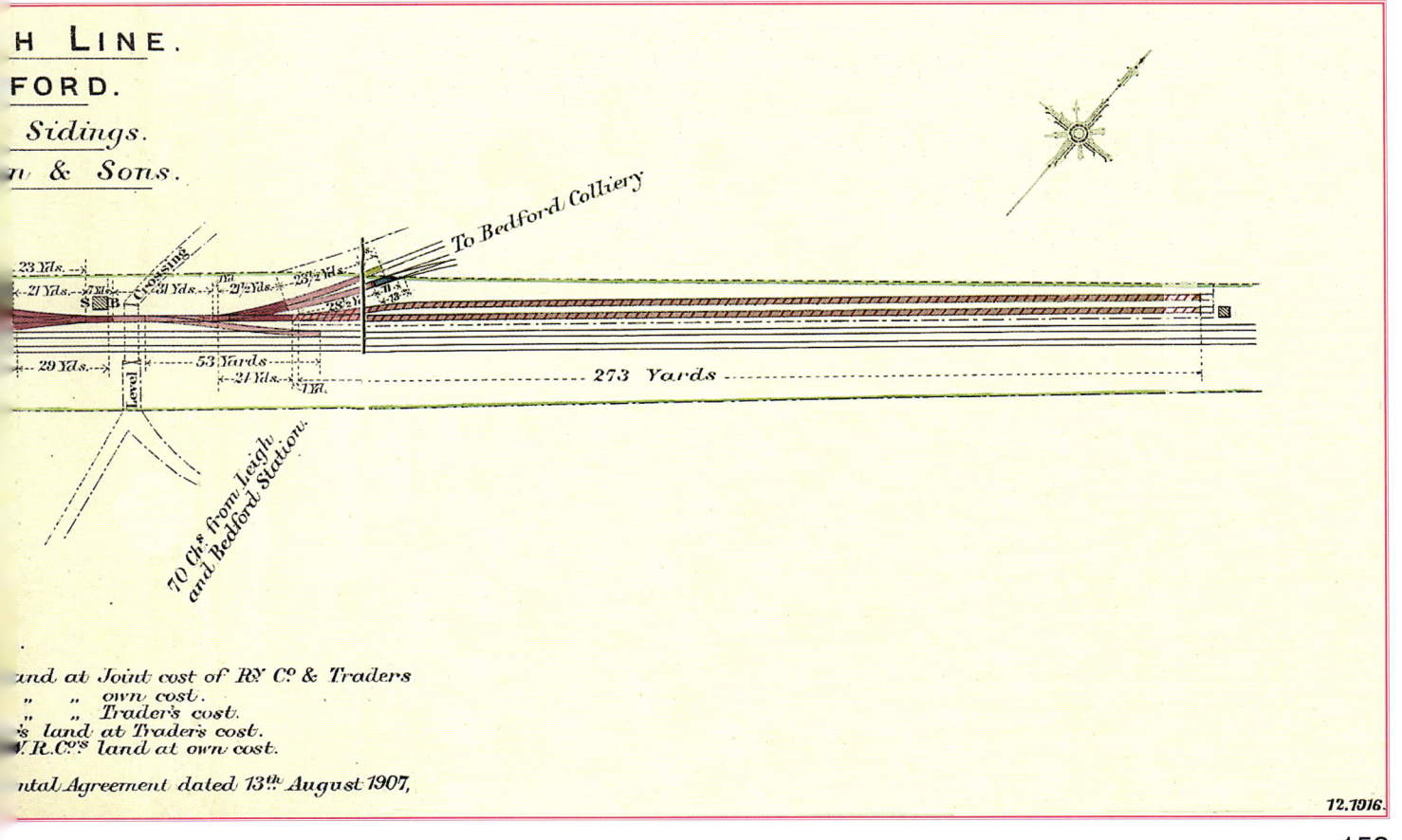

Plate 220. A diverted Liverpool Lime Street-Newcastle train hauled by Type '4' No.D1614 approaches Iron Bridge near Speakman's Sidings on 13th October 1968. The locomotive is in the early two-tone green livery and the stock in blue & grey livery which all appear to be of the B.R.Mark 'I' type. *Gerry Bent.*

Plate 221. At the same location is a six car Trans-Pennine express with a week-end diversion off the Chat Moss route having worked via Kenyon and Pennington Junctions. *Alf Yates.*

Plate 222. Having crossed Holden Road bridge, the L.C.G.Bs *Manchester Terminals Farewell Railtour* of 3rd May 1969, runs alongside Rosebury Avenue heading towards Tyldesley. *Gerry Bent.*

Plate 223. A 6 car DMU, Nos. NE50163, 59534, 50280, 50151, 59092 and 50242, passes Rosebury Avenue on the approach to Leigh Station on 12th November 1967. Bedford Colliery can be seen in the background.
Ian Isherwood.

Plate 224. An incredibly dirty photograph of a departure from Leigh Goods Yard which appears to be mid-1920s. The brake van is Lancashire & Yorkshire and the locomotive, although difficult to fully identify looks to be a 0-6-0 tender type of the same company. The wagons are loaded with farming equipment from Harrison-McGregors Leigh works probably working via Tyldesley through Manchester Victoria on ex Lancashire & Yorkshire metals. This would have to be after the Grouping in 1922/3 and economy of working this traffic has manifested itself in this manner. With a former London & North Western pilot on the footplate to Manchester, the train could work through to its destination without a change of engine or crew.
Author's Collection.

LEIGH

The Leigh station as seen in the accompanying photographs is not that as originally opened in 1864. Evidently that was a much more spartan affair, situated atop an embankment approached by 43 steps, with the booking office at street level under one of the arches. There was a small waiting room on each platform constructed, like the platforms themselves of timber, open to the mercy of the elements.

By 1870 the number of passengers using the station was in excess of 45,000 and by 1875 the number had risen to 75,000. These figures, presented to the London & North Western Railway at London Road, Manchester, in March 1875, formed part of a petition in the hope of getting some improvements carried out at Leigh Station by a deputation led by Mr.J.Jones Chairman of the Railway Improvement Committee accompanied by other prominent personages of Leigh including;- Mr.T.T.Hayes, Mr.T.Howcroft, Mr.Wm.Guest and Mr. Smith Lancaster.

Particular points put forward to the Company were the erection of first and second class waiting rooms at Bedford-Leigh and the complete relocation of the station at Bedford-Leigh to Queen Street, that the Station Staff are provided with readily identifiable uniforms; that the company runs more through services to Liverpool and Warrington, either London & North Western or Great Western. The latter must have made the company directors present choke in consternation!

The Leigh Board had become increasingly irritated that repeated requests to the Company for improvements at Leigh & Bedford Station, (renamed 1st August 1876) failed to have any effect. However, to go some way towards meeting the grievances of the Board, the London & North Western spent £1,500 in 1891 on platform and waiting room improvements only to have much of it undone by a fire shortly afterwards which necessitated additional moneys being spent. See *Fig 39.*

In June 1892 a meeting took place at Euston between the Leigh Local Board and the London & North Western Directors following which, plans were prepared by the Company and sent to Leigh for consideration by the Local Board on 5th November 1892. Evidently, this plan was not to the liking of the Leigh group and was rejected.

On the 12th January 1893, a deputation from Leigh Local Board again met with the Company Directors at Euston and came to an agreement whereby the London & North Western would carry out certain alterations at Leigh costing £5/6,000, plus the contribution of an additional £2,000 towards the construction of an approach road. That latter figure, though, had a spike in its tail.

This refers to a plot on the west side of Dukinfield Street occupied by a corner shop and seven terraced houses and the necessity to 'free the Company from the obligation of providing dwellings for the labouring classes' which the London & North Western would have to do if they had sought the necessary powers to acquire the land. In other words, the railway company wanted the Local Board to demolish the properties and re-house the occupiers. This sort of practice was, it appears, common place when the railways needed to obtain land. It mattered not to them because the tenants of such were at the bottom end of society. It was quite a different story when they were up against the landed gentry!

Plate 225. One of the new generation DMUs calls at Leigh on 31st August 1959 working to Scarborough via Manchester Victoria, Rochdale and the Calder Valley route.
Peter Johnson.

A further proposal by the London & North Western envisaged a new station between Leigh & Bedford and Pennington Stations. This too was rejected by the Leigh Board, and also by the Board of Trade as the platforms would have been on too steep an incline. Had this plan gone ahead Leigh & Bedford and Pennington Stations would have been closed.

November of 1894 saw the proposal of the Leigh & South Central Lancashire Railway put forward by a number of local businessmen. This would have cut a swathe across Leigh and the surrounding area, particularly around the major coal producers sites where strategically placed junctions were planned to siphon off coal traffic from under the noses of the London & North Western Railway.

This proposal was bitterly opposed by the latter, and the Lancashire & Yorkshire Railway and news of its defeat in May 1895 was reported with some despondency by the local press. Yet, it was perhaps because of its defeat and the realisation that the London & North Western were now committed to spending thousands on a new station, some relief, because the company had given an assurance that if the Bill were to fail, a new station would be forthcoming!

Further contact between Leigh and Euston towards the end of May 1895 resulted in plans for the new station being forwarded to Leigh. These were to include a new approach to the station on Princess Street.

On 27th October 1895, a delegation left Leigh for Euston taking with them a six-point plan for the railways in the area; that the London & North Western site the new station in Brown Street; the new bridge for Holden Road be at right angles to the railway; a bridge to be provided over the railway at Kirkhall Lane (Bolton-Kenyon line); better goods accomodation at Leigh; and a new station to be built at Dangerous Corner, (between Hindley Green and Howe

Plate 226. This pre-W.W.II. view at Leigh Station from the 1930s is a microcosm of the annual 'Wakes Weeks' annual holidays when almost everyone went by train, the happy smiling faces anticipating the journey ahead. Of course, it may not be the annual event, perhaps some special occasion, as the gent, centre stage, shakes the hand of the little girl. Whichever it is, the older generation will remember scenes like this.
Author's Collection.

157

Bridge). The latter was a renewed request of an earlier proposal by the Leigh Local Board.

These requests only met with partial success as the Company did not feel it desirable to construct a station alongside Brown Street due to much greater expense and the suggestion of a bridge at Kirkhall Lane received short shrift. They agreed to construct the bridge for Holden Road and to consider the station at Dangerous Corner which, in the event, was never built. Mr. Stevenson, for the Company, submitted amended plans to the delegation which were said to resemble those put forward some years before by the Leigh Local Board, giving an assurance that pledges made when the Leigh & South Lancashire Railway Bill was rejected, in regard to new facilities at Leigh, would be honoured.

Two further plans were drawn up by the London & North Western only four days later for consideration by Leigh District Council. Known as the 'July' and 'October' plans of 1895 respectively, the July plan was, with some detailed alteration, that as proposed on 21st July which included a new approach road of 80 yards in length from a junction with East Bond Street and Princess Street and, the demolition of the properties in Dukinfield Street. A new booking office, covered inclines, a station canopy and a subway would be built and the platforms extended towards Tyldesley.

Where the October plan differed from the July plan was that the approach road would be steeper and begin at Lord Street South which would preclude vehicular access under the bridge on East Bond Street.

In early November 1895, Leigh District Council approved the July plan, receiving a reply from Euston on the 13th inst. to the effect that the Company had given instructions to their engineers to proceed with the work. They 'regretted' however, that at present they could not see their way into constructing the station at Dangerous Corner.

Work began on the new Leigh & Bedford Station on 26th March 1896 receiving favourable comment in the local press: *The old wooden erection which has done duty for so many years past has not been very convenient but it is anticipated that the new and substantial station will answer all our requirements and will be an honour to the town.* So said the *Leigh Chronicle* Editorial the following day.

The rebuilding of Leigh & Bedford Station had cost some £17,000, eventually opening on 1st April 1898 but why had it taken so long to complete? It may be that the London & North Western were stalling as the extended platforms were not yet completed, nor were the lifts.

Nevertheless, when compared to the old station the new one must have been quite impressive with its broad gentle approach from Princess Street, the well lit booking office at its summit, together with totally enclosed passenger ramps and subway and, a canopy covering a considerable length of the platforms. It was certainly more in keeping with the expanded status of Leigh the population of which had gone from 10,000 in 1864 to around 35, 000 and would continue to expand reaching 50,000 in the early

Plate 227. The eastern end of Leigh Station from 'lovely Alley' in 1969. The Alleyway was built during the station rebuilding period and ran alongside the railway embankment from the top end of the station approach to Pownall Street. *David Norman.*

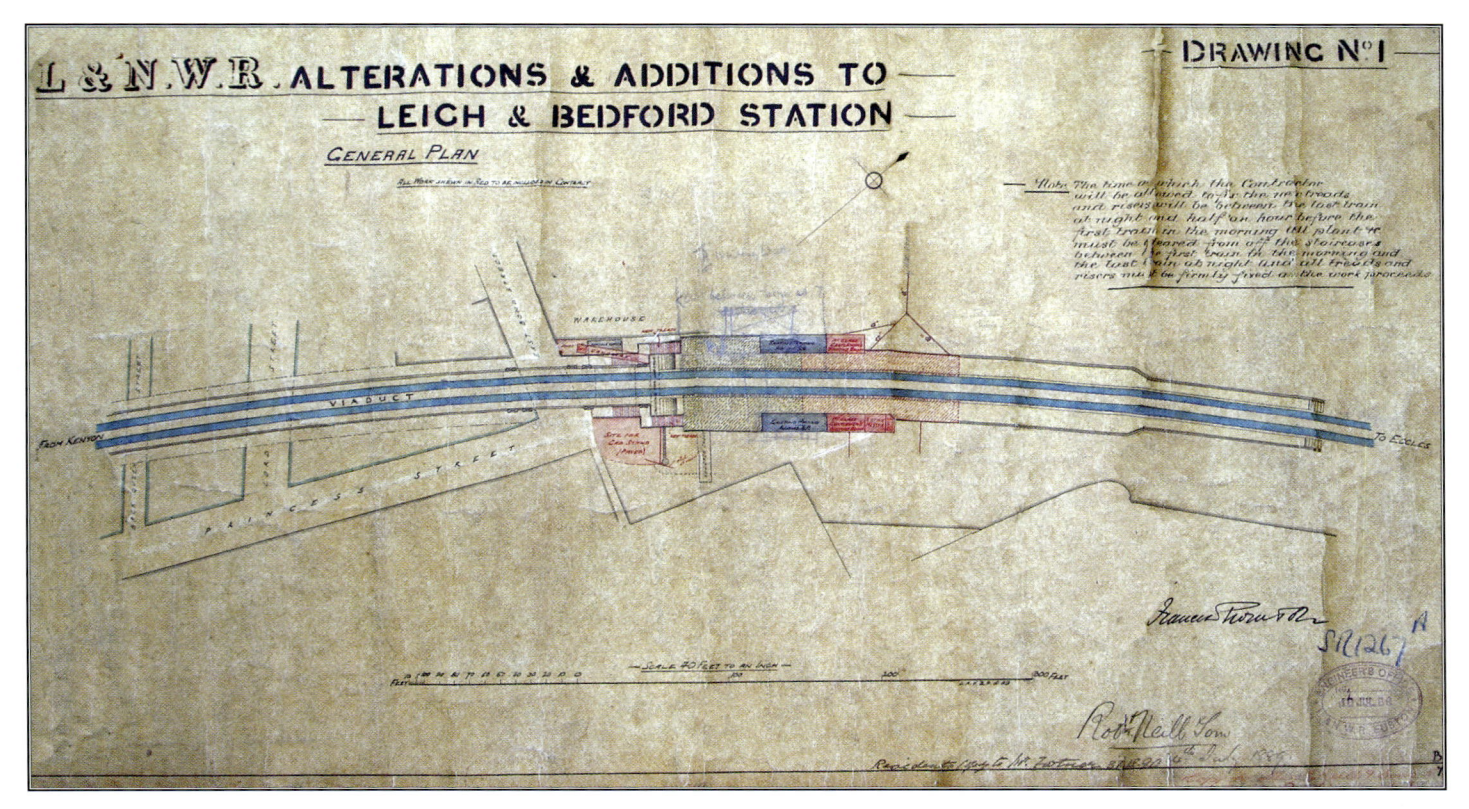

Fig 39. Alterations to Leigh & Bedford Station dated 1888/9. These are the modifications carried out in 1891, namely, new 1st class waiting rooms on up and down platforms; new Station Master's room on down platform; a paved cab stand area at the foot of down platform steps at the junction of East Bond Street and Princess Street; a canopy covering the lower flight of up platform steps and new treads and risers to both upper flights of steps. The notes, top right hand read:- *The time at which the Contractor will be allowed to fix the new treads and risers will be between the last train at night and half hour before the first train in the morning. All plant etc must be cleared from all staricases between the first train in the morning and the last train at night and all treads and risers must be firmly fixed as the work proceeds.* Therefore a night shift was in operation. The drawing is signed by Francis Stevenson.

Courtesy, Tim Oldfield.

Plate 228. Leigh Signalbox, with the letter 'I' missing is pictured shortly after closure of the route in 1969. Sections of the line had recently been re-ballasted as in evidence here. Bedford 'Wood End' Colliery forms the backdrop. *Peter Hampson.*

159

Plate 229. By the mid-1960s, expanding car ownership and coach travel had made serious inroads into British Railway's excursion traffic but it was still possible, during the annual 'Wakes' holiday weeks, for holidaymakers to travel from local stations to the seaside for their yearly intake of the 'ozone'. The Leigh holidays consisted of the last week in June and the first week in July, overlapping with Bolton's second week in June and Wigan's first in July. On 25th June 1966, Stanier Class '5' No.45208 is seen arriving at the eastern end of Leigh Station bound for the resorts of North Wales. The style of dress has changed somewhat, particularly for young women like the girl, right, whose passion for mini-skirts were a delight for any red-blooded young male. OOooooh! *Peter Eckersley.*

Plate 230. On the final day of working, D220 *Franconia* arrives at Leigh Station with the 09.38 British Insulated Callenders Cables Special to Blackpool North on 3rd May 1969. These works specials had run for many years but when the last of these returned on the evening of the 3rd Leigh was to lose its rail connection. Closure of the route is officially given as the 5th Inst. *Gerry Bent.*

160

ENGINEER'S OFFICE,

EUSTON, July 15th 1897

Leigh & Bedford Station.

Dear Sir,

As the new approach road to our Leigh & Bedford station is now almost complete, I shall be glad if you will arrange to form the portion of the roadway between this and Princess Street, shown coloured red on the accompanying plan, this being a part of the public road.

Kindly give this matter your early attention, as we are anxious to bring the improved access to the Station into use as soon as possible.

Yours truly,

Francis Stevenson

The letter sent from Euston, signed by Francis Stevenson, requests that the ground be cleared for the station approach road as the re-built station at Leigh & Bedford nears completion in 1897.
Courtesy, Peter Hampson.

Plate 231. This photo gives a good view of the track curvature at Leigh as Class '5' No.45208 gets away from Leigh Station with the holiday special to North Wales. The train would work via Pennington South Junction to Kenyon joining the historic Liverpool & Manchester Railway as far as Earlestown; thence via the Warrington & Newton Railway of 1831 and by way of Winwick Junction, gain access to the North Wales route at Warrington Bank Quay.

The engine carries a '56D' Mirfield shedplate. For its last days it was transferred to Low Moor shed from where it was withdrawn on 1st October 1967.
Peter Eckersley.

Plate 232. In the late 1960s a DMU approaches Leigh Station from Pennington. The station approach road is visible next to Brook Mill and to the right of that, Bedford Colliery headgear in the distance. *Eddie Bellass.*

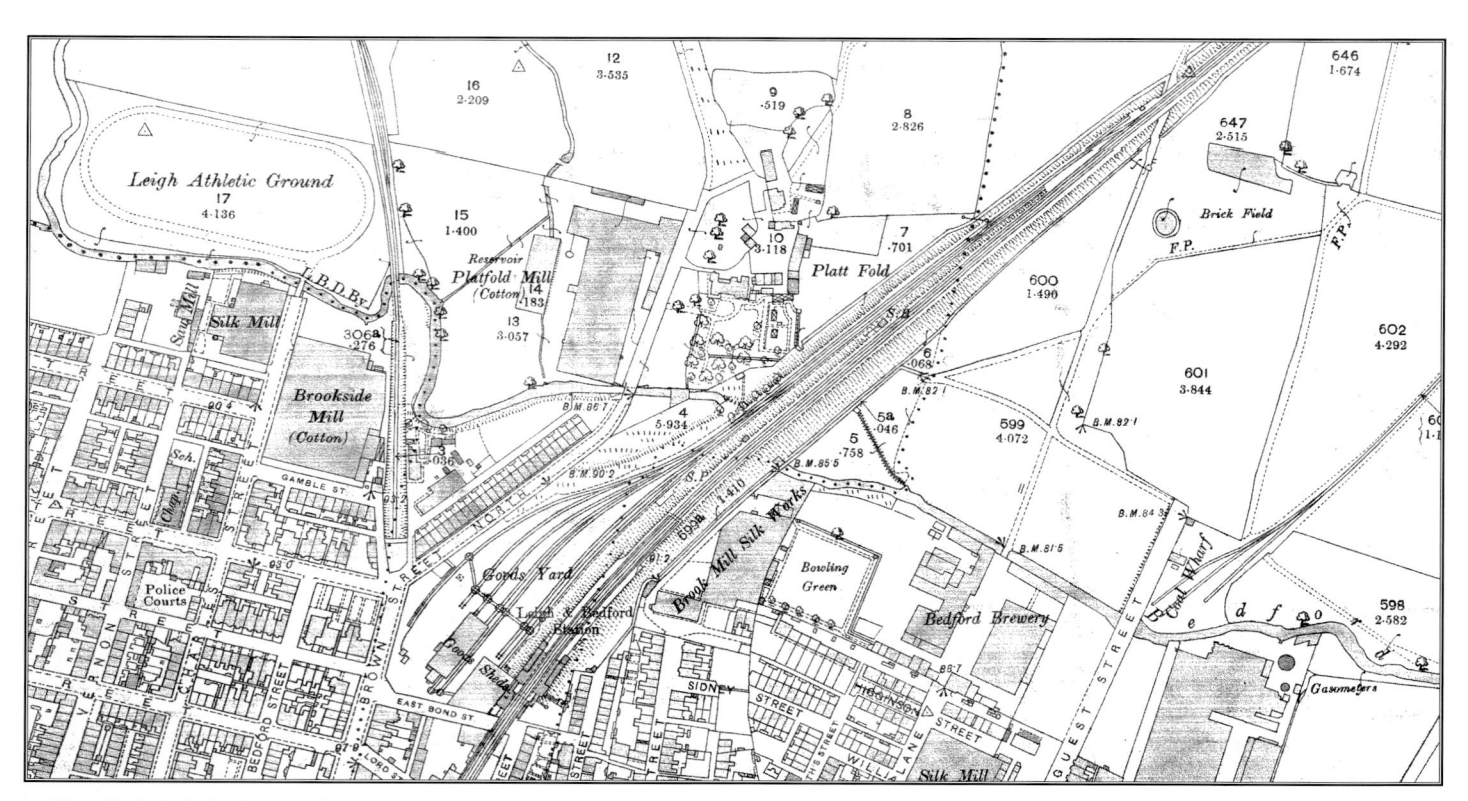

Fig 40. Leigh Station and surrounding area from the Ordnance Survey of 1888/1892 which shows the station as built in its original form. The railway at bottom right is the colliery line from Bedford Colliery to their landsales yard on Guest Street. Note that at this period Holden Road has not been built and when constructed in 1905, it would pass over these lines by a level crossing. Even today, when the tarmac at this location gets worn, the rails are exposed.

Plate 233. A crossover at the eastern end of Leigh Station facilitated the movement of trains terminating at Leigh. On 2nd May 1969, a two car DMU from Manchester Exchange crosses before reversing into the Up platform for its return to Manchester. *David Norman.*

Plate 234. The western end of Leigh Station is seen from the junction of Princess Street and East Bond Street shortly after closure. Note that the large station sign as seen in **Plates 231 & 232** has been removed. I wonder if someone locally got it!
David Norman.

Plate 235, below. Shortly after *A Lancashire Triangle Part Two* was published, a gentleman sent me a photo of this sign which had occupied the right-hand corner of the subway at the bottom of the ramp to the Down platform and although he didn't get the full extent of the signboard on film, I think you will get the gist of it. Of particular interest is the *Trains for Wigan via Plank Lane* part of it, which means it was installed for the opening of passenger services via the Pennington Loop lines as from 1st October 1903. Plank Lane Station was short lived, closing in 1915.
Author's Collection (A.M.Davies).

163

Plate 236. The demolition of Leigh Station is well underway in October 1969. Officialdom stated that the route would be left intact for about a year or two should the need for reopening materialise. However, the haste to rid the area of the railway infrastructure between Kenyon and Eccles junction proceeded rapidly indicating that there was never any intention of reopening taking place.
Author's Collection.

Plate 237. The bridge which carried the railway towards Pennington from Leigh Station crossed St. Helens Road at its junction with Bonnywell Road. Affectionately known as 'Lanry Bridge' for obvious reasons (although there were other bridges which carried the same advert). A rhetorical question was often answered; "It says Lanry on Pennington Bridge but they don't sell it"! *David Norman.*

Plate 238. As a prelude to the commencement of construction of the 'misguided' busway more of the old remaining railway arches between Spinning Jenny Way and Bradshawgate were demolished in November 2011. It was under these arches that the railway tunnel from the Atherton Collieries of John Fletcher & Others made its way from Platt Fold Street to Bedford Basin on the Bridgewater Canal, opening in September 1857. The arches on the extreme right hand are still in situ, a poingant reminder of what we have lost. *John Eckersley.*

Plate 239. Leigh Station arches alongside Princess Street as track lifting takes place. *John Eckersley.*

Plate 240. Track lifting at Pennington, St Helens Road 'Lanry Bridge' c1969 as viewed towards Leigh. Such was the haste by the authorities to prevent any possible re-opening of the route the entire track over the branch from Kenyon to Eccles was lifted in eleven months. It was supposed to have been left in situ for two years. *John Eckersley.*

Plate 241. This aerial view of Leigh dates from the early 1960s with the still operative railway entering at bottom left and exiting at middle top. At bottom centre is Bedford Basin, once used by John Fletcher & Others/ Fletcher Burrows for the discharge of coal from their Atherton Collieries transported by rail which passed under the London & North Western's Railway arches on Chapel Street. The wharfing area is apparently being used to store cable drums. The Police Station is brand new, as are the houses on Brunswick Street which border the canal and Henry Street, the last house on which is right up to the canal bank next to Bedford Wharf. At top right, the landsale yard on Guest Street still has a few wagons in, brought from Bedford, Wood End Colliery by rail, crossing Holden Road on the way. Come to think of it, there's not much left of what's on this photo. *Courtesy, Alan Davies Collection.*

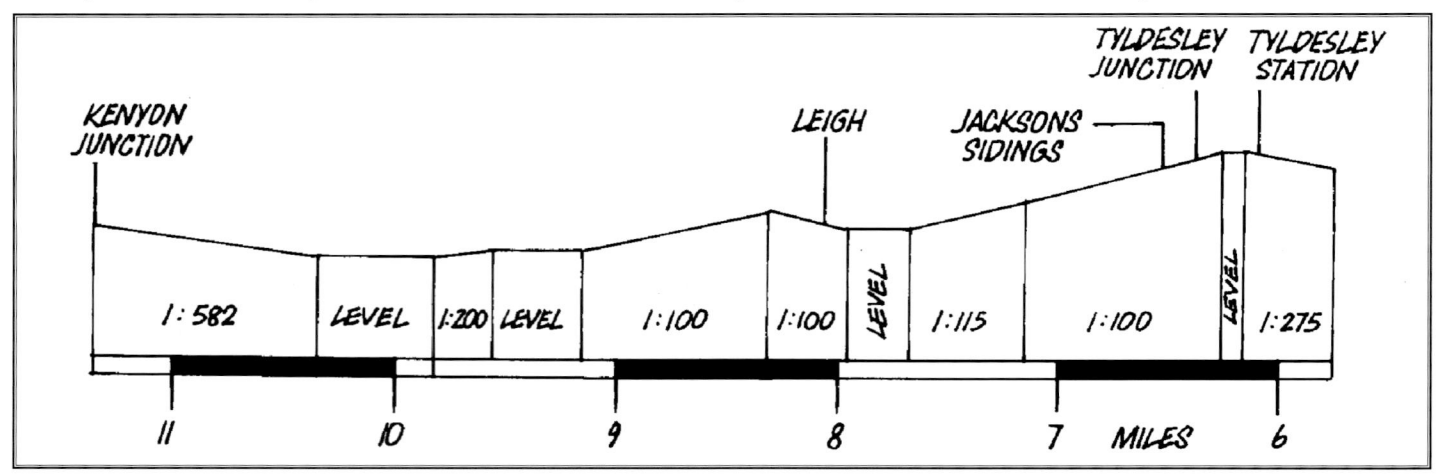

Fig 41. Gradient Profile Kenyon - Tyldesley.

Plate 242. This is a view of the railway arches at Leigh on Sunday 14th December 1986 from the corner of Princess Street and Lord Street looking south towards the BICC water tower. For a time, the arches on the extreme right were used by the contractor Maxwell as a plant yard for building machinery. *Author.*

Plate 243. A Liverpool bound DMU seen passing 'Taylors Hole' on the approach to Pennington Junctions c1968. *John Eckersley.*

Plate 244. Pennington Bridge which carried the A572 over the railway, replaced an earlier level crossing here. The old Turnpike Road is still traceable on the south-east side of the present A579 Atherleigh Way. The bridge itself, seen here after closure of the Leigh Branch, was demolished for the first section of the A579 which opened in 1985 from a junction with the A577, Wigan Road at Atherton, to Pennington. *John Eckersley.*

PENNINGTON JUNCTIONS

Plate 245. A 5 car Trans-Pennine set emerges from under Pennington bridge in April 1969 with a diverted week-end Newcastle-Liverpool Lime Street service. Just a month to go now before closure of this route yet its usefulness as a diversionary line must have cause a few reservations amongst the operating powers. *Gerry Bent.*

Plate 246. 'Peak' No.D173 pictured between Pennington Junctions and the A580 overbridge on 20th April 1969 with another Newcastle- Liverpool Lime Street diversion. The dip in the track caused by mining subsidence is noticeable to the rear of the train. *Gerry Bent.*

Plate 247. This is definately one of the last trains to be seen on the Kenyon & Leigh Railway, or at least the trackbed of it, as 37 298 passes through Pennington on 11th August 2005 en-route from Springs Branch to Booths Yard at Rotherham for scrapping. *Alan Hart.*

A junction had been formed at Pennington by the construction of the branch from Tyldesley via Leigh which met the former Kenyon & Leigh Junction Railway north of Pennington Station in 1864. Concomitantly, the then single track of the Kenyon & Leigh line was doubled from Kenyon to the new Pennington Junction at a cost of some £7,000. The remainder of the route to Bolton Great Moor Street would not finally receive double track until 1885, although there were a number of passing loops provided along the route at various locations.

In 1879, the London & North Western Railway had deposited plans with Parliament for a second junction at Pennington, Pennington North, by the construction of their Railway No.1 of the proposal, from a point north the first junction, which became Pennington South Junction, to meet up with the Ackers-Whitley private railway on the north bank of the Leeds-Liverpool Canal, Leigh Branch, some 200 yards south-east of the Ackers-Whitley's railways junction with the Wigan Junction Railway at Plank Lane. Railway No.2 of the proposals was an extension of Diggle's Westleigh Railway which ran from his Higher Hall Colliery at Bickershaw, via Lower Hall Colliery at Westleigh, to a wharf, also on the northern bank of the canal, south of Firs Lane. This new branch would be some 220 yards in length and meet with Railway No.1 approximately 170 yards south of Davenport House Farm. (Effectively Diggle's Branch Junction) These proposals were authorised by Parliament in 1880.

However, conscious of the efforts being made by the newly opened (1879) Wigan Junction Railways to siphon off coal traffic in the area the London & North Western Railway obtained Parliamentary approval to purchase outright the Ackers-Whitley branch railway in 1881 and also to construct a short curve at its northern end from Hindley Field (Jct) to a junction with the Tyldesley-Wigan line; namely Bickershaw West Junction. See also *Fig 5*.

Under the same Parliamentary Act which saw the purchase of the Ackers-Whitley branch railway, authorisation was also given to the London & North Western to purchase the short Scowcroft's Branch from Hindley Field to Scowcroft's Junction with the Tyldesley route, a junction since opening in 1864. The total length of the route from Pennington to Bickershaw West Junction was some 3½ miles, opening to freight traffic only on 9th March 1885.

The next phase of operations at Pennington concern the Pennington Loop lines proposed by the London & North Western Railway in late 1885. These consisted of Up and Down loops between a new junction at Pennington East on the Leigh line, and a new junction at Pennington West, on the Bickershaw Branch. Diggles' Branch connection *
Continued on page 171

Plate 248. A view of the L.C.G.Bs *South Lancashire Limited Railtour* as it approaches Pennington South Junction on 21st September 1963 hauled by '8F' No.48178. Other engines used on this tour were:- '4F' No.44501, '3F' No.47378 and '8F' No.48115.

The footbridge in the background was known locally as Robin Hood Steps. A later publication by the L.C.G.B. in its description of the tour commented that the branch from Bickershaw Junction to Pennington was the *most decrepit track* ever traversed by passenger rolling stock!

The tour had begun at Liverpool Road Goods Depot working via Eccles, Tyldesley and Howe Bridge to Bolton Great Moor Street and then a jolly jaunt to Little Hulton.

After working back to Crook Street Yard the train made its way via Howe Bridge East and Bickershaw Junctions to Wigan Central and after running round and making its way back to Bickershaw traversed the latter branch throughout. On reaching Kenyon and going via Parkside East and Golborne Junctions the through lines at Bamfurlong were taken to give access to the Whelley route at Amberswood, then via Haigh Junction to Adlington and Horwich Works. Here No.44501 was attached to work the special via Horwich South - Hilton House - Crow Nest and Hindley No. 2 Junctions, arriving at De Trafford Junction, running round, and via Amberswood East, take the former Wigan Junction line to Lowton St. Mary's where another run round was necessary to traverse the branch to St. Helens Central. Returning to Lowton the final leg was via Glazebrook Moss and West Junctions to terminate at Manchester Central.

Plate 249. This is the view from a few yards south of the A580 bridge looking towards Pennington Bridge in 1970 at the same location as *Plate 246,* with the Up line lifted. Again, note how the trackbed dips with subsidence. *John Eckersley.*

Plate 250. This view is taken midway between Pennington South Junction and the A580, East Lancashire Road overbridge which is seen in the background. The track has been lifted and the signal stands as a solitary reminder of what once was a busy railway. Until the extension of Atherleigh Way from Pennington to form a junction with the A580 opened the trackbed was a handy cycle track to Kenyon but was often used by the horse-riding fraternity and became in parts, a sea of mud, much to the annoyance of walkers and cyclists.

From this point in the foreground the new road was elevated towards the A580 to such an effect that today you would not believe that a railway ever passed this way. Only by standing on the extant overbridge at Kenyon can you perceive its former alignment. *John Eckersley.*

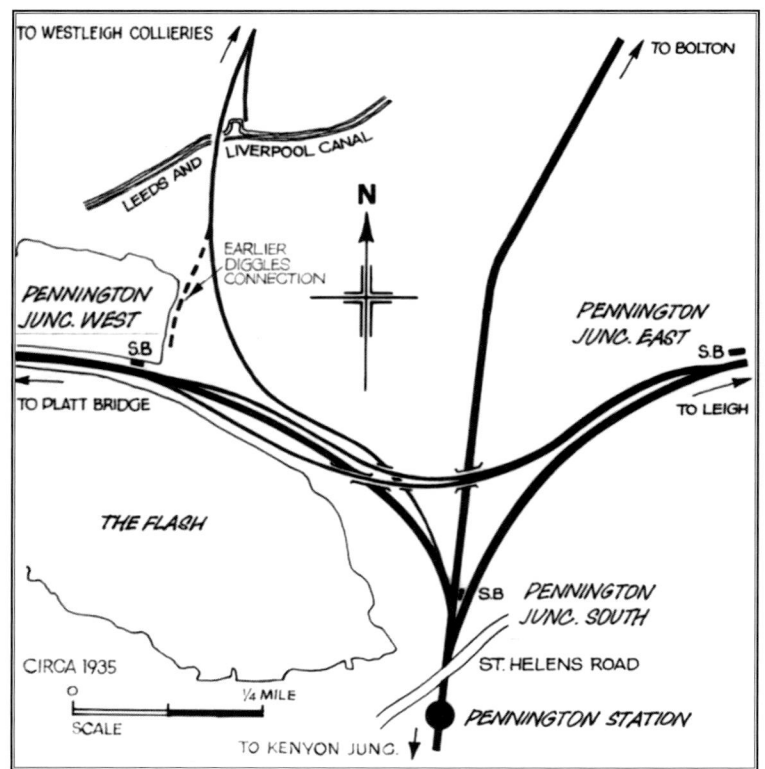

Fig 42. The Pennington area layout after the loop lines were constructed showing Diggle's new connection with Pennington South Junction. The earlier Diggle's connection to the Bickershaw Branch was sited much further west as shown at what became Pennington West Junction. *John Eckersley.*

170

would require moving south-west, much nearer to Pennington Junctions to allow these loops to be built and this was announced under extension proposals in November 1898. This made the earlier connection with Diggle's Branch under the 1880 Act, Railway No.2, redundant.

Beginning at Pennington East Junction the new lines ran side-by-side and crossed the Kenyon-Bolton line by a new overbridge and then split to cross the relaid Diggle's Branch by independent bridges, with yet another new bridge to carry the Down line over the Bickershaw lines in order to make a connection at Pennington West Junction, opposite the Up lines connection.

The loop lines opened for freight traffic on 2nd June 1903, and to passenger traffic on 1st October inst.

The Bickershaw Branch had been brought up to passenger line standard and a new station, Plank Lane, situated on the north side of Crankwood Road, also opened on 1st October, the first train departing Leigh & Bedford for Wigan North Western at 6.43a.m. with, according to the press reports, one passenger. Not a good omen!

Plank Lane Station was to close on 22nd February 1915 although through services from Manchester Exchange to Blackpool Talbot Road continued to use the route, as did 'local' trains calling at Leigh and Tyldesley to Wigan up to 4th May 1942. The loops continued to be used by freight trains, P.W. workings and holiday specials to Blackpool from Leigh and Tyldesley until 1953 when the signal box at Pennington East closed, Pennington West having closed two years earlier. In their latter years of operation these two boxes had been opened on a only 'as required' basis.

Diggle's collieries had closed in the late 1930s but the branch was used for wagon storage, often cripples before they were taken to Earlestown Works by special workings.

Plate 251. Pennington Station as viewed south towards Kenyon c1912. This section of railway, originally single track with a level crossing over the Bolton & St Helens Turnpike Road, was doubled concomitantly with the works for the Leigh Branch in 1864, the first section of the Bolton-Kenyon route to receive a double line of railway. The station here was originally named Bradshaw Leach, becoming Pennington on 1st February 1877.
Author's Collection.

171

KENYON JUNCTION

Kenyon Junction was sometimes referred to as Bolton Junction Station in the early years and is listed as such in Osbornes *Guide to The Grand Junction Railway c.* 1838.

The original station here was a source of much criticism in the early years of the railway and the local papers were littered with complainants letters of 'poor facilities" and yes, wait for it, 'missed connections' when travelling to or from Manchester. The railways did eventually respond to this adverse publicity and a number of timetable alterations appear in print as they attempt to get it right. Waiting rooms as such had again been described as "sheds" offering little shelter, if any, from the elements. The station was officially named Kenyon Junction in July 1843.

A two road engine shed at this location appears to have been provided about 1840 and was large enough to hold six locomotives. It seems to have closed prior to 1870, possibly when the engine shed at Tyldesley was built in the late 1860s, or perhaps the engines were being transferred to Ordsall Lane, Salford?

In November 1879 the London & North Western had announced their intention to seek powers to make a new railway from the Winwick Branch, south of its crossing by the Liverpool & Manchester Railway, to connect with the Kenyon & Leigh Junction Railway at Kenyon. This was included as part of the plans for the Bolton & Leigh deviations and called "The Winwick and Kenyon Junction Railway". In the event the branch was never built being dropped before the Bill came before Committee.

In late 1882 the contract for the re-construction of the station as seen in the accompanying photographs was let, and by mid 1883 the old station had been demolished, new platforms constructed with the complete re-building of station accommodation on an altogether more grandiose scale taking place. Sidings capacity here was quadrupled to cater for the immense goods and minerals traffic now working via Kenyon. Other works undertaken here during the station re-building included the abolition of the level crossing at Wilton Lane, the lane itself being re-routed and carried

Plate 252. Kenyon No.2 signal box was positioned on the north side of Wilton Lane overbridge, alongside the Up line, opening in June 1883. This view dates from 1967. In 2013, Network Rail carried out a major refurbishment of Wilton Lane bridge.

Peter Hampson.

Plate 253. A view looking north towards the A580 bridge which can just be seen at top left as a two car DMU approaches Kenyon No.2 signal box on 10th June 1967, photographed from Wilton Lane bridge. Kenyon No. 2 was to close on 17th December 1967 being demolished in January the following year.   *Gerry Bent.*

over the Kenyon & Leigh Junction Railway by a new bridge.

Over the years Kenyon Sidings continued to handle their fair share of goods traffic. Coal from Bag Lane and Westleigh as already mentioned, along with trip workings from Bickershaw & Abram Collieries, Speakman's or Jackson's Sidings. Edge Hill traffic worked via Kenyon Yard, as did traffic from Chester and North Wales. St. Helens Junction to Patricroft trains working viaABCDE called at Leigh and Tyldesley en-route to shunt the goods yards. In addition there were through coal trains from the local collieries, working through to Warrington or Widnes. Sometimes if shunting operations were required at Kenyon and no trip locomotive was available the Yard Foreman would summon a locomotive from Springs Branch.

In the mid 1960s the only coal traffic working via Kenyon was from Jackson's Sidings at Tyldesley and some from Parsonage Colliery at Westleigh. The closure of many of the local collieries and the increasing competition from road transport brought about the closure of Kenyon Goods Yard on 1st. August 1963. The passenger station had closed on 2nd January 1961.

Kenyon No.1 was a Class '2' signal box situated alongside the Down Liverpool-Manchester line and controlled the junction for the Bolton and Tyldesley routes and the western end of Kenyon Sidings. Kenyon No 1 also employed a Telegraph Lad and because of its important location a telephone concentrator panel had been installed here with lines to Tyldesley, Earlestown, Deal Street (Manchester), the water softening plant situated east of Brosely Lane, Pennington South & Bickershaw Junctions, Barton Moss, Bag Lane, the PW office and the Yard Foreman at Kenyon. Although every signal box was connected to Control, they were not all connected to each other. However, it was possible for some cabins fitted with the appropriate switch apparatus to act as a go between. For example, Springs Branch No. 1 Signalman could, by contacting the Signalman at Howe Bridge West and asking him to turn his switch, speak to the Signalman at Fletcher Street, Bolton, or vice-verca, thus keeping each other informed of any operating problems.

Kenyon No.2 was a Class '3' cabin sited on the north side of Wilton Lane bridge and had control of the northern end of Kenyon Yard and the Loop, or "Field Road" as the railwaymen called it.

The Station Master's house was situated on the south side of Wilton Lane, between the goods yard access road and the running lines, as were cottages for the Assistant Line Manager and Mechanical Chargemen, who, *c.* 1940's were Bert Bromley and Maurice Griffiths. Platelayer, Arthur Butler and Porter, Tom Foster, employed at Kenyon at the same period, also resided in railway cottages here as did Peter Hampson who began work at Kenyon No.1 box in 1965.

For a moment though, let us return to the very beginnings of the railways hereabouts and refer to the writings of Monsieur P. Moreau as published in 1833. Entitled; *Description of the RAIL ROAD from LIVERPOOL TO MANCHESTER By P. MOREAU, ENGINEER. Together with a HISTORY OF RAIL ROADS AND MATTERS CONNECTED THEREWITH. Compiled by A Notre, from the works of Messers WOOD and STEPHENSON and from information furnished by the latter.*

Plate 254. This was the scene on the north side of Wilton Lane bridge at the Kenyon No.2 site in 1969 with track lifting in progress as a section of track is loaded. A sad sight to any railway enthusiast.

Track lifting began almost immediately after closure, from each end of the line simultaneously, working towards Tyldesley. From there it was loaded for dispatch by road transport for smelting. *Gerry Bent.*

The work, freely available on the Internet, was translated from French into English by one J.A.Stocker Jr, Civil Engineer, published in Boston in 1833 by Hillard, Gray & Co., and a copy, by Act of Congress, entered the library of Stanford University from which the following extracts are taken.

Initially, the work deals with the evolution of early railways and plateways in general from early in the eighteenth century, particularly their establishment in England; the road or 'rail-road', a distinctly American term, upon which the steam engine ran, together with the steam engines of Trevethick and Stephenson and their development, all leading up to Moreau's journey over the Liverpool & Manchester Railway pre 1833.

Monsieur Moreau's journey begins at Wapping, then the extent of the railway from Manchester, describing enroute the topography of the landscape and the peculiarities of the railway.

It is on the approach to Kenyon Junction though that, as far as railways in this book are concerned that Moreau's writings have the most profound implications and I quote:-

A little beyond Newton, the main line is joined by the branch lines to Newton and to Wigan, and immediately after, the great Kenyon excavation commences, the work which has required the greatest labo(u)*r. About seven hundred thousand cubic yards of sand and clay were excavated and used for the construction of the nearest embankments. Numbers of bridges have been built to unite the two banks; one of which, that might almost be called a tunnel, from its width, has been filled up above the arch with earth covered with sods; the road which passes over it, is secured on each side with wooden barriers. The view of a large bank of verdure in such a position, has something in it striking as well as agreeable.*

Towards the end of the excavation, the Kenyon and Leigh branch road (railway) *joins the main line, by two tracks, one directing towards Liverpool and the other towards Manchester. This road* (railway) *joins also with that of Bolton and Leigh, near the latter town.*

The latter sentence describes the meeting of the Kenyon & Leigh Junction Railway with the Bolton & Leigh Railway at Twist Lane, Leigh.

Many a railway historian has mooted the possibility, or not, of rails being laid on this east facing curve to Manchester and as yet, no positive proof has come to light. Are we to believe Monsieur Moreau's account of its existence? If rails had been laid, why were the rails then removed at some undetermined date? On the 1849 Ordnance Survey, shown opposite in *Fig 43,* the trackbed is still clearly discernable and uninterrupted,

Although Moreau's continued writings of the Liverpool & Manchester route are beyond the parameters of this book, his account of Chat Moss gives further insight into the early activity on the moss.

Upon entering this desolate waste, the appearance is cold and melancholy; but in the middle, it becomes more varied, and the view more extensive. On each side can be seen, at two miles distant, the carriages on the road; and the surrounding country presents an agreeable panorama. On the north, can be distinguished the peak of Rivington, surrounded by mist; and in fine weather Black Stone Edge can be seen in front; a little to the left is Tildsley (Tyldesley) *church with its gothic steeple; and a little beyond, the village of Astley; further on, to the past, upon a wooded* eminence, stands Worsley castle, belonging to Mr. R. H. Bradshaw, who has established in the marsh and near the road, a plantation, of birch and other trees, to which he has given the name of Botany Bay.

On the east, the country is richly wooded, and on the right a manufactory, situated at Patri Croft, shows its walls, pierced with numerous windows, and surmounted by a bell; and on the south, the marsh is surrounded with trees in the bosom of which are many farms.

In the same direction after passing the twenty-fourth mile, it may be seen that a great part has been put under cultivation. Long avenues of trees newly planted, divide the ground, and on the borders of one farm, many houses have been erected. One of these is the residence of Mr. Reed, director of an extensive and productive farm, entirely reclaimed from a spot formerly abandoned.

This establishment owes its existence to several enterprising persons, who have constructed a private Rail Road, leading from the principal line, as far as the river Irwell, crossing at about two miles the Warrington and Manchester road, at eight miles from the latter town. Two hundred acres of land have been reclaimed in eighteen months; wheat of as good quality, as can be found elsewhere in the county, was collected in 1830, from twenty acres, in addition to eight acres of beans, and twenty acres of apples, of superior quality. The road, of which we have just spoken, is constructed with moveable rails, twelve feet in length, resting on wooden supports; their place is changed according to the direction to be given to the cars carrying the marl, for the preparation of the soil. The earth is divided into different portions by deep cuts, in which smaller ones are made, covered over with turf; and receiving the superabundance of water from the upper layer. This farm is an example, which will tend, sooner or later, to encourage the cultivation of the remainder of the marsh.

Note the splitting of Patricroft.

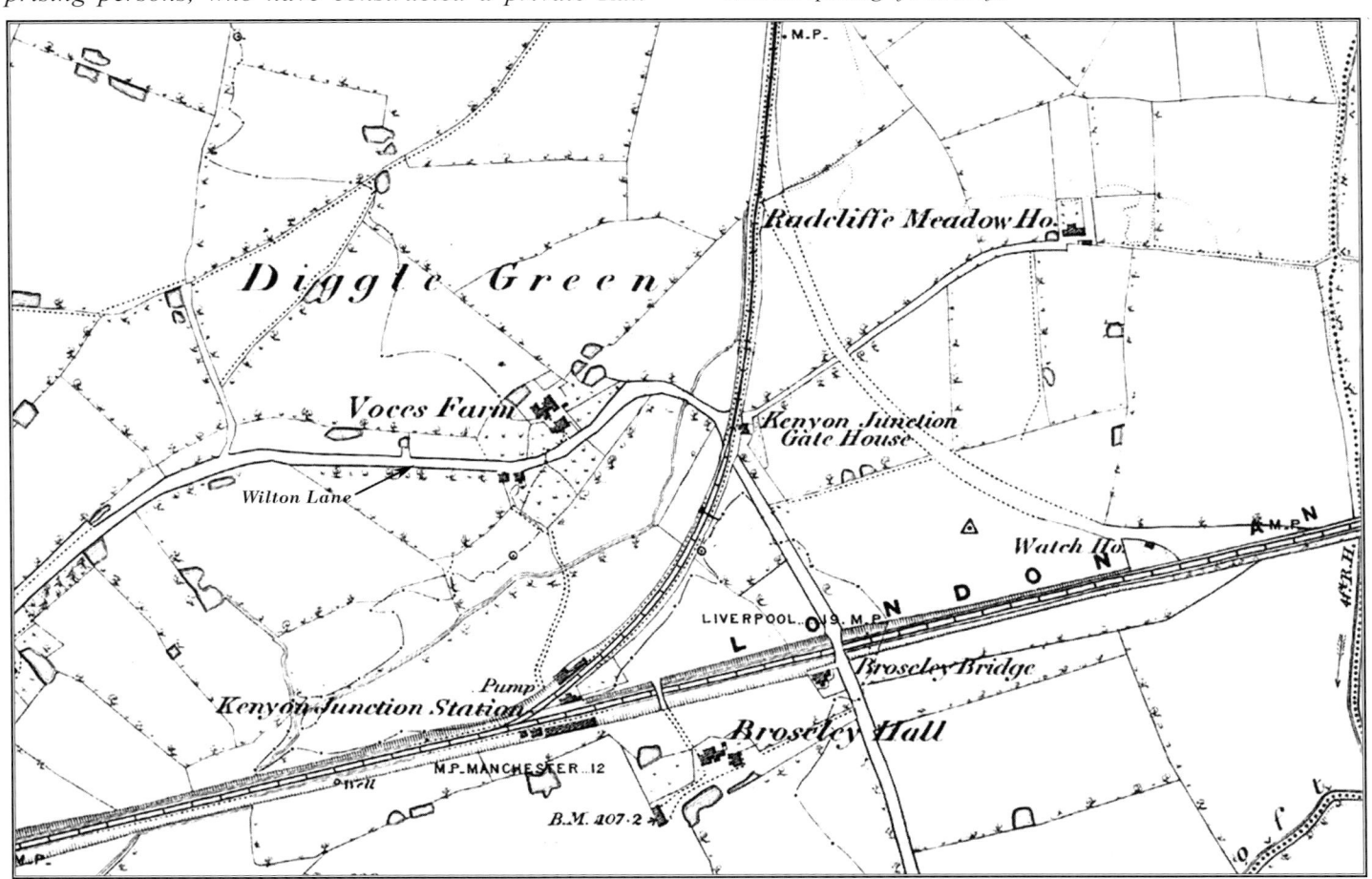

Fig 43. Kenyon Junction c1849, showing a section of the double line Liverpool & Manchester Railway just over a mile in length. It will be noted that there is a short section of the Bolton line from Kenyon Junction to Wilton Lane, which was crossed on the level, is also double. The east facing curve earthworks are also clearly seen and, over the years there has been much speculation as to whether lines were actually laid. However, the writings of Messuir P. Moreau c1833 recounting his journey over the Liverpool & Manchester line seem to confirm that rails had been laid. Note the Gate House at the level crossing.

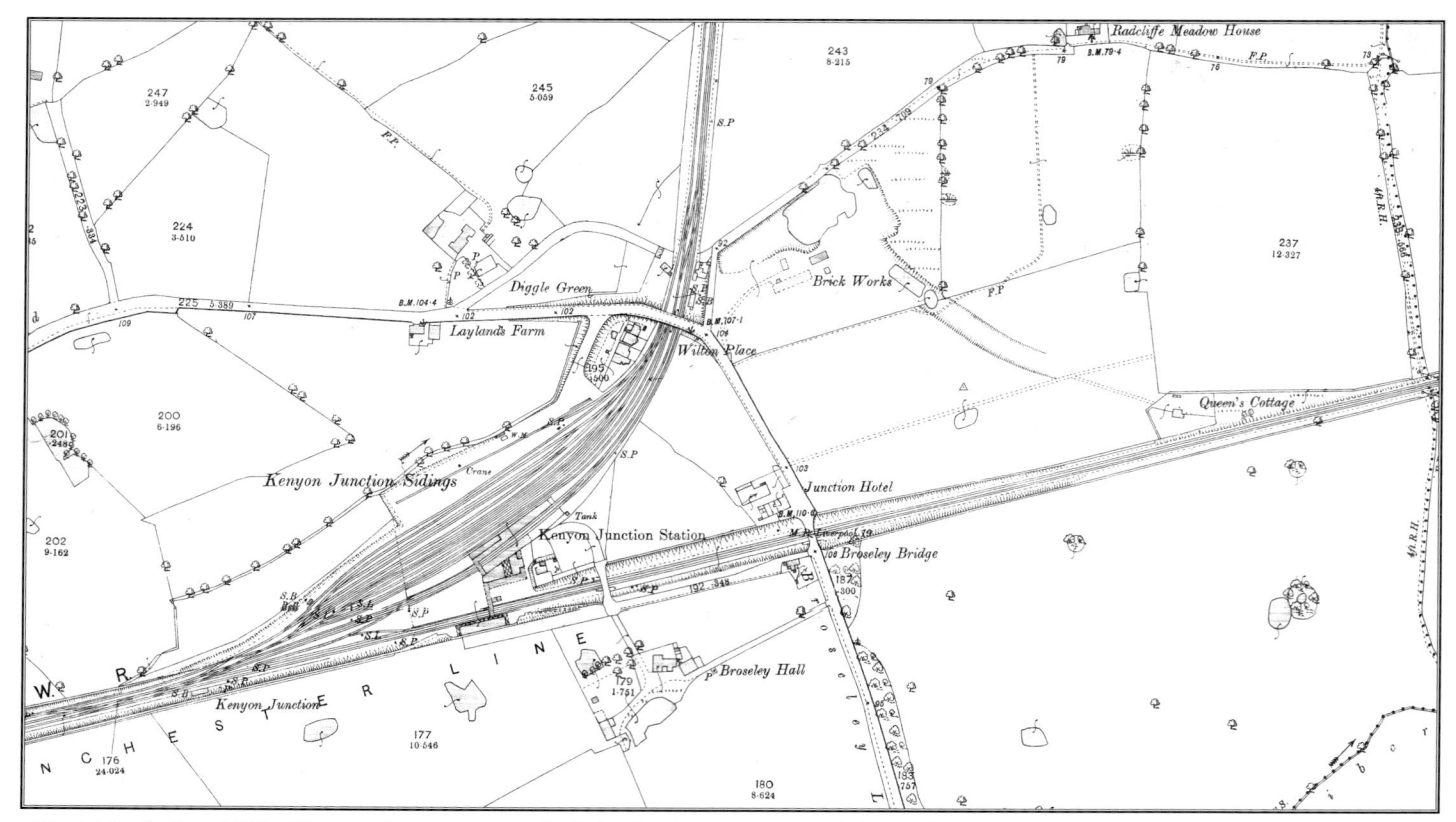

Fig 44. In the late 1880s, Kenyon Junction was rebuilt having been at the receiving end of complaints regarding facilities here for years. This Ordnance Survey is c1892, clearly showing just how much work had been carried out. A large array of sidings has been constructed and a bridge on Wilton Lane now spans the tracks near No.2 signal box. Note that much of the east curve earthworks have been taken over by a brickworks and a cottage built near the former junction with the Liverpool-Manchester lines. Note also the new section of Wilton Lane and the approach road to Kenyon Yard, which, as recently as 2014, had been used by Network Rail to bring in materials for the elecrtification of the Liverpool-Manchester lines.

Plate 255. London & North Western 4-6-0 Prince of Wales class No.5723 *Stentor* calls at Kenyon Junction's platform 2 with a westbound train c1932. Built as L&NW No.522 at Crewe in 1919 the locomotive was scrapped in 1936.

There's a train in the station for the Tyldesley branch and plenty of freight in the goods yard.
C.M & J.M.Bentley.

Plate 256. '8F' 48453 is seen in Kenyon Yard c1967. The water softening plant was situated on the east side of Broseley Lane overbridge alongside the Up line. The vans contain sacks of chemicals to treat the water.
Peter Hampson.

Plate 257. In L.M.S. days ex-London & North Western 4-4-0 No.5323 *Henry Ward* is seen at the western end of the goods yard about 1930. Built in November 1910 as LNW No. 1583 it was withdrawn in September 1939.
C.M & J.M.Bentley.

Plate 258. A westbound freight hauled by '8F' No.48520, passes through Kenyon Junction in July 1949. The tender sports the legend of its new owners British Railways. It would be a few years though before all locomotives and stock were defrocked of their old LMS insignia.
Cooperline, (W.D.Cooper).

Plate 259. The L.C.G.Bs. brake van tour of 15th June 1963 with '8F' 48663, is seen ready for departure from Kenyon Junction.
John Ryan.

Plate 260. Kenyon Station frontage as facing the Liverpool-Manchester lines viewed looking north west.
Eddie Bellass.

Plate 261, below. A DMU for Liverpool stops at platform 3 in December 1960. Far left are the railway cottages and adjacent to Wilton Lane bridge, the latter constructed during the rebuilding of Kenyon in the 1880s.
Eddie Bellass.

Plate 262. A busy scene at Kenyon Junction as Stanier 4-6-0 No.44936, with a self-weighing tender, draws a coal train out of the yard, probably bound for Garston Docks in December 1960. There is an unidentified W.D. 2-8-0 shunting the yard which is overflowing with wagons before the wholesale closures of local mines had such an adverse effect on traffic. *Eddie Bellass.*

Plate 263. In August 1967, type '3' diesel No.D6947 passes Kenyon Junction No1 box with the prototype 'DP2' in tow after the latter had been involved in an accident at Thirsk on 31st July 1967. Not actually owned by B.R., the locomotive is enroute to Vulcan Works where it was built in 1961/2 to undergo assesment for possible repair. Unfortunately, it was cut up in 1970 but its power unit was used in class '50' No.D417, also being built at Vulcan Works at the time. *Peter Hampson.*

Plate 264. Stanier class '5' No. 45348 passes through Kenyon Junction on 4th September 1965 with a special excursion with the demolition of Kenyon station well underway, a sight all too familiar on Britain's railways at the time. *Peter Eckersley.*

Plate 265. A deserted Kenyon Yard c1967. Demolition now completed, only the platforms remain to remind us that there had been a station here at all. The first station was built for the opening of the Kenyon & Leigh Junction Railway in 1831 then, often refered to as Bolton Junction. It would be 50 years before a new one was built in the early 1880s as the railways continued to expand; now in reverse, nothing it seemed could curtail the wholesale destruction of the nation's assets as motorway construction consumed all in its path.
Peter Hampson.

TIME TABLES & APPENDICES

The first Summer of passenger timetables in the new British Railways era from 31st May 1948 to September 26th inc.

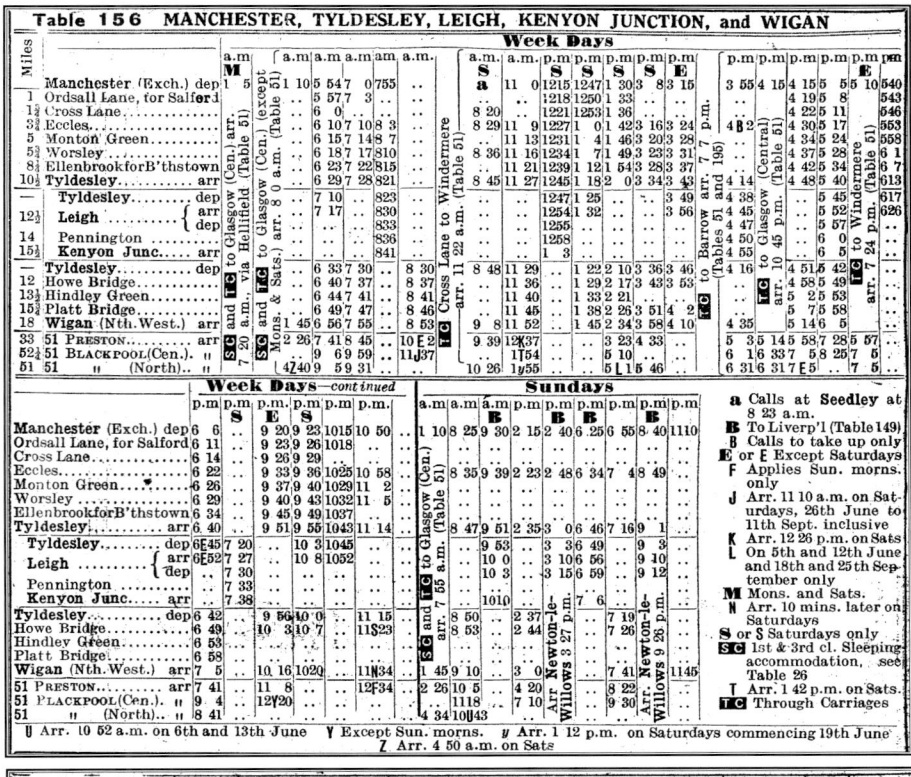

Manchester — Patricroft — Tyldesley — Leigh — Liverpool

Train Services 3 July 1967 to 5 May 1968

This page and opposite are the timetables for the Liverpool - Tyldesley Manchester Exchange route from 3 July 1967 to 5th May 1968.

Passenger services to Wigan over the route ceased in November 1964.

Manchester → Patricroft → Tyldesley → Leigh → Liverpool

Weekdays

	Manchester Exchange	Eccles	Patricroft	Monton Green	Worsley	Tyldesley	Leigh	Newton-le-Willows	Earlestown	St. Helens Junction	Rainhill	Huyton	Roby	Broad Green	Edge Hill	Liverpool Lime St.	
	06.40	06.48	→	06.52	→	07.02	07.10	07.20	07.24	07.30	07.38	07.43	07.45	07.49	07.53	07.59	
	07.00	07.08	→	07.12	07.15	07.24	07.32										
	07.10	07.18	07.21	→				07.34	07.38	07.44	07.52	07.57	07.59	08.03	08.07	08.13	
	07.25	07.33	→	07.37	07.40	07.49	07.56	08.07	08.11	08.17	08.24	08.30	08.32	08.35	08.40	08.45	
	07.38	07.46	07.57	→				08.11	08.16								
	07.40	07.48	→	07.52	07.55	08.04	08.12										
	08.15	08.23	→	08.27	08.30	08.39	08.46	08.58	09.02	09.08	09.15	09.21	09.23	09.26	09.31	09.36	
	08.30	08.38	08.41	→	→	→	→	08.54									
	09.00	→		→	→	→	→	→	09.19	09.24	→	→	→	→	→	09.42	
	09.10	09.18	→	09.22	09.25	09.34	09.41	09.52	09.56	10.02	10.09	→	→	→	→	10.25	
SO d	09.20	09.29	SO d					10.19	10.25							10.42	
	10.00																
	10.10	10.18	→	10.22	10.25	10.34	10.41	10.52	10.56	11.02	11.09	11.15	11.17	11.20	11.25	11.30	
	10.40	10.49	→					11.07	11.12								
SO a	11.30	→						11.50	11.55	→	→	→	→	→	→	12.12	
	11.40	→						12.02	SO a								
SX	12.00	12.08	→	12.12	12.15	12.24	12.31	12.42	12.46	12.52	12.59	13.05	13.07	13.10	13.15	13.20	SX
	12.08	→						12.30	12.37	→	→	→	→	→	→	12.53	
	12.14	→						12.34	12.38								
SO	12.18	12.26	→	12.30	12.33	12.42	12.49	13.04	13.17	13.23	13.25	13.28	13.33	13.38	SO		
	13.00	→		→	→	→	→	→	13.19	13.25	→	→	→	→	→	13.42	
	13.30	13.38						13.56									
SO a	13.55	14.03u	→					14.17	SO a								
	14.15	14.23	→	14.27	14.30	14.39	14.46	14.57	15.01	15.07	15.14	15.20	15.22	15.25	15.30	15.35	
	14.10	→							14.29	14.36	→	→	→	→	→	14.52	
	15.00	→							15.19	15.25	→	→	→	→	→	15.42	
SX	15.10	→						15.31	SX								
	15.10	15.18	→	15.22	15.25	15.34	15.41	15.52	15.56	16.02	16.09	16.15	16.17	16.20	16.25	16.30	
	16.00	→						16.19	16.25	→	→	→	→	→	→	16.42	
	16.15	16.23	→	16.27	16.31	16.40	16.47	16.57	17.01	17.07	17.15	17.20	→	→	→	17.32	
SO	16.30	→						16.51	SO								
	17.00	→						17.19	17.25	→	→	→	17.38	17.43			
SX	17.05	17.13	→	17.17	17.20	17.29	17.37	SX									
SX	17.07							17.28	SX								
	17.10	17.18	17.21					17.34	17.38	17.44	17.52	17.57	17.59	18.03	18.07	18.13	
	17.20	17.28	→	17.32	17.35	17.44	17.52										
SX	17.40	17.48	→	17.52	17.55	18.04	18.11	18.22	18.26	18.32	18.39	18.45	18.47	18.50	18.55	19.00	SX
	17.47	→	17.56					18.10	18.14								
	18.00	→						18.19	18.25	→	→	→	→	→	→	18.42	
	18.15	18.23	→	18.27	18.30	18.39	18.46	18.57	19.01	19.07	19.14	19.20	19.22	19.25	19.30	19.35	
	19.08	→						19.27	19.34	→	→	→	→	→	→	19.50	
	19.45	19.53	19.56					20.09	20.13								
	20.15	20.23	→	20.27	20.31	20.40	20.47	20.57	21.01	21.07	21.15	21.02	21.22	21.26	21.30	21.36	
	20.08	→							20.27	20.34	→	→	→	→	→	20.50	
	21.00	→							21.19	21.25	→	→	→	→	→	21.42	
	21.10	21.18	→	21.22	21.25	21.34	21.41	21.52	21.56	22.02	22.09	22.15	22.17	22.20	22.25	22.30	
	21.31	21.39	21.42	→				21.55	21.59								
	22.35	22.43	→	22.47		22.57	23.05	23.15	23.19	23.25	23.33	23.38	23.40	23.44	23.48	23.54	

Sundays

v	09.25	09.34	09.37	→	→	→	→	09.51	09.55							
v	09.30	09.39	→			09.53	10.00	10.10	10.14	10.20	10.28	10.33c	→	→	10.41	10.46
c v	09.50	09.59	10.02	→	→	→	→	10.16	10.20							
v	14.00	→						14.21	14.29	→	→	→	→	→		14.45
v	14.10	14.19	→					14.33	14.37							
v	15.55	16.04														
v	18.30	18.39	→	→		18.53	19.00	19.10	19.14	19.20	19.28	19.33c	→	→	19.41	19.46
v	19.25	→						19.45	19.50	19.56	→	→	→	→		20.09
v	19.30	19.39	19.42					19.56	20.00							
v	21.00	21.09	→	→		21.22	21.30	21.40	21.44	21.50	21.58	22.02c	→	→	22.10	22.15
v	21.38	→	→	→	→	→	→	22.00	22.07	→	→	→	→	→		22.23

For notes see over →

182

Liverpool → Leigh → Tyldesley → Patricroft → Manchester

Weekdays

Liverpool Lime St.	Edge Hill	Broad Green	Roby	Huyton	Rainhill	St. Helens Junction	Earlestown	Newton-le-Willows	Leigh	Tyldesley	Worsley	Monton Green	Patricroft	Eccles	Manchester Exchange	
				06.20	→	→	→	06.30	06.37	06.43	06.48	06.52	07.02	07.10	07.19	07.22		07.26	07.35	
07.00	07.04	07.09	07.12	07.14	07.21	07.27	07.32	07.36	→	→	→	→	07.49	07.52	08.00	
									07.46	07.53	08.02	08.05		08.09	08.19	
SX 07.25	07.29	07.34	07.37	07.39	07.46	07.52	07.57	08.01	→	→	→	→	08.14	08.17	08.25	SX
							SX	08.00	08.08	08.16	08.19		08.23	08.32	SX
07.45	07.49	→	→	07.55	08.00	08.07	08.11	08.15	→	→	→	→	08.27	08.29	08.37	
									08.20	08.27	08.36	08.39		08.43	08.52	
													08.44	08.47	08.55	
08.15	08.19	08.24	08.27	08.29	08.36	08.42	08.47	08.51	09.01	09.09	09.18	09.21		09.25	09.34	
							09.04	09.08	→	→	09.18		09.21	→	09.31	
09.00	→	→	→	09.18		09.21		09.43	
09.00	09.04	09.09	09.12	09.14	09.21	09.27	09.32	09.36	09.46	09.54	10.03	10.06		10.10	10.19	
							09.51	09.55	→	→	→	→	10.08	10.11	10.19	
10.05	→	→	→	→	→	10.21	10.26	→	→	→	→	→			10.46	
							10.51	10.55	→	→	→	→	11.08	11.11	11.19	
10.30	10.34	10.39	10.42	10.44	10.51	10.57	11.02	11.06	11.16	11.24	11.33	11.36	→	11.40	11.49	
11.00	→	→	→	→	→	11.16	11.20	→	→	→	→	→			11.41	
							SO a	11.41					11.57	12.05	SOa	
12.00	→	→	→	→	→	12.16	12.21	→	→	→	→	→			12.41	
							SO a	12.25	12.30	→	→	→	→	12.45	12.29	12.39	SO b
								12.51	12.55	→	→	→	→	12.45	12.58	SO a
													13.08	13.11	13.19	
12.05	12.09	12.14	12.17	12.19	12.26	12.32	12.37	12.41	12.51	12.59	13.08	13.11	→	13.15	13.24	
13.00	→	→	→	→	→	13.16	13.21	→	→	→	→	→			13.41	
							13.51	13.55	→	→	→	→	14.08	14.11	14.19	
13.35	13.39	13.44	13.47	13.49	13.56	14.02	14.07	14.11	14.21	14.29	14.38	14.41	→	14.45	14.54	
14.00	→	→	→	→	→	14.16	14.21	→	→	→	→	→			14.41	
15.00	→	→	→	→	→	15.16	15.21	→	→	→	→	→			15.41	
15.05	15.09	15.14	15.17	15.19	15.26	15.32	15.37	15.41	15.51	15.59	16.08	16.11	→	16.15	16.24	
							15.51	15.55	→	→	→	→	16.08	16.11	16.19	
16.05	→	→	→	→	→	16.21	16.26	→	→	→	→	→			16.46	
							17.00	17.04	→	→	→	→	SX 16.45	16.47	16.56	SX
													17.17	17.20	17.28	
16.20	16.24	16.29	16.32	16.37	16.44	16.50	16.55	16.59	17.09	17.17	17.26	17.29	→	17.33	17.42	
17.00	17.04	17.09	17.12	17.17	17.23	17.30	17.35	17.39	17.55	18.06	18.14	18.17	→	18.21	18.30	
17.05	→	→	→	→	17.21	17.51	17.55	→	→	→	→	→		17.43	17.52	
													18.08	18.11	18.19	
													18.12	18.15	18.23	
SX 17.40	17.44	17.49	17.52	17.54	18.01	18.07	18.12	18.16	18.26	18.34	18.43	18.46	→	18.50	18.59	SX
18.00	→	→	→	→	→	18.16	18.21	→	→	→	→	→			18.41	
18.20	18.24	18.29	18.32	18.34	18.41	18.47	18.52	18.56	19.06	19.14	19.23	19.26	→	19.30	19.39	
19.00	→	→	→	→	→	19.16	19.21	→	→	→	→	→			19.41	
19.25	19.29	19.34	19.37	19.39	19.46	19.52	19.57	20.01	20.11	20.19	20.28	20.31	→	20.35	20.44	
							20.04	20.08	→	→	→	→	20.25	20.30	20.39	
20.20	→	→	→	→	→	20.36	20.41	→	→	→	→	→			20.01	
21.05	21.09	21.14	21.17	21.19	21.26	21.32	21.37	21.41	21.51	21.59	22.08	22.11	→	22.15	22.24	
							22.15	22.19	→	→	→	→	22.33	22.41	
22.50	22.54	22.59	23.02	23.04	23.11	23.17	23.22	23.26	23.36	23.44	→	→	→	→	00.05	

Sundays

07.35	07.39	→	→	07.47c	07.54	08.00	08.05	08.09	08.19	08.27	→	→	→	08.40	08.50	v
							08.26	08.30	→	→	→	→	08.44	→	08.54	v
09.05	09.09	→	→	→	→	09.22	→	→	→	→	→	→	→		09.47	v
							10.50	→	→	→	→	→	→	11.06	11.14	v
12.10	12.14	→	→	12.20c	→	12.29	12.34	12.38	→	→	→	→	12.50	13.00	v
													14.58	15.08	v
15.00	15.04	→	→	15.12c	15.19	15.25	15.30	15.34	15.44	15.52	→	→	→	16.05	16.15	v
				c		17.24	17.28	→	→	→	→	17.41	17.44	17.53	v c
							18.42	→	→	→	→	→		18.59	19.08	v
18.30	18.34	→	→	18.42c	18.49	18.55	19.00	19.04	19.14	19.22	→	→	→	19.35	19.46	v
19.20	→	→	→	→	→	19.36	→	→	→	→	→	→			20.01	v
							19.53	19.58	→	→	→	→	20.12	20.17	20.27	v
21.00	21.04	→	→	21.12c	21.19	21.25	21.30	21.34	21.44	21.52	→	→	→	22.05	22.14	
							22.37	22.41	→	→	→	→	→	22.55	23.03	
23.38	→	→	→	→	→	→	→	→	→	→	→	→	→	→	00.26	v

NOTES

a From 17 June until 2 September
b From 24 June until 26 August
c From 18 June until 3 September
d From 17 June until 26 August
u Stops to pick up only
v Manchester Victoria
SX Saturdays Excepted
SO Saturdays Only

For complete service between Liverpool and Huyton see TABLE 89 LMR Timetable.

The British Railways Board accept no liability for any inaccuracy in the information contained in this leaflet which may be altered at any time without notice.

LIVERPOOL AND DITTON TO SPRINGS BRANCH, AND MANCHESTER (EXCHANGE), AND BRANCHES—continued

SPRINGS BRANCH No. 1 TO ECCLES JUNCTION.

Additional Running Lines	Stations and Signal Boxes, etc.	Distance from place next above (Miles)	Distance from place next above (Yards)	Lie-by Sidings and holding capacity (No. of Wagons) Up Side / Down Side	Runaway Catch Points — Where Situate	Line	Approx. Gradient 1 in	Engine Whistles UP — Main, Fast or Passenger Line	Engine Whistles UP — Slow or Goods Line	Engine Whistles DOWN — Main, Fast or Passenger Line	Engine Whistles DOWN — Slow or Goods Line	To	Speed Restrictions MPH Up	Speed Restrictions MPH Down
●	Springs Branch—No. 1. *See page 17.*	—	—											
	Between Springs Branch Junction and Platt Bridge Junction												25	25
	" Crompton's Siding	—	197						3 and 1 crow			Engine shed or sidings from down goods		
									5 short			Lancashire Union line from east loop		
									4 and 1 crow			Up goods loop from down goods		
									1 and 1 crow			Crompton and S. siding from down goods		
									2 crows and 1			Engine shed or sidings from east loop		
●	Platt Bridge—Junction	—	555					p2 1 crow	p2 1 crow			Bickershaw branch		
									3 short 3 long			Down goods		
									3 crows and 2			Down goods for engine shed or sidings at Crompton's sidings		
									p1 crow and 2			North sidings, Springs Branch		
									1 long 3 short			Trains with through loads for beyond Ince Moss		
									p2 crows and 1			Trains having shunt wagons to detach at north sidings, Springs Branch		
									2 and 2 crows			Springs Branch Incline		
									3 short			Fir Tree House Junction		
	" §Station	—	576											
	Hindley Green—Bickershaw Jn. (continued on page 77)	1	99					5 and 1 crow	5 and 1 crow			Moss Hall and vice versa		
								5	5			" from Bickershaw branch and vice versa		
								p4				Trains for Bolton branch		
	Hindley Green—Bickershaw Jn. (continued from page 76)								p1 crow and 1			Fir Tree House Junction		
									1 crow and 2			North sidings, Springs Branch		
									2 and 1 crow			Springs Branch Incline		
	Through junction and round Hindley Curves to and from Hindley & Platt Bridge (L.N.E.)												20	20
	" " to and from Pennington West Junction												20	20
	" Scowcroft's Sidings	—	690											
	" Station	—	1477											
	Howe Bridge—West Junction	1	170		*314 yards in rear of Atherton Junction home signal	Up branch	216	p4				Trains timed to pass Tyldesley		
	Through Howe Bridge West Junction to and from Atherton Junction												20	20
	" East Junction	—	730		*360 yards in rear of Atherton Junction home signal	Down branch	171	p4	p3			Hindley & Platt Bridge (L.N.E.) Through trains, Patricroft and beyond		
									p1 long 1 crow			Passenger trains not timed stop Wigan		
									3 short			Bolton branch		
	Through Howe Bridge East Junction to and from Atherton Junction												20	20
	" Chanter's Siding	—	1000											
	Tyldesley—No. 2	—	1597											
	Through Tyldesley No. 2 Junction to and from Wigan												35	35
	" " " " Leigh												30	30
	" No. 1	—	513											
	" Hough Lane	—	917											
	Ellenbrook—Station	1	763											
	Worsley—Roe Green Junction	1	952		44				p2 crows			Trains via Wigan not stopping Tyldesley		
	Through junction to and from Wigan												50	50
	" " " " Bolton												35	20
	" Sanderson's Siding	—	756						2 crows			Freight trains not requiring loop at Monton Green		
	" Station	—	671											
	Monton Green—Station	—	1526						2			Bolton line		
	Patricroft—Eccles Junction. *See page 63.*	—	1106											

Sectional Appendix c1937.   *Courtesy, John Hall.*

LIVERPOOL AND DITTON TO SPRINGS BRANCH, AND MANCHESTER (EXCHANGE), AND BRANCHES—continued.

ADDITIONAL RUNNING LINES.	STATIONS AND SIGNAL BOXES, ETC.	Distance from place next above. Miles.	Distance from place next above. Yards.	UP LINE.	Lie-by Sidings and holding capacity. No. of Wagons. Up Side.	Lie-by Sidings and holding capacity. No. of Wagons. Down Side.	RUNAWAY CATCH POINTS. WHERE SITUATE.	LINE.	Approximate Gradient. 1 in	ENGINE WHISTLES. UP. Main, Fast or Passenger Line.	ENGINE WHISTLES. UP. Slow or Goods Line.	ENGINE WHISTLES. DOWN. Main, Fast or Passenger Line.	ENGINE WHISTLES. DOWN. Slow or Goods Line.	TO	SPEED RESTRICTIONS. MILES PER HOUR. UP.	SPEED RESTRICTIONS. MILES PER HOUR. DOWN.
No block or bell.							**AMBERSWOOD JUNCTION EAST TO BICKERSHAW JUNCTION (VIA HINDLEY & PLATT BRIDGE, L.N.E.).**									
	Springs Branch—Amberswood Jn. East See page 56.	—	—													
	Hindley and Platt Bridge—Station (L.N.E.)	—	912				Near signal box	Down main	Level	2				New line to Amberswood Jn. West		
							120 yards west of signal box	Down goods	75	3 6 short 3 short				New line to Amberswood Jn. East Goods yard siding Down line sidings, North and main line		
							*270 yards in rear of Bickershaw Jn. distant signal	Up	91	5 and 1 crow 5		5 short		" " South " " Main line and Moss Hall and vice versa Pennington Jn. and Moss Hall and vice versa		
	Hindley Green—Bickershaw Jn. See pages 76 and 77.	—	1396				All lines at Hindley and Platt Bridge (L.N.E.)								10	10
							HINDLEY & PLATT BRIDGE (L.N.E.) TO AMBERSWOOD JUNCTION WEST (GOODS LINES).									
No block or bell.	Hindley & Platt Bridge—Station (L.N.E.) See above.	—	—													
	Springs Branch—Amberswood Jn. West See page 56.	—	912													
							BICKERSHAW JUNCTION TO PENNINGTON SOUTH JUNCTION									
	Hindley Green—Bickershaw Jn. See pages 76 and 77.	—	—				Through Hindley Field Junction								20	20
	" Hindley Field	—	674													
●	Pennington—Abram North (Level Crossing)	—	1231							2				Via Leigh		
	" Bickershaw Colliery	—	1251				Passing Bickershaw Colliery signal box								25	25
	Pennington—West Junction	1	301													
	" South Junction See page 70.	—	1040				Through Pennington West Junction to and from Leigh								40	40
							PENNINGTON SOUTH JUNCTION TO TYLDESLEY No. 2									
	Pennington—South Junction See page 70.	—	—													
	" East Junction	—	866				* 254 yards in rear of starting signal	Down	100							
							Through Pennington East Junction to and from Pennington South and West Junctions								25	25
	Leigh—Station	1	103								2 short			Bickershaw curve. To be given at Jackson's Siding when this signal box is closed.		
							Through Leigh station			1					40	
													1	All trains approaching Guest's occupation crossing between these places must give a warning whistle.		
	Speakman's Siding	—	1346													
	Tyldesley—Jackson's Siding	—	1197				594 yards in rear of home signal	Up	100					See Leigh Station		
	" No. 2 See page 77.	—	597													
							MOSS HALL BRANCH—BICKERSHAW JUNCTION TO MOSS HALL COLLIERY—(SINGLE GOODS LINE.)									
Staff	Hindley Green—Bickershaw Jn. See pages 76 and 77.	—	—													
	" §Moss Hall Coll'y	—	1212													
							HINDLEY FIELD TO SCOWCROFT'S SIDINGS—(GOODS LINES.)									
No block or bell.	Hindley Green—Hindley Field See page 78.	—	—													
	" Scowcroft's Sidings See page 77.	—	577													
							DIGGLES BRANCH—PENNINGTON SOUTH JUNCTION TO WEST LEIGH COLLIERY SIDINGS—(SINGLE GOODS LINE.)									
Staff	Pennington—South Junction See page 70.	—	—													
	" §West Leigh Colliery Sidings	—	1622													

Sectional Appendix c1937.   *Courtesy, John Hall.*

Description of Block Signalling on Main Lines. (Dots indicate Block Posts)	Stations and Signal Boxes	Distance between signal boxes M	Distance between signal boxes Yds	Additional running lines Up	Additional running lines Down	Loops and Refuge Sidings Description	Loops and Refuge Sidings Standage Wagons E. & V.	Permanent speed restrictions, miles per hour Down	Permanent speed restrictions, miles per hour Up	Catch points, spring or unworked trailing points Position	Gradient (Rising unless otherwise shown) 1 in	Engine Whistles L—long S—short C—crow Down Main or Fast	Down Slow or Goods	Up Main or Fast	Up Slow or Goods	For
	HOWE BRIDGE WEST JUNCTION TO SPRINGS BRANCH No. 1—*Continued*															
●	Springs Branch Crompton's Siding	—	595													
●	No. 1 (See page 8)	—	197					25	25	Between Springs Branch No. 1 and Platt Bridge Junction Through junction						
	PENNINGTON SOUTH JUNCTION TO BICKERSHAW JUNCTION (THROUGH SIDINGS)															
	PENNINGTON SOUTH JUNCTION TO BICKERSHAW JUNCTION							45	45	MAXIMUM PERMISSIBLE SPEED						
● NB	Pennington South Jn. (Central Lines)	—	—			URS	74	20	20	Through junction						
● NB	Bickershaw Colliery	1	1341	Up Through Siding No. 2 NB	Down Through Siding No. 2 NB			25	25	Passing Bickershaw Colliery box						
● NB	Abram North (Level Crossing)	—	1251										*Drivers must whistle when 1 mile distant from Abram North Level Crossing.*			
●	Bickershaw Jn. (See page 145)	1	145					20	20	Round curve between 3 m.p. and junction and through junction						
	MOSS HALL BRANCH—MOSS HALL COLLIERY TO BICKERSHAW JUNCTION (SINGLE GOODS LINE)															
One engine in steam	MOSS HALL BRANCH—MOSS HALL COLLIERY TO BICKERSHAW JUNCTION							15	15	MAXIMUM PERMISSIBLE SPEED						
●	Moss Hall Colliery	—	—													
●	Bickershaw Junction (See page 145)	—	1212													
	HINDLEY GREEN, BICKERSHAW JUNCTION TO AMBERSWOOD JUNCTION EAST (VIA HINDLEY SOUTH)															
	BICKERSHAW JUNCTION TO AMBERSWOOD JUNCTION EAST (via HINDLEY SOUTH)							15	15	MAXIMUM PERMISSIBLE SPEED						
●	Hindley Green Bickershaw Junction (See page 145)	—	—						15	Through junction						
●	Hindley South Station (Midland Lines)	—	1396	NB	NB			10	10	All lines and over East Curves C. Down main, near signal box. C. Down line to Amberswood Jn. East 53 yards after passing signal box. C. Up Branch, 270 yards in rear of Bickershaw Jn. distant signal.	Level 75 94					
●	Amberswood Junction East (See page 36)	—	912	●	●			15		Through junction						
	AMBERSWOOD JUNCTION WEST TO HINDLEY SOUTH STATION (DOWN THROUGH No. 1 AND UP THROUGH No. 2 SIDINGS)															
	AMBERSWOOD JUNCTION WEST TO HINDLEY SOUTH STATION							15	15	MAXIMUM PERMISSIBLE SPEED						
● NB	Amberswood Jn. West (See page) 36	—	—													
●	Hindley South Station (Midland Lines)	—	912							C. Down line, 120 yards west of signal box.	75					

Sectional Appendix c1960. *Courtesy, John Hall.*

FREIGHT TRAINS, HINDLEY GREEN TO HOWE BRIDGE WEST

Guards must leave control of their trains entirely to Drivers, and must not apply the hand brake except when the Driver whistles for it, or on account of fixed signals being at Danger.

Drivers must shut off steam after having gained sufficient speed to carry the entire train well on the rising gradient approaching Howe Bridge West Junction, and must not apply steam until the whole of the train is on the bank and all the couplings are extended.

CROMPTON'S SIDING

Hodgson & Co. Ltd. Private Siding.—Trips to and from Hodgson & Co. Ltd. Private Siding must **not** cross Warrington Road until two hand Signalmen, provided by the firm, are in attendance to protect the Public Highway.

BICKERSHAW BRANCH

Park Lane Crossing.—Up trains stopping at Bickershaw Colliery must leave Park Lane level crossing clear.

MOSS HALL BRANCH

The crossing gate at the railway boundary must be kept locked, except when in use. Guards having wagons to work to Moss Hall Colliery must obtain the key from Bickershaw Junction, and afterwards return it to that place.

Freight trains assisted in rear.—When trains are assisted in rear from Moss Hall Colliery to Bickershaw Junction the Train Staff must be carried by the assisting engine in rear and the Driver of the leading engine must assure himself that the Train Staff is in possession of the Driver of the assisting engine.

BICKERSHAW JUNCTION

Freight trains from Bickershaw Junction to Amberswood Junction East, via Hindley South.—Guards must apply the van brake in travelling down the bank, in order to keep the couplings tight and steady the train.

Extracts from the 1960 Sectional Appendix & Local Instructions.
Courtesy, John Hall.

ATHERTON BAG LANE JUNCTION TO HOWE BRIDGE WEST JUNCTION

Location		Yards			Speed	Notes				
ATHERTON BAG LANE JUNCTION TO HOWE BRIDGE WEST JUNCTION					20	20	MAXIMUM PERMISSIBLE SPEED			
Atherton Bag Lane Junction (See pages 37 and 42)	—	—				20	Through junction CW. Down line, 237 yards before reaching Howe Bridge West Jn. home signal	253		
Howe Bridge West Junction (See page 39)	—	574				20	Through junction CW. Up line, 314 yards before reaching Atherton Jn. home signal	216	1L 1S / 1L 1C	Hindley South Passenger trains not timed to stop at Wigan.

TYLDESLEY No. 2 TO LEIGH, PENNINGTON SOUTH JUNCTION

Location		Yards			Speed	Notes		
TYLDESLEY No. 2 TO PENNINGTON SOUTH JUNCTION				45	45	MAXIMUM PERMISSIBLE SPEED		
Tyldesley No. 2 (See page 39)	—	—				30	Through junction	
Jackson's Siding	—	597					C. Up line, 594 yards before reaching home signal	100
Leigh Speakman's Siding	—	1197						
Station	—	1346						
Pennington South Jn. (See page 38)	1	969			25 / 20	25	Round curve, between ¾ m.p. and Pennington South Jn. Through junction	

LEIGH, PENNINGTON SOUTH JUNCTION TO BICKERSHAW COLLIERY

Location		Yards			Speed	Notes
PENNINGTON SOUTH JUNCTION TO BICKERSHAW COLLIERY				45	45	MAXIMUM PERMISSIBLE SPEED
† Leigh Pennington South Jn. (See page 38)	—	—	URS	74	20	Through junction
Bickershaw Colliery (Western Lines)	1	1341				

† Up line only.

187

Special Instructions. From WTT 9.9.63 to 14.6.1964 *Courtesy, John Hall.*

ELLENBROOK.

N.C.B. Sidings:—

Guards must, on completion of work, leave the tumbler points fixed at the siding leading to the middle road, on the station side of the box, set for that road.

TYLDESLEY.

Trains setting back:—

When a train requires to set back from up goods to up main line at No. 1 box, the Guard, or Fireman in case of a light engine, must go to the box and wait there until permission can be given to set back, when he must call the train back.

JACKSON'S SIDING.

Guards and Shunters must exercise great care when shunting. When it is necessary to place wagons on the line leading to the colliery, they must secure the wagons by means of sprags, so as to prevent them running into the siding where the N.C.B. engine is shunting.

HOWE BRIDGE.

Fog signalling arrangements, Chanter's Siding up distant signals:—

The up outer distant signals for Chanter's Siding box from Wigan and Bolton direction, fixed underneath the home signals for Howe Bridge East Junction box, will be fog signalled by the man at the down home signals for Howe Bridge East Junction box at a point immediately opposite the last mentioned signals.

FREIGHT TRAINS, HINDLEY GREEN TO HOWE BRIDGE WEST.

Guards must leave control of their trains entirely to Drivers, and must not apply the hand brake except when the Driver whistles for it, or on account of fixed signals being at Danger.

Drivers must shut off steam after having gained sufficient speed to carry the entire train well on the rising gradient approaching Howe Bridge West Junction, and must not apply steam until the whole of the train is on the bank and all the couplings are extended.

Date.	Locality.	Lines Affected.	Particulars of Work and Instructions.
	BICKERSHAW JUNCTION, PENNINGTON (W. & E.) AND TYLDESLEY (exclusive).		
Until further notice	Bickershaw Branch, between 3¼ and 3 m.p. and 2 and ¼ m.p.	Up and Down	Subsidence. Speed not to exceed 15 MILES PER HOUR when flagmen are out.
Until further notice	Between Leigh and Tyldesley, 2¾ and 1¾ m.p.	Up and Down	Subsidence. Speed not to exceed 15 MILES PER HOUR when flagmen are out.
Until further notice	Between Leigh Station and Speakman's Siding Signal Boxes, 2¼ and 1½ m.p.	Up and Down	7.30 a.m. to 5.0 p.m. Lifting subsidence. BETWEEN TRAINS. Speed not to exceed 15 MILES PER HOUR day and night. Warning Boards and **C** and **T** Indicators provided.
	FLETCHER STREET JUNCTION AND ROE GREEN JUNCTION.		
Until further notice	Between Plodder Lane and Little Hulton, 3 and 2¾ m.p.	Up and Down	Subsidence. Speed not to exceed 15 MILES PER HOUR when flagmen are out.
	BOLTON AND KENYON JUNCTION AND BRANCHES.		
Sunday, Feb. 5	Bolton, Fletcher St. Jn.	All	9.0 a.m. to 6.0 p.m. Renewing levers and quadrants, tumbler apparatus. Locking disarranged and points and signals disconnected as required.
Feb. 6 to 10	Kirkhall Lane Crossing	All	8.30 a.m. to 4.30 p.m. Repairing gate connections. Gates and signals disconnected as required.
Until further notice	Between Chequerbent and Atherton, 6½ and 5 m.p.	Up and Down	Subsidence. Speed not to exceed 15 MILES PER HOUR day and night when flagmen are out.
Until further notice	Chequerbent Bank, between 5½ and 6 m.p.	Down	Subsidence. Speed not to exceed 20 MILES PER HOUR day and night Warning Boards and **C** and **T** Indicators provided.
Until further notice	West Leigh, between 2¼ and 2½ m.p	Up and Down	Repairing Bridge No. 7. Speed not to exceed 10 MILES PER HOUR day and night. Warning Boards and **C** and **T** Indicators provided.
Until further notice	Pennington Station, between 1¾ and 1¼ m.p.	Up and Down	Subsidence. Speed not to exceed 15 MILES PER HOUR day and night when flagmen are out.

Note that these instructions refer in particular to those lines affected by subsidence.

BIBLIOGRAPHY

A Lancashire Triangle Part One. D.J.Sweeney. Triangle Publishing 1996.
The Wigan Branch Railway. D.J.Sweeney. Triangle Publishing 2008.
Article, The Hunslet Austerity 0-6-0STs. Don Townsley. Locomotives Illustrated, Ian Allan 1988.
LMS Engine Sheds Vol 1. C.Hawkins & G.Reeves. Wild Swan Publishing 1981.
Railways of Great Britain & Ireland. Francis Whishaw. 1842.
The Industrial Railways of the Bolton, Bury and Manchester Coalfield Part Two.
    C.H.A.Townley, F.D.Smith & J.A.Peden. Runpast Publishing 1992.
Clinker's Register of Closed Passenger Stations. C.R.Clinker. Avon-Anglia Publications 1988.
Description of the railroad for Liverpool to Manchester. P.Moreau. Hillard Gray & C. Boston 1833.
Guide to the Grand Junction Railway. E.C & W.Osborne 1838.

ABBREVIATIONS

B.R.	British Railways
B.R.C.W.	Birmingham Railway Carriage & Wagon Co.
C.WT.	Hundredweight
D.M.U.	Diesel Multiple Unit
L.C.G.B.	Locomotive Club of Great Britain
L.M.S.	London, Midland & Scottish (Railway)
L&N.W.	London & North Western (Railway)
L&Y.	Lancashire & Yorkshire (Railway)
M.G.R.	Merry-Go-Round
M.o.D	Ministry of Defence
M.o.S.	Ministry of Supply
N.C.B.	National Coal Board
P.W.	Permanent Way
R.C.T.S.	Railway Correspondence & Travel Society
R.E.C.	Railway Executive Committee
R.O.F.	Royal Ordnance Factory
S.B.	Signal Box
U.K.	United Kingdom
S.LS.	Stephenson Locomotive Society
S.T.	Saddle Tank
S & T.	Signal & Telegraph
W.C.M.L.	West Coast Main Line
W.D.	War Department
W.T.T.	Working Time Table
W.W.II.	World War II.

Locomotive Builders

HC.	Hudswell Clarke & Co. Leeds
HE.	Hunslet Engine Co. Leeds

Imperial to Metric Conversion

1in (inch) = 25.4mm.
1ft (foot) = 304.8mm.
1yd (yard) = .944 metres. (22yds = 1 chain).
1 statute mile = 1.6093 kilometres.
1 acre (4,870 sq yds) = .4097 hectares.
20 cwt (hundredweight) = 1 ton = 1.016 tonnes.

FURTHER READING from TRIANGLE PUBLISHING

The Lancashire Union Railway, D.J. Sweeney.

Promoted by Wigan coal proprietors as a means of greater access to the markets of East Lancashire this railway had the nominal support of the London & North Western Railway and was to be worked by them. The Lancashire & Yorkshire Railway opposed this, coming up with their own proposals. The result was a compromise, some sections jointly worked. Today only the St. Helens-Ince Moss section survives. In its heyday the route by-passed Wigan providing a relief line known as the 'Whelley' much used by WCML diversions. 168PP, 235 illustrations, some in colour, with numerous maps etc. Hardback. ISNB 978-09550030-42. priced £25.00

Plodder Lane for Farnworth, Bert Holland.

Plodder Lane was situated on the London & North Western's Roe Green -Bolton Great Moor Street branch which opened in 1874 for mineral traffic and passengers from 1875. This is a thoroughly absorbing history of the route, the author receiving much praise for his efforts. Bert was a local lad attending school adjacent to the railway which kindled his interest in the route. After university, Bert emigrated to Canada taking up the post of Professor of Organic Chemistry at Brock University, Ontario; never though did he forget his roots at Plodder Lane. Sadly, Bert died soon after publication but this work has become the standard on its subject matter, a fitting tribute to a really nice man. 160pp, 114 illustrations, TTs, maps etc. Hardback. ISBN 0 952 9333 65. Price £18.95

The Wigan Branch Railway, D.J.Sweeney.

A relatively short branch line from Parkside to Wigan this railway was the final link that connected all the major industrial towns of South Lancashire and was to become an integral part of the WCML. It is described from it earliest days until modern times with a wealth of detail. Complete with a fold-out map of Wigan N.W. c1941. 200pp, 240 illustrations, line maps diagrams etc. Hardback. ISBN 978 09550030 35 Priced at £28.00

A Trolleybus to the Punch Bowl, Phillip J.Taylor

The South Lancashire Transport Co. Ltd. had their headquarters at Howe Bridge, Atherton, its venerable trolleybuses serving the old industrial towns of Bolton, Leigh, Swinton, St. Helens, Farnworth, Tyldesley etc. Route by route the author takes the reader on a nostalgic journey beneath the wires of this fondly remembered system. 200pp, 394 illustrations, some in colour, large fold-out map. ISBN 0-9529333-73 Price £32.00

Top, Punch Bowl at Atherton

Left, Bolton's old bus station.

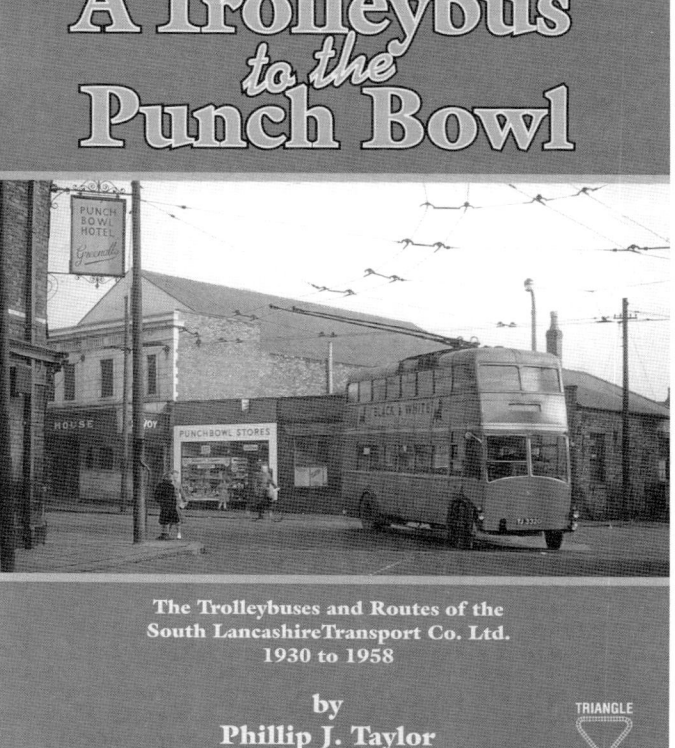

The Wigan Junction Railways, D.J.Sweeney.
Late arrivals on the scene in this part of South Lancashire, the Wigan Junction Railways were attracted to the large coal deposits to be found south of Wigan. Any incursion though into this London & North Western stronghold would be problematic and so it proved. Without the financial clout of the Manchester, Sheffield & Lincolnshire Railway the Wigan Company would have floundered. Opened in 1879 in part for freight and to passengers in 1884; more grandiose schemes to reach the Lancashire coast never got of the ground. 126pp, 139 illustrations, some in colour, line maps etc.
ISBN 978 09550030 59. Priced at £24.00

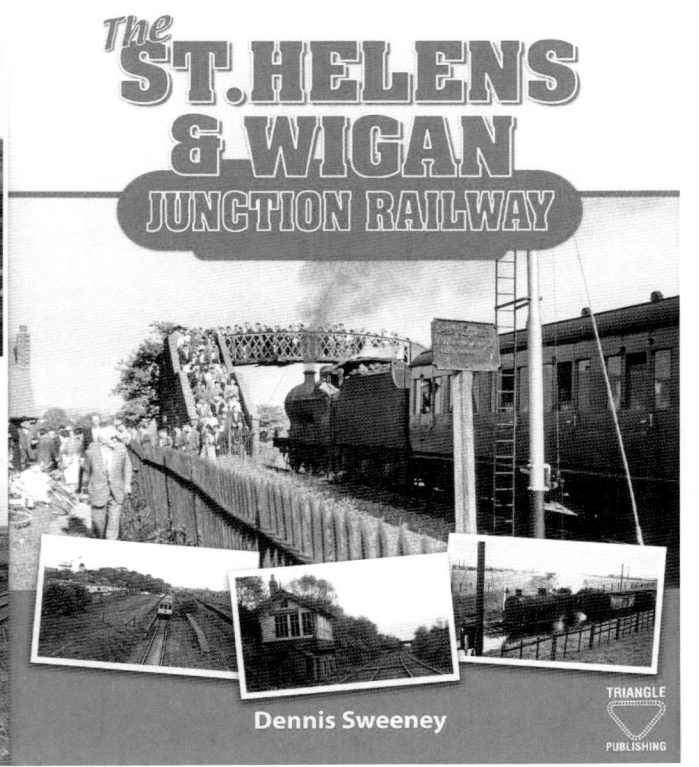

The St. Helens & Wigan Junction Railways, D.J.Sweeney.
The Companion to the Wigan Junction Railways, this book tells the story of the trials & tribulations of proposals & constructing a railway in the London & North Western dominated St. Helens area. Once again the support of The Manchester, Sheffield & Lincolnshire Railway was forthcoming, albeit the railway had a long gestation period. 120pp, 144 illustrations including colour sections. Line maps, TTs, etc.
ISBN 978-09550030 66 Priced at £24.00